MASTERING GRID COMPUTING

Scheduling and Resource Management

MASTERING GRID COMPUTING

Scheduling and Resource Management

Ankita, PhD

Sudip Kumar Sahana, PhD

APPLE ACADEMIC PRESS

First edition published 2025

Apple Academic Press Inc.
1265 Goldenrod Circle, NE,
Palm Bay, FL 32905 USA

760 Laurentian Drive, Unit 19,
Burlington, ON L7N 0A4, CANADA

CRC Press
2385 NW Executive Center Drive,
Suite 320, Boca Raton FL 33431

4 Park Square, Milton Park,
Abingdon, Oxon, OX14 4RN UK

Apple Academic Press exclusively co-publishes with CRC Press, an imprint of Taylor & Francis Group, LLC

Library and Archives Canada Cataloguing in Publication

CIP data on file with Canada Library and Archives

Library of Congress Cataloging-in-Publication Data

CIP data on file with US Library of Congress

ISBN: 978-1-77491-875-3 (hbk)
ISBN: 978-1-77491-874-6 (pbk)
ISBN: 978-1-00359-840-4 (ebk)
DOI: 10.1201/9781003598404

About the Authors

Ankita, PhD
MTech Computer Science, Pranveer Singh Institute of Technology, Kanpur, Uttar Pradesh, India

Ankita, PhD, is currently working as an Assistant Professor at the Pranveer Singh Institute of Technology (PSIT), Kanpur, India, in the Department of Computer Science and Engineering. Her fields of interest are grid computing, artificial intelligence, and computational intelligence. She has authored research papers on computer science and has been assigned as a reviewer for several SCI-indexed journals and IEEE conferences. She received her bachelor's degree (BE) in Computer Science and Engineering from Nagpur University and her MTech and PhD degrees from Birla Institute of Technology, Mesra, Ranchi, India.

Sudip Kumar Sahana, PhD
Department of Computer Science and Engineering, Birla Institute of Technology, Mesra, Jharkhand, India

Sudip Kumar Sahana, PhD, is currently working as an Associate Professor in the Department of Computer Science and Engineering at the Birla Institute of Technology, Mesra, India. His major field of study is in computer science. His research and teaching interests include soft computing, computational intelligence, distributed computing, and artificial intelligence. He has authored numerous articles, research papers, and books in the field of computer science and has been assigned as an editorial team member and reviewer for several reputed journals. He also holds several patents. He is a lifetime member of the Indian Society for Technical Education (ISTE) and fellow of the Institution of Electronics and Telecommunication Engineers (IETE), India. He received his BE degree in Computer Technology from Nagpur University, India, and MTech degree in Computer Science from the Birla Institute of Technology, Mesra, Ranchi, India, where he was awarded his PhD (Engineering) as well.

Contents

Abbreviations

ABC	Artificial Bee Colony
ACO	Ant Colony Optimization
ACOthresh	Threshold-Constrained Ant Colony Optimization
AI	Artificial Intelligence
AMU	Average Machine Utilization
APGrid	Asia Pacific Grid
API	Application Programming Interface
ARPANET	Advanced Research Projects Agency Network
AS	Ant System
AST	Actual Start Time
ATC	Apparent Tardiness Cost
BGS	Best Gap Search
BIRN	Bioinformatics Research Network
C-DAC	Centre for Development of Advanced Computing
CPU	Central Processing Unit
CR	Cluster Resource
CRU	Cluster Resource Utilization
CSO	Cat Swarm Optimization
CSOA	Chicken Swarm Optimization Algorithm
DAG	Direct Acyclic Graph
EGEE	Enabling Grids for e-Science Projects
EGI	European Grid Infrastructure
ESA	Elephant Search Algorithm
ETC	Expected Time to Compute
FCFS	First Come First Serve
FSA	Fish Swarm Algorithm
GA	Genetic Algorithm
GBC	Genetic Bee Colony
Gfarm	Grid Datafarm
GMA	Grid Monitoring Architecture
GRACE	Grid Architecture for Computational Economy
GRAMP	Grid Resource Access and Management Protocol
GRM	Grid Resource Management
GSSIM	Grid Scheduling Simulator
GWO	Grey Wolf Optimization
IaaS	Infrastructure as a Service

ICT	Information and Communication Technology
IoT	Internet of Things
LAN	Local Area Network
LHC	Large Hadron Collider
MCT	Minimum Completion Time
MET	Minimum Execution Time
MSG	Message Passing
NAREGI	National Research Grid Initiative
NDFS	Nearest Deadline First Scheduled
NetSolve	Network Solver
NGI	National Grid Infrastructure
NP	Non-deterministic Polynomial
OGSA-DAI	Open Grid Service Architecture Data Access and Integration
PaaS	Platform as a Service
PB	Petabytes
PSO	Particle Swarm Optimization
QoS	Quality of Service
REST	Representational State Transfer
RPC	Remote Procedure Call
RU	Resource Utilization
SaaS	Software as a Service
SD	Standard Deviation
SJF	Shortest Job First
SJF-ACOthresh	Shortest Job First combined with ACOthresh
SJF-GA	Shortest Job First combined with Genetic Algorithm
SLA	Service Level Agreement
SOA	Service-Oriented Architecture
SOAP	Simple Object Access Protocol
SWF	Standard Workload Format
TCT	Total Completion Time
WOA	Whale Optimization Algorithm

Acknowledgments

The book incorporates different scheduling algorithms, including traditional and non-traditional (bio-inspired) methods, to solve grid scheduling problems. Our special thanks to MetaCentrum, the Czech National Grid Infrastructure (NGI), for providing the workload traces to test new algorithms and compare their performance with other reference algorithms. We sincerely thank all our colleagues for positively supporting our research and directly or indirectly contributing to the case studies presented in the book.

The primary driving force behind the creation of this book has been the consistent support and unwavering motivation provided by Punam Sharma, my mother. We appreciate and acknowledge the encouragement of our family members, including Ravi Kumar Gautam, Kumar Pratyush, and Arun Sharma.

We would like to extend our gratitude to the members of Apple Academic Press for their ardent support and guidance throughout the course of book preparation and for assisting us at different times during the book preparation and for bringing the process of publication into motion.

Preface

The last two decades have seen grid computing as one of the major computing platforms that has contributed to the development of various computer science domains by ensuring resource availability to a wide community of users and bridging geographical gaps. The widespread usage of the internet and the availability of pervasive devices are rapidly transforming the way we connect, handle our lives, do business, and access and deliver services.

The focus of computing has shifted from personal to data-centric because of the reduced communication and computation costs. Different grid computing infrastructures have been utilizing computational resources all around the globe while exploring new dimensions of parallelism. The idea of serving computing in the form of a model consisting of commoditized services has revolutionized the entire concept of service delivery. This type of model allows the user to access services irrespective of their geographical location. Not only grid computing, but there are various computing platforms assuring the vision of utility computing.

Though there are several computing technologies such as cloud computing and the use of dedicated high-performance (HPC) infrastructures for parallel computation, grid computing continues to be the prevalent technology well used for scientific computations by the research community in Europe. Job scheduling is an important task in a grid computing environment. The primary objective of grid scheduling is to create an optimal mapping of jobs on the available resources in a network. A large number of scheduling algorithms are available, but choosing an optimal algorithm is important. In this book, we have studied several scheduling algorithms such as First Come First Serve (FCFS), Shortest Job First (SJF), Ant Colony Optimization (ACO), Particle Swarm Optimization (PSO), Genetic Algorithm (GA), and a few hybrid algorithms. The efficiency of these algorithms has been calculated using a standard workload, and a comparative analysis has been carried out to study the behavior of all these algorithms under different job counts. There are several simulation toolkits available for setting up (designing) a grid computing environment to evaluate real-world complex computational problems. Some of the notable grid simulators are GridSim, MicroGrid, Alea, and SimGrid toolkits.

In this book, the scheduling algorithms have been implemented in a simulation environment using the Alea simulator. A wide range of grid computing applications is available in different fields such as life sciences, engineering, the gaming industry, health, education, business, and entertainment. Grid computing technology enables every computer to act as a supercomputer by allowing them to access enormous storage and processing power through various resources. The book contains all the major grid applications in different domains and their future prospects. In order to utilize the full potential of grid computing, it is required to ensure that the target users are well-educated, and they must understand the advantages of grid computing. It is the responsibility of grid practitioners and researchers to make the potential users aware of the benefits of grid computing technology.

Introduction

This book begins with the introduction to grid computing, covering the basic idea, definition, characteristics, and other associated paradigms. This book features grid computing and its history in the computing world. The need to switch to grid computing and how it serves the modern needs of computing in today's world is discussed. The book presents a classical evolution of grid computing, starting from distributed computing to service-oriented computing. The book contains chapters describing the architectural models of grid computing and various elements present in a grid infrastructure. It discusses various classifications of grids and major grid developments all around the world.

Scheduling of jobs and resource management are two major concerns of grid computing. Job scheduling has become a non-trivial issue in grid computing due to the increased number of users and their job requests. It is important to complete the execution of these jobs in minimum time and manage the grid resources at the same time. The book incorporates different scheduling algorithms, including traditional and non-traditional (bio-inspired), to solve grid scheduling problems. Various research-based case studies to solve grid scheduling problems have been included in this book to analyze the efficiency of scheduling algorithms. These case studies will help the users figure out the system of grid computing and various scheduling algorithms so that they can utilize them in their personal endeavors. Also, the book covers major grid applications and upcoming new computing technologies in the field of computer science.

The book consists of eight chapters which are arranged into three different parts:

- Part 1: Foundations
    - Chapter 1: Introduction to Grid Computing
    - Chapter 2: Scheduling: Conventional and Bio-Inspired Algorithms
    - Chapter 3: Work Done Using Conventional and Bio-Inspired Algorithms

- Chapter 4: Scheduling Algorithms: Modified and Hybrid Algorithms

➢ Part 2: Implementation of Scheduling Algorithms in grid environment using ALEA and performance comparison of algorithms

- Chapter 5: Research-Based Case Study to Solve Grid Scheduling Problem Using FCFS, SJF, ACO, PSO, and GA
- Chapter 6: Research-Based Case Study to Solve Grid Scheduling Problem Using Modified and Hybrid Algorithms: ACOthresh, SJF-ACOthresh, and SJF-GA

➢ Part 3: Performance Comparison of Algorithms and Emerging Computing Technologies in the Field of Computer Science

- Chapter 7: Comparison of Conventional, Bio-Inspired, and Hybrid Algorithms: A Review
- Chapter 8: New Computing Platforms for Solving Convoluted Engineering Problems: A Review

Grid scheduling is an intrinsic component of grid computing infrastructure. The problem of grid scheduling is NP-complete and therefore requires an intelligent algorithm to solve this problem. This book addresses the grid scheduling problem and provides promising solutions using modern and powerful metaheuristics. The use of metaheuristics (bio-inspired) improves the performance results of grid scheduling and paves the way to solve other NP-complete problems in the future. The basics of grid computing, different bottlenecks, formulation of solution strategies, implementation, and case studies are the appealing and unique features of this book. The book will guide new researchers and learners to understand the concept of grid computing from a broader perspective. Starting from the basic definition of the grid and its architecture to the complex hybridized model of scheduling, this book is a comprehensive resource on grid computing, grid scheduling, and grid resource management. This book explores basic understanding, in-depth exploration, and future research directions on grid computing.

PART I
FOUNDATIONS

CHAPTER 1

Introduction to Grid Computing

1.1 GRID COMPUTING

In a world of high-speed internet, modern devices, an increased number of users, and voluminous data, there is a need to manage, handle, and provide hassle-free services to the users. The advent of parallel and distributed computing has changed the whole dimension of computing. Due to low computational as well as communication costs, a new computing paradigm called grid computing has brought about a radical change in the computing industry. The transformation of computing into a commercial model of delivering services is quite equivalent to delivering basic utilities such as water, gas, and electricity to the users. Therefore, the services provided by information technology (IT) are being charged and delivered to the users as computing utilities. This chapter highlights the salient features of grid computing. A grid is defined as a collection of resources such as servers, databases, processors, and networks. These resources (homogeneous or heterogeneous) are scattered over different geographical regions.

It covers the basics of the grid computing environment. This chapter describes the layered architecture of the grid computing environment. It also describes the requirements that any computing infrastructure must possess in order to build a grid environment. It deals with the categories of grids (classifications) available based on their applications (academic, commercial, scientific, and hybrid) and functionalities (data, computational, utility, and real-time). Academic grids can be useful in sharing information among educational institutions spanning different geographical locations. It also provides insight into the introduction of grid computing and its classical evolution in the computing world. Several types of grids based on their functionalities and applications have been developed, and

Mastering Grid Computing: Scheduling and Resource Management.
Ankita & Sudip Kumar Sahana (Authors)

researchers are still developing hybrid grids that can serve disparate user requests. Notable grid developments in different parts of the world are discussed and studied in this chapter. The notion of distributed computing and other computing paradigms is also discussed. Various advantages as well as limitations of the grid computing platform in comparison to other computing environments are also discussed in this chapter.

The concept of the grid in the computational network (Foster and Kesselman, 2003b; Foster et al., 2001) has been presented by Foster, Tuecke, and Kesselman. The primary aim is to create the illusion of an extremely large and powerful virtual supercomputer that contains heterogeneous and homogeneous systems with a wide variety of shareable resources.

There are various applications handled by grid computing systems, such as partitioning of applications, scheduling of jobs, result management, and sharing experimental results among a number of researchers across the world, as well as ascetic properties, for example, self-optimization, self-configuration, and self-management. The model of grid computing also facilitates on-demand computing, which benefits enterprises by helping them meet their fluctuating demands efficiently.

One of the most challenging issues of grid systems is job scheduling because of the distributed and dynamic nature of the grid, as well as the heterogeneity of the computing components. Improving efficiency and reducing job completion time are the major goals of any scheduling policy in a grid environment.

1.1.1 IDEA OF GRID COMPUTING

During the 1990s, the computational needs of the users forced researchers to develop a computing network that could provide easy and transparent access to resources. Additionally, the researchers needed a computing network through which they could coordinate and share the results of their experiments with other collaborators almost instantaneously. These reasons facilitated the development of a new computing infrastructure called grid computing infrastructure (Buyya and Venugopal, 2005), which enables the cooperative and pervasive use of computing resources for users to solve their complex problems.

Resources in an organization are often underutilized or overutilized at some locations, which leads to poor utilization. These resources can be connected in a grid network that will prioritize the underutilized resources and make them available for future use by the end users in a grid computing network.

The status of these resources is always changing, which exemplifies the non-trivial need for resource management in a grid computing environment. The network size increases with the escalating user requests. New resources are added to the existing grid infrastructure to meet the growing needs of the users. Hence, proper resource management is necessary to ensure minimum waiting time for jobs and enhance resource utilization (RU).

Resource management is concerned with the selection and allocation of suitable resources for the required job. The resources are assigned to different jobs based on some scheduling techniques, which can be conventional or non-conventional. The stand-alone conventional algorithms are no longer sufficient to solve complex NP-complete problems. They can be combined with other non-conventional algorithms to form a strong scheduling algorithm. The process of merging two or more algorithms is called hybridization. The current research trend shows that the hybridized approach to scheduling is gaining popularity in solving complex optimization problems.

1.1.2 DEFINING GRID

In simple words, a grid is defined as a collection of resources such as servers, databases, processors, and networks. These resources (homogeneous or heterogeneous) are scattered over different geographical regions. There are multiple administrative domains that own and share these resources to provide a ubiquitous and transparent computing service for a variety of applications (Figure 1.1).

1.1.3 CHARACTERISTICS OF GRID COMPUTING

Grid Computing is designed to meet the dynamic demands of users by providing common access to computational resources that are networked together and act as a virtual supercomputer. The resources are broadly classified into three categories:

1. **Communication Resources:** These resources specify the network bandwidth of the grid, that is, the data transfer rate of the machines and other communication paths of the grid.

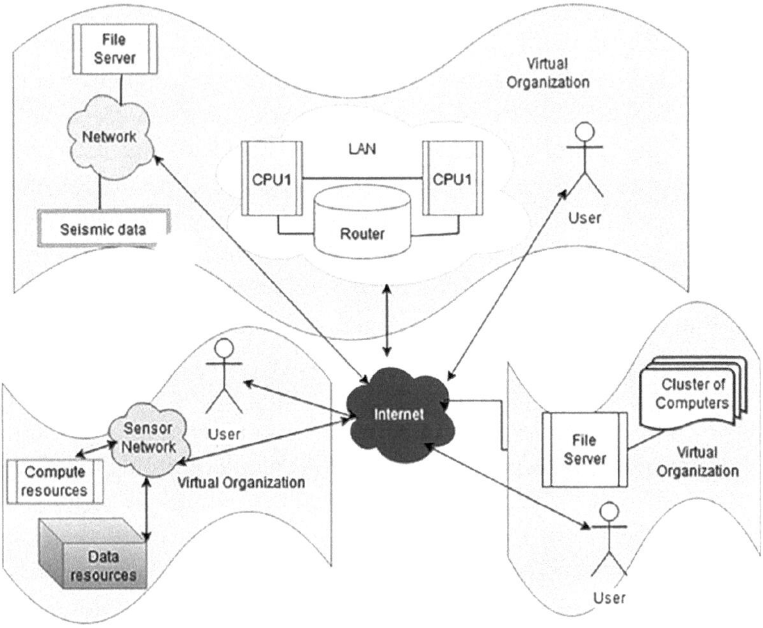

FIGURE 1.1 Structure of a grid.

2. **Computation Resources:** These resources specify the processing capacity of the resources or the machines of the grid. They are also known as processing resources. Processing resources can be renewable or nonrenewable, depending upon their usage. If the resource is exhausted after a job uses it and cannot be used again by other jobs, then it is a nonrenewable resource. A resource is said to be renewable if the usage of the resource is limited to one job at a time but becomes available for other jobs after it is released by the job using it.
3. **Storage Resources:** These resources specify the amount of storage provided by the machines of the grid storage manager whose integrated view is given by the grid with an aim to increase the capacity and sharing of data.

The management of these resources is a key functional requirement of any grid system. Some of the important features in grid resource management (GRM) are discussed below:

- A grid network may contain homogeneous as well as heterogeneous resources. Also, the applications or the demands of the end users are of varied types, and therefore it is required to allocate suitable resources for a particular job. Hence, the task of resource management becomes a critical issue.
- The members of the grid must be trustworthy for secure communication, and hence the users are validated before they can submit jobs to the grid system.
- An interface is provided to the users so that they can submit as well as track the status of their previously submitted jobs. Also, it provides a medium for the resource administrators to check the current status of the resources.
- The resources are registered in a central server, which consists of a list of available resources and their current status.
- The resources are selected and allocated to the job based on the chosen scheduling policy.
- The execution of the job takes place over the selected resource. The job scheduler manages the waiting jobs in the queue based on the selected scheduling technique.

1.1.4 CLASSIFICATION OF GRIDS

The grid computing platform is a popular platform among users due to its capacity to handle large and complex jobs without compromising the performance of the grid environment. The performance metrics, such as response time, wait time, completion time, and load distribution, determine the behavior of the overall grid environment. Grids can be classified based on their applications and functionalities.

1.1.4.1 CLASSIFICATIONS BASED ON APPLICATIONS

Types of grids available according to their applications are listed below:

1. **Commercial Grids:** Grid computing has gained the attraction of different communities all over the world due to its low cost and high-performance computing results. For example, in the business world, the demands of customers are increasing rapidly, which requires instant and fast responses to serve the customers and understand the market dynamics to stay competitive in this area.

2. **Scientific Grids:** Grid computing has made a remarkable contribution to the field of science and technology, and it is creating new advancements and developments to this day. Standard scientific projects related to astronomy, quantum physics, and nuclear science have their grid systems exclusively for their needs.
3. **Academic Grids:** The grids can be useful in sharing information among educational institutions spanning across different geographical locations. Students from different places might get involved in a common project and can collaborate and exchange information while working in a grid environment. This will eventually bring two academic or research communities together, irrespective of their geographical locations.
4. **Public Grids:** These are the non-commercial grids offering services to general public issues. The concept of public grids depends on the availability of unused CPU cycles and data storage to solve public problems.
5. **Health Science Grids:** The role of grid computing in health science is significant in terms of finding new, accurate, and fast methods of diagnosis. Doctors have a huge amount of data, and their analysis will greatly help in finding cures and treatments for patients, irrespective of their geographical locations.
6. **Hybrid Grids:** There are several grids that are not dedicated to a single application. Instead of providing services to specific applications, some grids are diverse and provide services in multiple domains. TeraGrid is a kind of grid that is used in academic, health science, and research activities.

1.1.4.2 CLASSIFICATIONS BASED ON FUNCTIONALITIES

Types of grids available according to their functionalities are listed below:

1. **Computational Grids:** These are the compute-intensive grids that serve the computational needs of the clients. The CPU cycles are the main resources provided by computational grids. These grids provide combined CPU cycles from various resources located at different sites to satisfy user requirements. Applications such as

weather forecasting, nuclear simulation, and complex business analysis use computational grids for implementation.

2. **Data Grids:** The data-intensive grids are useful in performing operations on massive amounts of distributed data. Different types of data around the globe are placed in data repositories, digital libraries, and data warehouses, which are scattered over multiple administrative sites located in different geographical regions. Data grids are intended to provide a safe and reliable mechanism for data transfer, data filtering, and an overall data management system. CERN is a widely known data grid that deals with the development of huge data organizations.
3. **Utility Grids:** The job of utility grids is to pool the dynamically accessible resources to meet the needs of the given application. This helps in combining resources from multiple machines dynamically and providing services that are not possible with a single machine.
4. **Real-Time Grids:** Real-time applications have various requirements that are not supported by traditional computational or data grids. These real-time grids provide a virtual workspace to enable interactions between the clients and applications. Real-time applications such as disaster management are handled by real-time grids.

1.2 CLASSICAL EVOLUTION OF GRID COMPUTING

The period of the 1990s witnessed the expansion of grid computing networks, a concept that had already been manifested long before by notable researchers like John (1961) and Leonard (1969) in their works. They believed that in the coming time, computing utilities would be provided to users in a seamless manner, similar to other essential services of mankind. High-speed networks such as US Gigabit testbeds have made it possible to combine resources located at different sites. Smarr and Catlett (1992) referred to this method of combining resources as metacomputing.

The results of the experiments (Messina, 1998) indicated that a new type of computational resource with unique abilities could be created by bringing together compute resources such as parallel and vector supercomputers for a designated application. However, this technology was designed for research-oriented applications, but it succeeded in generating interest in creating a platform for distributed applications of different types.

In Europe, a scientific group working on the large hadron collider (LHC) launched the EU DataGrid project. This project was developed because they realized that it was needed to distribute computing resources at multiple sites in order to evaluate petabytes (PB) of data generated by LHC experiments. Likewise, two projects were developed in the United States, forming the Open Science Grid and the European Grid Infrastructure (EGI) in Europe.

1.2.1 DISTRIBUTED COMPUTING AND ITS CHARACTERISTICS

Distributed Computing, as the name suggests, is a kind of computing that enables users to access the required services without disclosing the existence of several autonomous computers. The mode of interaction between the communicating entities in a network is known as message passing, based on standard protocols. Clusters, Clouds, Grids, and P2P networks (peer-to-peer) are popular distributed systems. The cluster computing system consists of closely connected computers, appearing as a single high-performance supercomputer to the users. Cluster computing is mainly used in scientific and engineering applications.

It also supports large-scale business applications. The grid computing system enables the collaborative sharing of diverse resources (such as data, files, computing entities, and different devices) located at different geographical locations to solve complicated problems in the science and business domains. Peer-to-peer networks are a special distributed system that supports online multiplayer gaming, fast messaging, and file sharing.

1.2.1.1 CHARACTERISTICS OF DISTRIBUTED COMPUTING SYSTEM

1. **Resource Sharing:** This is an intrinsic characteristic of all distributed systems, which enables users to access and cooperatively share remote resources in a regulated manner.
2. **Transparency:** The goal of distributed computing is to hide the complexities and the existence of associated computing devices and provide a hassle-free computing experience to users. Transparency comes in different forms, such as access, location, migration, concurrency, and failure.

3. **Acceptance (Openness):** The services provided by open distributed systems are standardized services that reflect the syntax, semantics, and definition of sent and received messages. These standards contain the necessary rules for the transmission of messages between computing entities. All these rules are interpreted in protocols.
4. **Extensibility:** The property of extensibility, generally called scalability, enables the distributed system to increase its computing power by deploying more systems and providing seamless services to users without fail.
5. **Reliability:** This in distributed computing ensures that the breakdown of some machines will not affect the working of the whole distributed computing system, and there will be systems available that can compensate for the failure of other machines.

1.2.2 SERVICE-ORIENTED COMPUTING

Service-oriented computing forms the backbone of a popular distributed computing system, that is, cloud computing. The underlying principle is to embrace the notion of services for application and system development. The service itself is an abstraction that has the capability to perform basic to complex tasks based on requirements, regardless of the programming language or computing platform. The platform's independence increases the service accessibility for a better reach for users. Hence, a large number of clients or users can be served in different situations. These services are merged in a single Service-Oriented Architecture (SOA). The SOA is a logical approach to organizing software systems and providing services to users through observable interfaces.

The two main services included in service-oriented computing are quality of service (QoS) and software-as-a-service (SaaS), which also form the base of cloud computing systems.

1. **Quality of Service (QoS):** It consists of functional and non-functional properties that measure the nature of service from several viewpoints. These properties are different performance metrics like scalability, response time, reliability, and availability. The service level agreement (SLA) sets an accord between the service provider

and service user over minimum values for QoS performance attributes which are required to be met once a service is called.

2. **Software-as-a-Service (SaaS):** The SaaS method enables the distribution of complicated business processes in the form of service to the user which can be accessed from every location.

1.2.3 NOTABLE GRID DEVELOPMENTS WORLDWIDE

With the onset of grid computing, it has always been a subject of curiosity among scientists and researchers around the globe. Overall, the grid projects are broadly divided into two categories:

1. The first category includes the setting up of hardware and various software installations and making administrative policies and mechanisms to facilitate scientists and researchers in carrying out their work. This category is known as Grid Infrastructure Development.
2. The second category focuses on investigating the evolution of software and policy plans that aid in recognizing the true potential of the grid computing environment. This category is called Grid Middleware Research.

Based on these categories, some of the prominent grid infrastructure and middleware projects are discussed below:

1. **TeraGrid:** The United States National Science Foundation has funded a grid infrastructure called TeraGrid that provides computing power of 40 teraflops and a storage capacity of 2 PB across eight grid sites in the United States. Grid3 is a major testbed covering 25 geographical sites in the US and Korea that are being used for operational areas such as astronomy, computational biology, and high-energy physics.

2. **Bioinformatics Research Network (BIRN):** It is a kind of testbed in biomedical science that facilitates data sharing stored in several repositories around America.

3. **NEESGrid:** This grid is meant to assist the scientists and researchers working in the earthquake engineering community

to demonstrate and perform experiments in diverse locations and investigate data through a common terminal.

4. **The Globus Toolkit:** The Globus Toolkit is a very popular grid middleware project developed by the Global Alliance conducted by the Argonne National Laboratory.
5. **Storage Resource Broker (SRB):** The SRB, led by the Supercomputing Center in San Diego, is a renowned grid middleware project that organizes dissimilar data repositories and handles data storage, access management, and data replication.
6. **Condor:** It is a grid middleware project developed at the University of Wisconsin, Madison, which supports high efficiency and throughput computing methods. This project supports the conversion of a collection of workstations and dedicated clusters into a distributed supercomputing facility.
7. **AppleS (Application Scheduling):** It is a grid middleware project developed at the University of California, San Diego, to support application scheduling.
8. **NetSolve:** Or GridSolve is a grid middleware project developed at the University of Tennessee, Knoxville, which aims to bring together different resources interconnected by a computing network. This middleware is an RPC-based client/server structure that facilitates user access to software as well as hardware components remotely.
9. **Grid Application Development Software:** This project, popularly known as GrAds, intends to create a framework to use grid resources in a much simpler manner.
10. **Enabling Grids for e-Science Projects (EGEE):** This, popularly known as the EGEE project, is one of the major grid initiatives in the development of grid computing infrastructure in current times. The European Union has funded this major data grid project, which associates more than 250 computing (resource) centers from 48 different countries to generate a reliable source of computing for European and global research groups.

11. **GridLab:** The European Union has funded the GridLab project that aims at developing a Grid Computing Software Infrastructure to serve the application communities. This project has collaborated efforts of system scientists, astrophysicists, and other researchers from different domains to enhance the effective usage of resources in the grid environment.

12. **GridSphere:** This is one of the eminent grid initiatives funded by the European Union, which aims at the creation of a web portal environment to facilitate the grid users.

13. **Cactus:** The design of the Cactus framework makes it an excellent choice as a testbed for the grid computing environment. It is another project funded by the European Union. This testbed mainly supports scientific programming.

14. **Open Grid Service Architecture Data Access and Integration (OGSA-DAI):** This, popularly known as OGSA-DAI, is a middleware solution that facilitates application developers by providing easy access to distributed data at multiple sites along with various local access mechanisms. Data integration can also take place at the server site, and output can be delivered with the help of several protocols and policies within OGSA-DAI. This middleware can accommodate data resources, such as relational databases, files, or XML databases, and can handle multiple operations, such as changing to disparate formats, with the help of a highly malleable and extensible framework.

15. **National Research Grid Initiative (NAREGI):** It is a popular grid program developed by the Japanese scientific and research community, which aims at building an R&D center of high performance to escalate scientific and engineering applications.

16. **Asia Pacific Grid (APGrid):** This, popularly known as APGrid, is an international collaboration that has initiated the testbed development in the Asia Pacific region. The aim of APGrid is to allow the sharing of resources, technologies, and knowledge, as well as to develop new grid techniques and technologies.

17. **Ninf:** It is a Japanese programming middleware solution based on the GridRPC (remote procedure call (RPC)) programming

structure. This middleware provides a user-friendly interface to access various software, hardware, and data resources, such as scientific data.

18. **Nimrod:** It is an Australian grid initiative project developed at Monash University. This project is designed to handle the complexities related to parametric computing on groups of distributed systems. Nimrod provides an elementary declarative language to express a parametric experiment. The plans for parametric computing can be created by domain experts, and the Nimrod runtime system can be used to execute different applications, such as bioinformatics, business process simulations, and operational research.
19. **Grid Datafarm (Gfarm):** The Japanese research and scientific community has developed the Gfarm project to support petascale data-intensive computing, enabling distributed resources in a vast area. The salient features of this framework are to (i) dedicate a Grid file system for integrating local disks of computing systems in the computational grid; and (ii) facilitate distributed and parallel computing by linking the Data Grid and Computational Grid.
20. **GARUDA:** It is an Indian National Grid Computing initiative launched by the Centre for Development of Advanced Computing (C-DAC) with the aim of providing solutions to different scientific and engineering problems. GARUDA is a collaborative effort of engineers, computer scientists, and researchers to develop a nationwide grid consisting of a large number of computational nodes, data storage resources, and other scientific instruments.

1.2.4 GRID APPLICATIONS

During the early computing days, sharing computational resources among different organizations was a troublesome task. Researchers all around the globe were seeking means to find a promising solution to facilitate the sharing of resources among different computing bodies. This solution came in the form of grid computing, which facilitated increased processing power to handle both simple and complex computational problems. Later, many scientific initiatives were projected to analyze grid computing in detail and understand different aspects to enhance scientific research. The whole idea of grid computing is based on dividing large, complex jobs into smaller jobs that can run on different machines connected to a common network in a grid. After the job has completed its execution, the results from different machines are combined as a final output. This output is delivered to the user, which finally completes the process of job execution. With the growing acclaim, grid computing has evolved as an eminent computing technology and is widely used in different areas of business, engineering, and biomedicine. In this chapter, we will see several grid applications in different areas of science and technology. There are several advantages of grid computing, including improved job performance and cost reduction. The performance of the grid can be visualized in terms of the total time taken by the job to complete its execution, waiting time, and RU. Presently, a good number of industries (finance, banking, science and engineering, biomedicine, and entertainment) are utilizing grid computing technology to solve complex engineering problems.

In this section, we will highlight the major grid applications and their utilities in the current scenario:

1. **Life Science and Engineering:** The area of life science is related to the study of living organisms such as human beings, plants, animals, and microorganisms. Computational biology in life science deals with the study of bioinformatics, genomes, and neuroscience, which has started to utilize grid computing. Medical practitioners often perform large-scale simulations to analyze the connection of remote devices to medical frameworks or infrastructure using grid computing. The data collected from different sources is assessed by a team of experts in the relevant field.

   Engineering applications are quite resource – and cost-intensive when performing a single unit of work. With the advent of grid computing, the cost of carrying out engineering applications has significantly reduced. The fact that the grid infrastructure is scalable and dynamic allows for the addition of any computing resource at any time according to the job requirements of the users. In this way, the cost of building a new infrastructure is saved, and the grid owner can use and update the existing computing infrastructure to accommodate increased job requests. This will eventually lower the overall costs of carrying out a complex engineering application and serve as an economical approach for grid organizations.

Engineering applications such as the automotive and aerospace industries essentially require testing facilities to carry out significant simulations. These industries have focused their attention on the evolving grid computing technology, which can serve their requirements and expedite time-intensive engineering tasks.

2. **Data-Oriented Applications:** A tremendous amount of data is being produced from several devices such as sensors, smart accessories, scientific equipment, and IoT devices. Grid computing plays an important role in collecting this data and performing necessary assessments to filter valuable information. Once the data is stored, grid computing can be used to interpret the data to analyze patterns in order to incorporate knowledge.
3. **Scientific Research and High-Performance Computing:** The modern approach to computing has brought scientists and researchers closer than ever, irrespective of their geographical locations. They can share data and solve computationally complex engineering problems using grid resources. For example, the data produced by the LHC at CERN is exceptionally large, and grid computing aids in analyzing this bulk of data. Grid computing is often used in bioinformatics for different applications, such as modeling genome behavior. It also helps in simulating the performance of massive nuclear explosions. As a result, huge amounts of data are generated that need to be stored and analyzed. Grid computing serves as an ideal choice for researchers to process and store data for future use. The computational resources provided by grid computing help carry out high data-intensive processing in a legitimate time frame. Grid computing also provides a secure means of transferring and accessing data, building a protected computing environment.
4. **Entertainment and Gaming:** Commercial applications in the entertainment and gaming fields rely on high computational resources and storage networks. Grid resources are chosen based on the computing demand of the grid computing framework. Resource selection is often driven by the number of participants

in the game and the amount of traffic volume being generated. Grid computing plays a crucial role in processing and distributing huge amounts of digital data, such as games, movies, and other special effects in motion films. It also helps store and manage digital rights management information.

5. **Trade Intelligence and Data Analytics:** Trade intelligence or business intelligence is a software-based approach to perform data mining and data visualization in order to make improved data-driven decisions. Grid computing can be used to process and evaluate large amounts of business data in real time. Later, it can be used to store the processed data and find useful patterns in the stored data that will eventually help the organization in making future decisions. An enterprise might utilize the grid computing framework to monitor its sales, client behavior, or changing market trends to make better and more informed decisions.

6. **Healthcare:** It is an emerging application of the grid computing environment. The medical industry is utilizing grid computing to store and process large amounts of patient data. As we know, a patient's medical record is sensitive data, so it requires a strong security mechanism to maintain its integrity and privacy. Grid computing provides an enhanced security mechanism so that the privacy of the patient's data is not compromised. The stored data is useful in many ways, such as developing personalized or customized medicines, carrying out medical research, and analyzing diseases in a thorough manner. This will eventually help in learning and finding new ways to detect and manage disease outbreaks.

7. **Weather Forecasting:** Weather or climate forecasting is an important application of grid computing. Weather sensors and satellites generate a large amount of data that requires real-time processing to make quick and accurate weather forecasts. Grid computing can process and analyze useful patterns in the data generated from the sensors and satellites in real-time to model weather patterns accurately.

8. **Government and Defense:** The growing digitalization has brought significant changes in different areas such as education, government, defense, business, and so on. Electronic government

(e-government) is a growing field that uses information technologies to carry out its activities and handle administration. In government offices, large paper files are now replaced by software files. Digital data is now abundant and needs to be stored and analyzed in an appropriate manner. Grid computing helps in handling and processing this data using its computational and data-intensive resources. Though security poses a big challenge in e-governance, the grid computing environment provides necessary user authentication and data protection mechanisms. Similarly, defense organizations generate huge amounts of data from satellites and other sensors, which require accurate and real-time analysis. It is not feasible to purchase a supercomputer, and leasing supercomputer resources incurs huge costs. In such cases, the grid computing platform serves as an excellent platform to carry out advanced modeling and simulation operations, data mining, and visualization.

1.2.5 SCOPE OF GRID COMPUTING

Grid computing offers enterprises and organizations immense computing power. The applications mentioned in the above section highlight the role of grid computing in different industries such as education, governance, finance, entertainment, life sciences, medicine, and scientific research and development (R&D). Grid computing helps organizations accelerate their overall growth and complete assigned jobs faster by distributing the jobs across different grid nodes, irrespective of their locations. With the growing popularity and evolution of grid computing, a large number of industries will adopt this technology to attain business growth.

1.3 DESIGNING GRID COMPUTING ENVIRONMENT

The core concept of grid computing is to build a distributed computing system that enables the sharing of resources in order to execute one or more applications. The underlying difference between grid and cluster computing lies in the nature and distribution of resources in the computing environment. The grid computing resources are geographically distributed and may be heterogeneous. The cluster computing resources are mostly homogeneous and localized, providing an efficient computing platform.

The grid resources are distributed and owned by multiple organizations. Therefore, a cordial relationship is strongly required among the grid resource owners for smooth application execution without compromising performance. It may happen that an application requires data resources available at different grid sites. The site owners must provide necessary resources within acceptable standard management policies to assure the performance of the grid environment.

A computing infrastructure is required to have certain properties in order to form and run a grid environment. These properties are listed below:

- Security in terms of user access authorization and standard authentication;
- Systematic access to available resources;
- Data storage and duplication of data sets;
- Service broadcasting and its access costs;
- Exploration of required computational resources;
- Exploration of applicable data sets using their standard global names;
- Job scheduling and assignment to proper resources;
- Job submission, examination, and handling job execution;
- Monitoring resource usage and availability of resources;
- Ensuring QoS requirements.

Any grid computing infrastructure must possess these properties to run scientific, engineering, and large-scale business applications. These components are formulated into layers where each layer has distinct functionality.

1.3.1 INTRODUCTION TO GRID COMPUTING ARCHITECTURE

The software and hardware infrastructure of Grid Computing has been the spotlight of research groups and scientific communities in the field of education and industry.

The Grid computing architecture consists of several layers where the lower layer provides services to the upper layer in the model, and the components lying at the same level interact with each other. The grid computing architecture (Figure 1.2) consists of five layers:

1. **Fabric Layer:** This layer is composed of resources such as networks, storage devices, and processors distributed across different grid sites. The computational resources, such as servers

and supercomputers, are required for running various operating systems. Other scientific devices, such as sensor networks, are helpful in providing real-time data for direct transmission to the intended computational sites.

2. **Connectivity Layer:** The authentication and communication protocols are provided by the connectivity layer for secure network transactions. It provides secure mechanisms to identify users and resources of the grid. Other services, such as access to storage resources, remote process management, and QoS constraints, are handled at this layer.

3. **Resource Layer:** This layer consists of resource-specific protocols, such as the grid resource access and management protocol (GRAMP), for allocation and monitoring of resources. It also contains some information and management protocols.

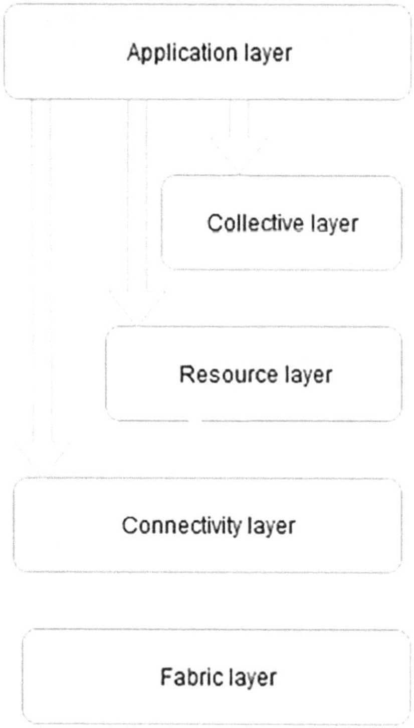

FIGURE 1.2 Layered grid architecture.

The information protocol helps to inquire about the state of the resources (by making a call to the fabric layer), and the management protocol helps in managing access to shared resources in the grid.

4. **Collective Layer:** This layer consists of protocols such as the Grid Resource Information Protocol, which enables information sharing across a group of resources. This layer includes resource brokers for resource management and scheduling jobs (applications) on the global computational resources.
5. **Application Layer:** The lower layer provides interfaces and a programming environment to build grid applications and portals. The grid portals support web-enabled application services, which enable a user to submit and get results for their submitted jobs on remote resources.

1.3.2 ELEMENTS IN GRID COMPUTING MODEL

The grid computing model is composed of several elements discussed below:

1. **Job:** A job submitted by the grid user to the grid system has a specific requirement for resources. The resource requirement can include storage, processing, software libraries, and so forth.
2. **Resource:** It is a scheduling entity where a job is scheduled and processed according to its requirements. There are several properties of a resource, such as its processing speed and memory. Resources in the grid are distributed across multiple sites, where each site has its own access rights and usage policies.
3. **A Scheduling Problem:** It consists of a set of jobs, resources, optimality conditions, working environments, and other constraints specified by the user and the resource provider.
4. **Specification:** The job requirements are written in a high-level language.
5. **Scheduler:** The job of a scheduler is to place the job over the resource based on the requirements of the job and track the status of the job and resource until it finishes its execution.

1.3.3 LIMITATIONS AND ADVANTAGES

In spite of the popularity of the grid computing network, there are certain limitations or challenges that need attention for the stable and efficient working of the grid environment. The availability of resources in the grid network is changing due to the dynamic nature of the grid environment. Resources may not work properly, or new resources may be added to the grid system at any time. These difficulties or challenges in resource management need to be addressed by the resource provider in a grid computing environment. The scheduling problem in the grid has been a common optimization problem studied by research groups.

The limitations or the challenges of a grid computing network are stated below:

1. **Autonomy:** The resources of the grid are spread across multiple locations for organizational use and are owned by different resource owners. It is very important to maintain a cordial relationship between the resource owners and the organizational bodies using the resources for continuous and effective usage of resources.
2. **Expansion of Grid:** The size of the grid may change over time, scaling from a few nodes or resources to thousands of resources. Therefore, it is required for the applications to be scalable; otherwise, it will lead to performance deterioration of the grid network.
3. **Diversity of Resources:** The resources in the grid network are of different types and hence can be used to serve a variety of applications. The management of different types of resources is a trivial task for the grid resource manager.
4. **Diversity of Jobs:** The jobs submitted in the grid system are of a diverse nature and have different resource requirements. Some jobs require processing resources, while others might require storage resources.
5. **Dynamicity of Grid:** It becomes very important for the grid resource manager to keep track of the available resources in the grid because the resources may fail, or some new resources can join the current grid network at any point in time.

6. **Security:** There are two components of security in the grid network. The first component concerns job security over the node, ensuring that the node will not look into the data used by the job. The second component of security ensures that the user who submitted the job over a node is not looking at or accessing other data in that node. The grid environment must be able to overcome these limitations so that grid users will have continuous access to the available resources and jobs are executed over appropriate resources in a legitimate time, which will eventually uplift the performance of the grid environment.

Some of the prominent advantages of grid computing are listed below:

1. **Cost-Effective:** Buying a number of large servers for complex applications is no longer needed because the applications can be divided and distributed to small-sized servers. Further, the results can be combined and provided to the user after the job completion.
2. **Utilization of Idle Resources:** The site administrator can make policies to direct jobs to lightly loaded or free resources in the grid environment. It balances the load among all the computing resources in the grid environment.
3. **Modular Computing:** Grid computing supports a model of modular computing. A computing paradigm with no single point of failure is considered modular, where multiple resources are available and can handle a job in the case of a single resource failure in the grid environment.
4. **Grid Policies:** There are some policies that govern the functionality of the grid. For instance, a client residing in each server sends information to the master regarding the availability and nature of resources to execute the incoming job.
5. **Scalability:** The design of the grid system enables the addition of new resources at any instant of time for more computing power. Also, it allows uninstalling or removing some resources from the grid as per requirement.

1.4 SUMMARY

Grid computing is a popular computing platform all around the globe. It is a new distributed computing paradigm with immense potential to solve complex optimization problems. Based on the type of problem, there are different classes of grids that can be used to serve user requests. Several classifications of grids have been studied to meet user requirements. The development of grid computing infrastructure such as NetSolve, TeraGrid, Condor, and many more shows the prevalence of grid computing platforms in the computing world. The fundamentals of distributed computing, its characteristics, and its evolution in the modern computing world have been covered in this chapter. The need to switch to grid computing and how it serves the modern needs of computing in today's world has been discussed here. With grid computing, the utilization of idle resources is possible, and scalability allows adding new resources at any point in time or cutting out any resource from the grid according to requirements. A grid computing model is a five-layered architecture, having the application layer at the top and the fabric layer at the bottom of the computing model. The grid computing model has several key elements, such as job, resource, specifications, scheduling problems, and scheduler.

Current research trends show that grid computing has managed to draw the attention of the science and research community around the world. Researchers and scientists are working on it to minimize its limitations and expand its capabilities.

KEYWORDS

- **dynamicity**
- **grid computing**
- **modular computing**
- **NetSolve**
- **resource utilization**
- **TeraGrid.**

CHAPTER 2

Scheduling: Conventional and Bio-Inspired Algorithms

2.1 RESOURCE ALLOCATION SCHEMES

Scheduling of jobs and resource management are two major concerns of grid computing. Job scheduling has become a non-trivial issue in grid computing due to the increased number of users and their job requests. It is important to complete the execution of these jobs in minimum time and manage the grid resources at the same time. The distribution of jobs among the processors has been a major concern in the grid environment, with a seemingly increased number of job requests.

In order to meet the ongoing demands of computing users, an intelligent algorithm must be developed to perform scheduling and resource management. The algorithm will not only meet the users' job requirements but also finish the job execution in minimum time. Two conventional algorithms and their implementation in a grid computing environment have been discussed in this chapter. Conventional algorithms are well suited to static problems, but they often fail to give the desired performance due to the dynamic nature of the grid environment, resource, and job heterogeneity. Due to the weak performance of conventional algorithms, researchers came up with a solution to handle job scheduling and resource management. The proposed solution belongs to a class of swarm-based and evolutionary algorithms. Two swarm-based algorithms, ant colony optimization (ACO) and particle swarm optimization (PSO), and one evolutionary algorithm, that is, genetic algorithm (GA), and their implementation in a grid computing environment have been discussed in this chapter. The performance evaluation of these algorithms will be covered in later chapters.

Mastering Grid Computing: Scheduling and Resource Management.
Ankita & Sudip Kumar Sahana (Authors)

The management of resources in a distributed computing environment (Peleg, 2000) like a grid is a complex issue because of the size of the grid and the increasing number of user requests. The changing state of the grid has elevated the complexities since a machine (resource) can be added or may stop working at any point in time in the grid environment. Moreover, it is important to maintain a balance between the needs and requirements of a resource provider and a resource user because of the changing availability of the resources. Therefore, proper resource management and uniform scheduling policies are required for the regular and successful functioning of the grid environment. The resource allocation schemes are divided into three categories:

1. **Centralized Approach:** The user requests are directed to a single, centralized scheduler, which schedules the submitted jobs over the available resources. Though the resources are scattered across several regions, the information regarding the state of the resources as well as the jobs is contained within a single position, that is, the centralized scheduler. Hence, the decisions of this scheduling model are optimal. However, they are prone to a single point of failure and are limited to small-sized grids.

2. **Decentralized Approach:** In a decentralized model of resource allocation, the user requests are scheduled at different sites by individual schedulers independently. The local schedulers maintain their table of information regarding the state of resources and jobs. Any update in the state of the resource has to be maintained across each site at every local scheduler to avoid any discrepancy among the schedulers while making scheduling decisions. The decisions of this scheduling model may or may not be optimal. It is difficult to attain efficient grid schedulers because of the independent grid sites. Though the decentralized approach is scalable and works well in the grid environment, it is less efficient than a centralized approach to resource allocation.

3. **Hierarchical Approach:** It is a combination of a centralized and decentralized approach to resource allocation. A hierarchy is maintained among the schedulers. The schedulers in a hierarchy can communicate directly with the other schedulers above or below them. The information regarding the state of the resource is present at the lowest level.

2.2 JOB SCHEDULING

The process of assigning appropriate resources to jobs is called job scheduling. Job scheduling (Figure 2.1) is a non-trivial issue because it affects the performance of any computing system or organization.

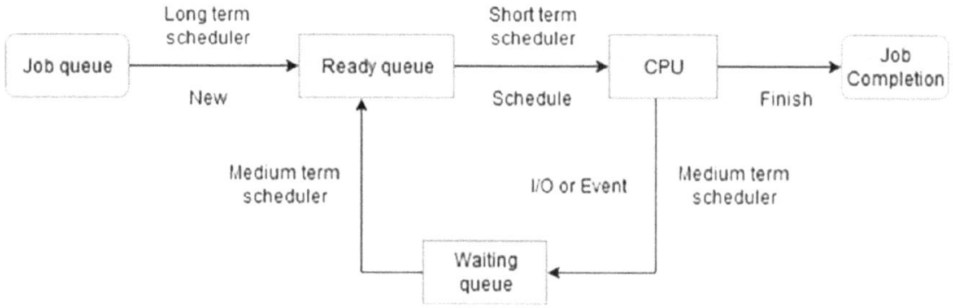

FIGURE 2.1 Process of scheduling.

2.2.1 *JOB SCHEDULING IN GRID ENVIRONMENT*

The proper assignment of the grid resources over jobs is a primary aspect of grid scheduling (Figure 2.2). Grid scheduling (Lu et al., 2010) involves making scheduling decisions for allocating the jobs over the grid resources.

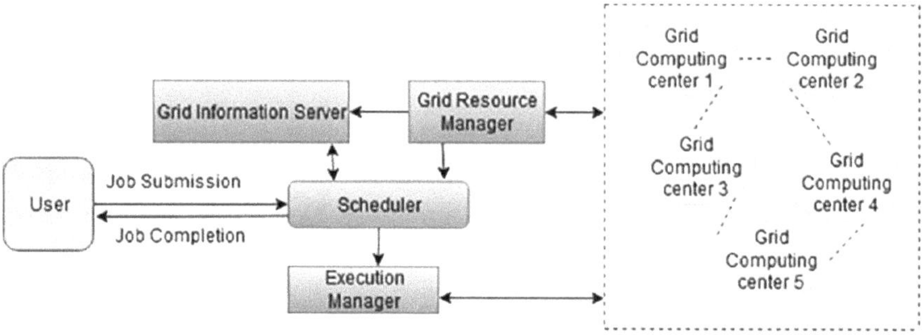

FIGURE 2.2 Grid scheduling.

Source: https://journals.plos.org/plosone/article?id=10.1371/journal.pone.0207596; https://doi.org/10.1371/journal.pone.0207596.g002.

The user submits the job to the grid scheduler through an interface or job portal. The Grid Information Server provides information to the grid scheduler. The Grid Resource Manager manages and monitors the status of the resources in the grid environment. The grid computing centers provide the necessary resources for job execution.

2.3 CONVENTIONAL ALGORITHMS

Conventional algorithms have been successful in finding solutions to simple and small sets of problems. These algorithms are incapable of dealing with large problem spaces and complex data sets. The next section discusses two conventional algorithms and their implementation for solving the grid scheduling problem. These algorithms are given in subsections.

2.3.1 FIRST COME FIRST SERVE (FCFS)

First come, first serve (FCFS) is one of the simplest and most conventional scheduling approaches, and scheduling decisions are made on the basis of the arrival time of jobs. FCFS is non-preemptive, such that a job, once assigned a resource, will never be preempted (leave the resource) until it finishes its execution. The sequence of arrival of jobs decides the running sequence of jobs, which means the job that arrives first (first come) will be scheduled first (first serve). The algorithm for FCFS in the grid computing environment is given in Algorithm 1.

Algorithm 1: FCFS in Grid Computing Environment

Input: Number of jobs and available resources.
Output: Allocation of each job to available resources.
begin

Initialize grid environment
Initialize scheduler components
g_i = next job in the job queue
r_i = next resource in the resource queue

while the queue of unscheduled jobs is not empty do

- **Step 1:** Add a new incoming job to the job queue of unscheduled jobs.

- **Step 2:** Select a job g_i from the job queue in the order of their arrival.
- **Step 3:** Select a resource r_i randomly from the resource queue.
- **Step 4:** if r_i is suitable and available to execute job g_i then Set job g_i to be scheduled on resource r_i

end if
end while

- **Step 5:** Repeat the above steps till all the jobs are scheduled over available resources.

end

A resource r_i is said to be suitable for executing a job g_i if r_i fulfills the processing requirement of g_i. The availability of resources indicates that the resource is ready to execute a job.

2.3.2 SHORTEST JOB FIRST (SJF)

Shortest job first (SJF) belongs to the conventional family of scheduling algorithms, which can be preemptive or non-preemptive. The jobs, in this case, are scheduled over the available resources based on their processing requirements. Jobs with low processing requirements are favored over jobs with high processing requirements.

The algorithm for SJF in the grid computing environment is given in Algorithm 2.

Algorithm 2: SJF in Grid Computing Environment

Input: Number of jobs and available resources.
Output: Allocation of each job to available resources.
begin

Initialize grid environment
Initialize scheduler components
g_i = next job in the job queue
r_i = next resource in the resource queue

while the queue of unscheduled jobs is not empty **do**

- **Step 1:** Add a new incoming job to the job queue of unscheduled jobs.
- **Step 2:** Select a job from the job queue in the ascending order of their job requirements.
- **Step 3:** **if** r_i is suitable and available to execute job g_i **then** Set job g_i to be scheduled on resource r_i

end if
end while

Repeat the above steps till all the jobs are scheduled over available resources.

end

2.3.2.1 SHORTCOMINGS OF CONVENTIONAL METHODS OF JOB SCHEDULING

Conventional methods like FCFS, SJF, Min-Min, and Max-Min algorithms are no longer suitable in modern times because of the increased complexities associated with jobs and resources. For example, FCFS is not a good approach for solving complex problems in modern times because it leads to poor resource utilization (RU; convoy effect) and high execution time. FCFS is non-preemptive, meaning that a job, once assigned a resource, will never be preempted (leave the resource) until it finishes its execution.

Conventional methods require complete information regarding the state of the system, which is not possible in a dynamic grid environment. These approaches provide an exact solution to the problem, which takes a considerable amount of time. There are cases when many mathematical programming methods have been incompetent in finding a good (optimal or near-optimal) solution to multi-objective optimization problems.

The conventional methods are not suitable for non-differentiable problems. It is notable that the problem of grid scheduling is NP-complete. The reason behind the shift from conventional to non-conventional modes of scheduling (Dave and Choudhary, 2016) has been witnessed because an approximate solution in less time to an NP-complete problem is sufficient in the current scheduling paradigm. The modern approaches are application-independent and can be applied to any kind of problem without having detailed information about the type of the problem or the state of the working environment.

A category of metaheuristics comprises population-based methods. These methods are inspired by nature and its phenomena, which have drawn the attention of researchers around the world. These methods are being used in different fields to solve multi-objective optimization problems. They are also known as bio-inspired methods and can be applied in a dynamic environment like a grid. In the context of finding solutions to the grid scheduling problem, the built-in structure of these methods can be used to adjust the convergence speed to reach an optimal solution.

2.4 BIO-INSPIRED ALGORITHMS

The shortcomings or disadvantages of conventional approaches have inspired the application of bio-inspired algorithms to solve multi-objective optimization problems. Though there are many complexities present in the diverse nature, natural phenomena or processes are balanced and follow an optimal plan. Non-conventional algorithms are recent advancements that have given researchers a new way of solving complex problems in science and engineering, especially NP-complete problems. These algorithms are based on the principles of nature as well as evolutionary theory and have been applied in different fields. The beautiful and competent design of nature has inspired researchers to mimic natural theory in technology. A mapping between these two, that is, nature and technology, can be easily done to understand the connection between them and solve the complex problems of computer science.

Bio-inspired algorithms are extensively used in the field of machine learning to solve complex problems in computer science and engineering. The nature of these problems is non-linear and has several non-linear constraints, which create various issues such as high dimensionality and time constraints to attain optimal solutions. Current research trends show that bio-inspired algorithms can provide potential means to handle such issues of traditional optimization algorithms and provide solutions to convoluted optimization problems. Bio-inspired algorithms have been used in many areas, including robotics, networking, gaming, data mining, and many more. Swarm algorithms and evolutionary algorithms together form a set of bio-inspired algorithms.

2.4.1 SWARM ALGORITHMS

Swarm intelligence (Blum and Merkle, 2008; Kennedy, 2006) is a subset of artificial intelligence (AI). It is generated in a decentralized and distributed environment with the help of the intelligence of the members of the swarm by replicating their behavior. This intelligence helps in designing more efficient algorithms that can find solutions to complicated real-world applications. These algorithms are popular because they are fast, robust, and cost-effective. The swarm algorithms discussed in this thesis are given in subsections.

2.4.1.1 ANT COLONY OPTIMIZATION (ACO)

Dorigo and Blum (2005) and his colleagues developed ant colony optimization (ACO) as a powerful metaheuristic to solve NP-complete problems at the beginning of the 1990s. Inspired by the indirect communication capability of ants, ACO is treated as a subgroup of the system of social insect approaches. The pheromone deposition of ants forms a pheromone trail, which is sensed by other ants in the search space to find food sources. It is notable here that the pheromone evaporates as time passes. Therefore, it can be said that ACO is a probabilistic approach because the path that leads the ants to the food source is highly dependent on the quantity of pheromones. The probability of the ants choosing a route is directly proportional to the quantity of pheromones deposited on that path. It has been applied in many application areas, such as routing, scheduling, assignment, and load balancing. We have chosen ACO, a powerful global optimizer, as our candidate solution to solve the job scheduling problem because of its suitability for solving NP-complete problems and its dynamic problem-solving nature.

The kth ant moves from state x to state y (Dorigo et al., 1996; Blum, 2005) using a probability value calculated from Equation 2.1:

$$P_{xy}^{k} = \frac{\left(\tau_{xy}^{a}\right)\left(\eta_{xy}^{\beta}\right)}{\sum_{z \in allowed_{y}} \left(\tau_{xz}^{a}\right).\left(\eta_{xz}^{\beta}\right)} \tag{2.1}$$

The pheromone update rule is given in Equation 2.2:

$$\tau_{xy} \leftarrow (1-\rho)\tau_{xy} + \Sigma_k \Delta\tau_{xy}^{k} \tag{2.2}$$

where; p_{xy}^{k} is the probability value that helps the ant to change its state; τ_{xy} is the measure of pheromone deposition of ants when it changes its location from one position to another. The basic theory of ACO states that the higher the pheromone deposition on a path, the higher the probability of that path being selected by the other ants; η_{xy} is the attractiveness of the move indicates the desirability of the ants to follow that path; α and β are the controlling parameters in ACO which regulate the value of other parameters. α controls the concentration of pheromones deposited by the ants (τ_{xy}) on the path it traverses. The value α is normally less than 1. β controls the attractiveness of the route. Length of the route is inversely proportional to the attractiveness of the route; ρ is the pheromone evaporation coefficient; τ_{xz} indicates the amount of pheromone deposited, that is, trail level for all other feasible state transitions; and η_{xy} indicates the attractiveness for all other feasible state transitions.

2.4.1.2 MAPPING OF ACO TO A GRID SCHEDULING PROBLEM

The mapping of ACO algorithms to a grid scheduling problem is given in Figure 2.3. In this figure, the ants are mapped to jobs, and the food sources are treated as resources. The scheduling policy (ACO conditions) decides

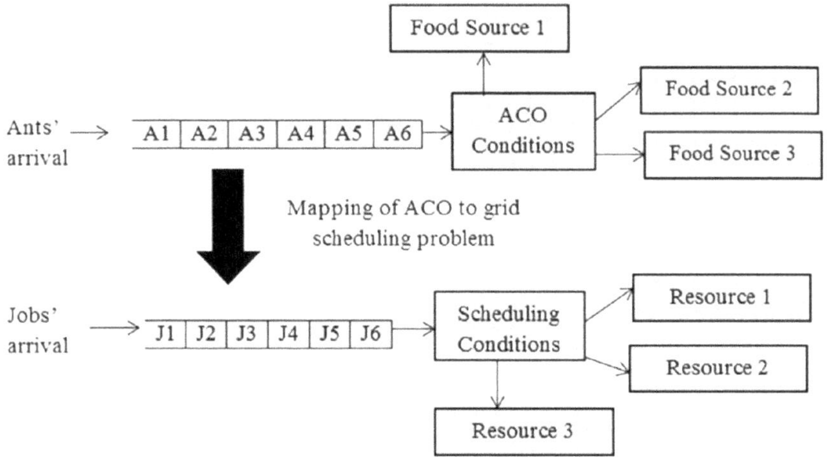

FIGURE 2.3 Mapping of ACO to a grid scheduling problem.

the allocation of a job to a resource in the grid computing network. An ant is created as soon as a job is submitted to the grid. Initially, the job (ant) randomly selects a resource (food) from the resource queue. The quality of the resource (food) is evaluated using its suitability and availability for an incoming job. The suitability of a resource indicates its computational capacity to execute a job. The resource with a higher pheromone value implies better computing capabilities. The pheromone value is calculated using Equation 2.2. The availability of a resource checks the current status of the resource (idle, busy, or not working).

The simple ACO algorithm in the grid computing environment is given in Algorithm 3.

Algorithm 3: ACO in Grid Computing Environment

Input: Number of jobs and available resources.
Output: Allocation of each job to available resources.
begin

Initialize grid environment
Initialize scheduler components (p_{xy}^{k} τ_{xy} $\eta\rho\alpha\beta$)
Initialize global best solution = s
Job list = add new job(), resource list= select resource()

while the queue of unscheduled jobs is not empty **do**

- **Step 1:** Add a new incoming job (ant) to the job queue of unscheduled jobs.
- **Step 2:** Generate the initial population of solutions in a random manner.
- **Step 3:** Calculate the probability value using Equation 2.1.
- **Step 4:** Check the availability and suitability of the resource (quality of food source).
- **Step 5:**

  if the resource is suitable for the job and available to execute **then**
  Update the pheromone values using Equation 2.2.

else
go to Step 1
end if

- **Step 6:** The job is scheduled over the selected resource.
- **Step 7: if** the value obtained in the current iteration is better than the global best solution **then**
Set s = current solution

end if
end while

- **Step 8:** Repeat the above steps till all the jobs are scheduled over available resources.

End

2.4.1.3 PARTICLE SWARM OPTIMIZATION (PSO)

Kennedy and Eberhart (1995) developed particle swarm optimization (PSO) by simulating the social (collective) behavior of living organisms, such as flocks of birds or schools of fish. Later, after much simplification of the algorithm, it was found that PSO works well for optimization problems and can be applied to large and complex data sets. There is no prior prerequisite for applying PSO to a problem, and hence it is a popular swarm-based metaheuristic for solving NP-complete problems. Initially, the particles in PSO are initialized with a set of possible solutions in a random manner. These solutions are called positions in PSO, and each particle has its velocity and position. They move through the search space to discover new solutions (positions) based on the fitness function.

The velocity and position update equation (Kennedy and Eberhart, 1995) of particles is given below (Equations 2.3 and 2.4):

$$v = \omega v + c1 * rand() * (pbest - present) + c2 * rand() * (gbest - present) \tag{2.3}$$

$$present = present + v \tag{2.4}$$

where; v denotes the particle velocity; and *present* denotes the current position of the particle.

For every particle, the *present* "value" is initially set by the algorithm, which is updated after Equations 2.3 and 2.4. *pbest* denotes "particle best" which denotes the best position acquired by an individual particle in the population space. *gbest* stands for "global best" which is the best position, that is, the best fitness value achieved by any particle in the population. *rand ()* introduces diversity in the search space, used to generate random numbers. ω is the inertia factor. c1 and c2 are learning factors. The inertia factor helps in controlling the effect of previous velocities over current velocity. The learning factors denote the social and cognitive components that inflect the movement of a particle towards its *pbest* and *gbest* positions.

2.4.1.4 MAPPING OF PSO TO GRID SCHEDULING PROBLEM

A simple representation of a PSO particle is given in Figure 2.4. The proper encoding of a problem solution to a PSO particle is the first requisite for the successful application of the PSO algorithm. Initially, all the particles (jobs) are randomly placed at different positions (resources). The velocity of the particle is updated using Equation 2.3, and the position of the particle is updated using Equation 2.4.

PSO Particle	J1	J2	J3	J4	J5	J6	J7
	R1	R2	R3	R4	R5	R6	R7

FIGURE 2.4 Mapping of PSO to a grid scheduling problem.

The PSO algorithm implemented in a grid environment to solve the job scheduling problem is given in Algorithm 4.

Algorithm 4: PSO in Grid Environment

Input: Number of jobs and available resources.
Output: Allocation of each job to available resources.
begin

Initialize grid environment
Initialize scheduler components
n = population size
G is the population of solutions.
joblist = add new job(), resourcelist = select resource()

while the queue of unscheduled jobs is not empty **do**

- **Step 1:** Add a new incoming job to the job queue of unscheduled jobs.
- **Step 2:**

for i = 1 to n **do**
Initialize G[i] randomly;
particle(job) velocity = v[i]=0;
particle(job) best = pbest[i]= G[i];
global best = gbest;

- **Step 3:** Find the fitness value of each particle.
- **Step 4:** Update the particle velocity v[i] using Equation 2.3.
- **Step 5:** Update the particle position (present) using Equation 2.4.

end for

- **Step 6: if** the fitness value of the particle, that is, fitness(present) > fitness(pbest) **then**
  update pbest = present

end if

- **Step 7: if** the fitness value of the particle, that is, fitness(present) > fitness(gbest) **then**
  update gbest = present

end if
return gbest;
end while
end

➢ **Fitness Function:** It is a parameter used to evaluate the fitness of the particles in the PSO. It determines the closeness of a given design solution in achieving certain objectives. In this case, the objective is to minimize the total completion time (TCT) of jobs and enhance RU. The fitness value in this case is expressed in Equation 2.5:

$$fitness = min\sum_{n=1}^{N}(TCT_{jobs}) + max\sum_{r=1}^{R}(RU_{resources}) \quad (2.5)$$

where *N* is a set of jobs and n ϵ *N*; *TCT* is the total completion time of the jobs; *R* is a set of resources and r ϵ *R*; and *RU* is the resource utilization.

2.4.2 EVOLUTIONARY ALGORITHMS

In the 1960s, Rechenberg introduced the notion of evolutionary computing for the very first time in the field of computer science and engineering. Evolutionary algorithms (Rechenberg, 1973) are a subset of non-conventional algorithms that are based on the principles of Darwinian theory of evolution. Like swarm algorithms, these algorithms are also problem-independent and do not require any prior information about the problem being solved. They involve several control parameters that affect the nature of the search process and their effectiveness. The evolutionary algorithm discussed in the thesis is given in subsections.

2.4.2.1 GENETIC ALGORITHM (GA)

The invention of GA is attributed to John Holland in Michigan in the 1960s. Later, he authored a book called "Adaptation in Natural and Artificial Systems," where he described natural evolution (inspired by Darwinian theory) and a foundation for transformation using GA. A candidate solution in a GA is represented by a chromosome. The GA operates on a group of solutions called a population rather than a single solution. Selection, crossover, and mutation are the three important parameters of GA.

The efficiency of GA depends on the following three aspects:

- Objective function (also known as fitness function);
- Genetic representation of the problem; and
- Genetic operators and their implementation.

2.4.2.1.1 Fitness function

The objective function in GA is called the fitness function. The fitness function evaluates the fitness of the candidate solutions for a problem. It helps in determining the chromosome that produces new children and continues into the next generation. A higher fitness value indicates a higher chance of survival for the chromosome. A fitness function is decided by the scheduler according to the requirements of the application.

2.4.2.1.2 Genetic representation of the problem and its implementation

The method of representing individual entities of the problem in GA is defined as genetic representation. A good genetic representation is important for formulating the problem and reaching better solutions. A representation of chromosomes is necessary to illustrate every entity in the population of GA. The two most popular chromosome representation schemes in GA, which are used for solving scheduling problems, are given below:

1. **Direct Representation:** It represents each solution as a list where the size of the list corresponds to the total number of jobs. The element [b] indicates the resource where job b will be allocated. The list contains integer values where the range of integers lies between [0, r – 1], where r is the number of resources.
2. **Permutation-based Representation:** The permutation-based representation also represents each solution as a list, but the size of the list is equal to the number of resources. In this case, the individual [b] indicates the resource which contains a list of jobs allocated to it. The list contains integer values where the range of integers lies between [0, n – 1], where n is the number of jobs.

2.4.2.1.3 Genetic operators and their implementation

There are three operators in a standard GA which include selection, crossover, and mutation.

1. **Selection:** The process of selection chooses solutions (parents) from the original population of solutions. The idea is to select good parent solutions that can survive into the next generation and reproduce new offspring. Some of the popular selection mechanisms are given below:
   1. **Roulette Wheel Selection:** This is a simple method of selecting an individual from the population of solutions. The chances of selection of an individual depend on their fitness. The probability of selection of an individual is high for fitter individuals. The slots in the wheel indicate the fitness value of the individuals.

ii. **Rank Selection:** In this method, the individual solutions are arranged in the order of their fitness values. Later, a rank is assigned to the individuals where the most fit individual has rank N (N is the highest rank) and rank 1 is assigned to the least fit individual.

iii. **Tournament Selection:** It is a popular selection method because it is easy to implement and gives better solutions to problems (Goldberg, 1989). This method involves the selection of individuals from the population of solutions that are set to compete against each other. The steps of the tournament selection are given below:

a. Tournament size is set such that $m \geq 2$.
b. A random permutation of chromosomes is generated in the population of solutions.
c. The fitness values of the first m chromosomes are calculated and compared with each other. The best values are copied into the next generation, and the rest of the string is discarded completely.
d. Another permutation is generated if the current permutation is completely exhausted.
e. The step from (c) to (e) is repeated till all the selections are done for the next generation.

iv. **Boltzmann Selection:** The selection rate is handled by a continuously changing temperature.

2. **Crossover:** The genetic information of the selected individuals is combined to form a new offspring. It enables exploration of the search space and finds unexplored regions to provide better quality solutions that can survive to the next generation. The selection of the crossover technique depends on the type of genetic representation chosen for representing the solutions in GA. The popular crossover methods are given below:

i. **One-Point Crossover:** A random position is selected in the two parent solutions, which serves as the swap point and divides the parents into two parts. The two-child solutions are generated by swapping the two parts of the parents (Figure 2.5).

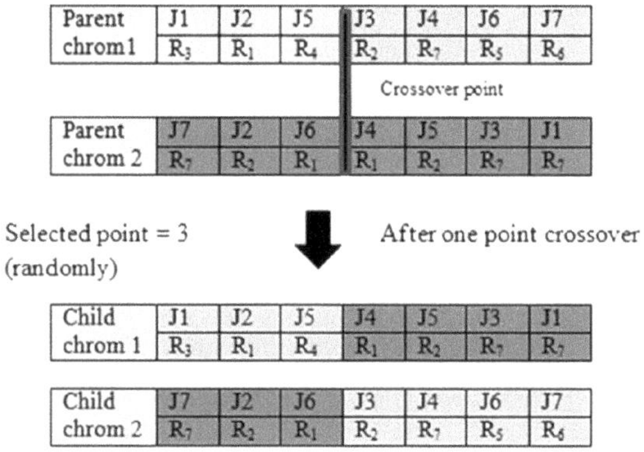

FIGURE 2.5 One-point crossover.

3. **Mutation:** The last operator, mutation, is optional and randomly modifies the offspring (child) generated in the crossover step of the GA (Figure 2.6). Mutation brings diversity in the GA which is required for the exploration of the search space.

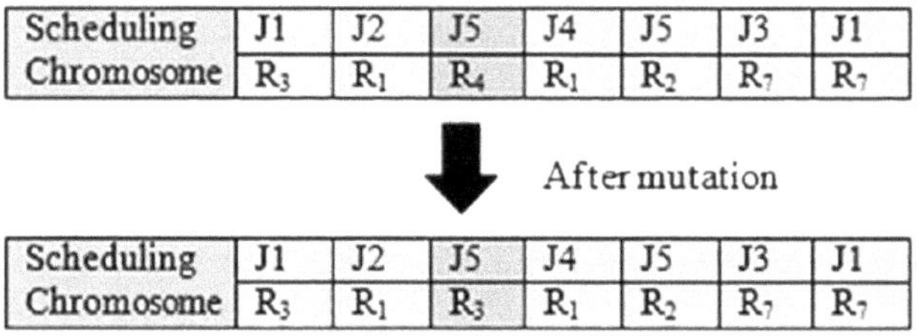

FIGURE 2.6 Mutation.

2.4.2.1.4 Mapping of GA to grid scheduling problem

During job scheduling in the grid environment, the GA allocates the job to the available processors in a random manner. It creates a population of solutions. The representation of the chromosome for the grid scheduling problem is shown in Figure 2.7. The chromosome contains the jobs (J1, J2, …, J7) which are positioned to the resources (R1, R2, …, R7) where these jobs will be executed. Here, the gene pool is a resource pool that consists of scheduling resources. The GA implemented in the grid environment to solve the problem of grid scheduling is given in Algorithm 5.

Jobs	J1	J2	J5	J3	J4	J6	J7	Resources	R_1	R_2	R_3	R_4	R_5	R_6	R_7

⬇

Scheduling Order	J1	J2	J5	J3	J4	J6	J7
Mapping	R_3	R_1	R_4	R_2	R_7	R_5	R_6

FIGURE 2.7 Mapping of GA to a grid scheduling problem.

Algorithm 4: GA in Grid Environment

Input: Number of jobs and available resources.
Output: Allocation of each job to available resources.
begin

Initialize grid environment
Initialize scheduler components
Probability of Crossover = p_c
Probability of Mutation = p_m
Number of generations = m

- **Step 1:** Add a workload containing a number of jobs
- **Step 2:** Initialize population of solutions R_y: Generation of the initial population of solutions in a random manner.

repeat

- **Step 3:** Selection operator ()
- **Step 4:** Crossover operator ()
- **Step 5:** Mutation operator ()
- **Step 6:** $R_{y'}$ is created containing chromosomes (job-resource assignment) with best fitness values
- **Step 7:** The jobs are scheduled over the first best-selected resource from R$_{y'}$ according to the fitness function.
- **Step 8:** Repeat until all the jobs are scheduled over the available resources.
- **Step 9:** Print the scheduling result.
- **Step 10:** Repeat until the number of generations

return the best solution
end

2.4.3 OTHER BIO-INSPIRED ALGORITHMS

Apart from the above-discussed swarm algorithms (Blum and Merkle 2008) and evolutionary algorithms (Coello et al. 2007), there are other prominent bio-inspired algorithms that offer promising solutions to a wide range of NP-complete or complex optimization problems. A review of the literature reveals a substantial number of bio-inspired algorithms developed in the last decade that imitate the biological behavior of living organisms to solve various optimization problems (Darwish 2018). Optimization is the process of finding the best possible solutions to a given problem. The next section summarizes some of the recent bio-inspired algorithms.

2.4.3.1 GENETIC BEE COLONY (GBC) ALGORITHM

GBC algorithm (Zhao et al., 2010) is a nature-inspired evolutionary algorithm that is capable of solving machine learning problems such as classification and selection problems. It is a combination of the traditional genetic algorithm (GA) and a new swarm algorithm, that is, the artificial bee colony algorithm (ABC). This algorithm (Ozturk et al., 2015) employs the qualities of both algorithms. The GA suffers from the problems of prematurity and local optima in the search space. The bee colony algorithm eliminates the problem of local convergence of the GA and helps in increasing the search speed and reducing the overall searching time. The ABC algorithm (Nseef et al., 2016) consists of three types of artificial bees: the onlooker bees, the employed bees, and the scout bees. The steps of the ABC algorithm are as follows:

1. **Setting Parameters of ABC:** At first, the parameters of the ABC algorithm, such as population size (PS), the limit parameter, and total numbers, are initialized.
2. **Population Size Initialization:** The solutions are generated randomly after the initialization of parameters.
3. **Assessment of Population Solutions:** The population of solutions is assessed using objective functions.
4. **Employee Bee:** The employed bees are a type of bee that is assigned a particular job to discover a new food source in its surrounding environment. After the discovery of the food source, the employed bee gradually moves into the category of candidate

neighbor solutions with its discovered food source in the neighboring environment. The employed bees carry the nectar amount from the discovered food sources, which is then evaluated by the algorithm. If the nectar amount collected by the employed bee from the newly discovered food source is greater than the nectar amounts available at the current food source, then the newly detected food source will be memorized.

5. **Onlooker Bee:** In this phase, the onlooker bees use the information provided by the employed bees to start their search process. They begin their food source search in the vicinity of the previously discovered food source by the employed bees and also cover other competent areas in the exploration process of the food source. Both types of bees (onlooker and employed) work on the betterment of their current solutions by exploring their nearby areas.

6. **Scout Bee:** After the successful detection of a food source, the employee bee converts into scout bees, and they again start the discovery of a new food source in the solution space. The increased number of scout bees can be controlled by setting a limit parameter to indicate the number of trials. When the current solution can no longer be improved, a random search may be applied to discover a new food source.

7. **GA Parameters:** The fundamental GA operators, such as crossover and mutation, provide a better option to solve binary optimization problems in comparison to the ABC algorithm.

   The combination of the ABC algorithm and GA can be performed in the given four steps:

   - In the vicinity of the currently available food source, two other new food sources can be selected randomly to identify a proposed solution.
   - The first operator and the two-point crossover operator are applied between the two current neighbors to develop food sources for children.
   - In the next step, the swap or mutation operator can be applied to the food sources of children to generate grandchildren's food sources.

- Out of the children's food sources and grandchildren's food sources, the best food source will be selected as a neighborhood food source of the computed solution.

In this manner, the ABC algorithm's performance can easily be enhanced in binary optimization problems.

2.4.3.2 FISH SWARM ALGORITHM (FSA)

The fish swarm algorithm (FSA) algorithm (Neshat et al., 2012) is one of the intelligent swarm optimization algorithms that have important attributes such as quick convergence speed as well as deep and efficient search mechanisms. This algorithm imitates the nature of fish, and each fish can conduct its search for food sources in different manners. The fish can exchange information with each other to reach global optimization. There are several phases of the FSA algorithm, which are briefly described below:

1. **Preying or Predacious Behavior Phase:** In the preying phase, if Ni represents the present position of the fish and the artificial fish performs a random selection and selects Nj from its visual range, then there are two possible cases: in the first case, if $f(Ni) < f(Nj)$, the artificial fish will proceed in the direction of (Nj–Ni) or from Ni to Ni. In the second situation, the artificial fish can continue random selection to choose the next state Nj.
2. **Swarm Behavior Phase:** In the next phase, the artificial fish will explore the central position of its present neighborhood fish.
3. **Following Behavior Phase:** The artificial fish, say Ni, will move towards the best fish found in its local neighborhood.
4. Random Behavior Phase: The artificial fish in this phase apply a random selection approach to select a position in its observable range and gradually drift towards that selected position.
5. **Best Behavior Phase:** In this phase, the finest behavior will be chosen to update the present state of the artificial fish. This is the last phase, which indicates the successful completion of the previous phases.

2.4.3.3 ELEPHANT SEARCH ALGORITHM (ESA)

The elephant search algorithm (ESA) (Deb et al., 2016) is a member of heuristic optimization algorithms (Deb et al., 2015), and it imitates the behavior and traits of elephants. It follows a dual search procedure where the search agents are partitioned into two groups. Usually, elephants tend to live in groups, where each group is segregated into one or more subgroups under the supervision of the oldest elephant in the main group. Socially, female elephants prefer to live in groups, while male elephants choose to live in isolation. The male members perform the task of exploration, while the female elephants are responsible for spatial enhancement. There are three important features of ESA as an efficient search optimization algorithm:

- In order to obtain an optimal solution, the search process repeatedly improves the current solution.
- The main female elephant carries out a comprehensive search locally at some places where the chances of getting the best solution are high.
- The male is assigned the responsibility of performing explorations out of local optima.

2.4.3.4 MOTH FLAME OPTIMIZATION (MFO)

The MFO (Mirjalili, 2015; Shehab et al., 2020) is a recent search optimization algorithm. Moths are identical to butterflies in their behavior. The moths follow their way of navigation and fly towards moonlight during nighttime. The technique followed by the moths to navigate during nighttime is called transverse orientation. Mathematically, moths indicate the candidate solutions, and the position of moths in solution space indicates the variables of the problem.

2.4.3.5 GREY WOLF OPTIMIZATION (GWO)

The grey wolf optimization (GWO) algorithm (Mirjalili et al., 2014) belongs to a group of the latest meta-heuristic algorithms (Faris et al., 2018) and has been motivated by the hunting and leadership attributes of grey wolves. These wolves are related to the Canidae family. The grey wolves tend to live in groups, which are led by the alpha wolf of the group. The alpha wolf is the leader of a particular group and is liable to make critical decisions such as hunting and sleeping areas. The beta wolf belongs to the second category of grey wolves, whose job is to assist the alpha wolf in making important decisions. The third category is omega wolves, whose job is to provide information to the other wolves. The rest of the wolves are called delta wolves and are pledged to dominate the omega wolves. The phases of the GWO algorithm can be formulated in three steps:

- Locate, quest, and reach the prey;
- Seek, encircle, and intimidate the prey; and
- Strike towards the prey.

Among all the solutions, the fittest solution is considered as alpha wolf. The second-best solution is known as beta and the third best solution is known as delta wolves. The remaining omega wolves belong to the other candidate solutions.

2.4.3.6 CHICKEN SWARM OPTIMIZATION ALGORITHM (CSOA)

The chicken swarm optimization algorithm (CSOA) (Meng et al., 2014) is a new swarm optimization algorithm that imitates the nature of chicken swarms and their ranking order. Lately, the literature study suggests that these algorithms have proven their potential in solving multi-objective optimization problems (Zouache et al., 2019). Different groups depict the swarm of chickens, where each group contains only one rooster and several chicks and hens. Competition takes place among different chickens with a given hierarchical order. The ranking order holds an important place in the swarm because it affects the social lives of chickens, hens, chicks, and mother hens. The nature of the chicken swarm changes with the presence of male or female chickens in the swarm. The leader rooster is responsible for searching for food and actively fights with other chickens in the vicinity of its search area, that is, around the group. The chickens that search for food will be persistent with the leader roosters, and some submissive chickens will be standing in the identical place of the group to find their food. The competition exists between the chickens, but the baby chicks find food around their mother hen. Mathematically, the CSOA can be formulated as follows: the swarm of chickens is composed of many groups, and each group comprises hens, chicks, and one rooster. The chickens with the best fitness values will be regarded as roosters, whereas the chickens with the worst values are considered chicks. The remaining chickens are considered hens, who are free to decide which group they want to live in.

2.4.3.7 CAT SWARM OPTIMIZATION (CSO)

The cat swarm optimization (CSO) algorithm (Chu et al., 2006) is a new optimization algorithm that impersonates the behavior of cats. In the last few years, CSO (Ihsan et al., 2021) has been used to solve optimization problems. There are different modes of cats in the CSO algorithm. The seeking mode signifies that the cats are resting, but they are still alert. In the tracing mode, the cats perform a local search to find the good (optimal) solution to the given optimization problem.

2.4.3.7.1 Seeking mode

The seeking behavior of cats in the CSO algorithm has four major factors:

1. **Seeking Memory Pool (SMP):** It indicates the size of the pool of seeking memory.
2. **Seeking Range of Selected Dimension (SRD):** It determines the value of maxima and minima of the seeking range.
3. **Count of Dimensions to Change (CDC):** It defines the number of dimensions that are possible to show variation in the seeking mode of the CSO algorithm.
4. **Self-Position Consideration (SPC):** It is a Boolean-valued variable. A mixture ratio (MR) is defined as a population fraction having a smaller value, which assures that most of the time, cats are in two states, namely observing and resting. The seeking process of the CSO algorithm has been briefly discussed below:
   - The MR value is selected randomly as a part of the population fraction n_p for the seeking cats in the algorithm.
   - In the next step, SMP copies are prepared for the ith cat.
   - The position of each copy is updated randomly in the form of a plus or minus SRD fraction of the value of the current position and replaced accordingly.
   - The evaluation of the fitness value of all the copies is completed.
   - The probability values of individual candidates from all the available copies are computed, and the copy with the best probability value is placed at the position of the seeking cat.
   - Step 2 – tracing mode is repeated to include all the seeking cats in the algorithm.

2.4.3.7.2 Tracing mode

In an optimization process, tracing mode is treated as an exploration technique where the cats chase the desired target with strong energy. The fast chase of a cat can easily be modeled in a mathematical equation by changing the cat's position.

2.4.3.8 WHALE OPTIMIZATION ALGORITHM (WOA)

The whale optimization algorithm (WOA) (Mirjalili and Lewis, 2016; Gharehchopogh and Gholizadeh, 2019) is another metaheuristic that provides solutions for complex engineering problems. Out of all the mammals, whales are the largest, and they are an extraordinary species. Some of the significant members of this class are killer, humpback, blue, and finback whales. Whales spend most of their time breathing in seas and oceans, which deprives them of getting sleep. They are a type of mammal whose only half of the brain can sleep. They may live in a group or can sustain themselves alone. Killer whales prefer to reside with their family, while humpback whales are known as the largest whales, and their main targets are small fish and krill species. The brains of whales contain distinct cells in precise regions. These cells govern different feelings, emotions, and aspects of human nature. Whales are smarter than humans because they have twice the number of cells as humans do, which contributes to their intelligence. Whales are capable of thinking, communicating, learning, and developing their dialects. A type of hunting technique used by humpback whales, known as bubble-net feeding, is a special feature of these whales.

2.4.3.9 ARTIFICIAL ALGAE ALGORITHM (AAA)

As the name suggests, the artificial algae algorithm (AAA) (Uymaz et al., 2015) is inspired by the living habits and nature of microalgae. It is a new bio-inspired algorithm that draws its inspiration from the lifestyles of algae, such as reproduction, algal habits, and adaptation to the neighboring environment to modify the main species. Hence, there are three important processes of algae, namely the process of evolution, helical movement, and adaptation. The population of algae is called algal colonies, and the cells in these colonies will develop to a larger size if they receive an adequate amount of sunlight. If the algae cells grow, it will lead to the growth of algal colonies. However, the process of growth of algal colonies may be affected due to insufficient light. In the next movement, that is, the helical movement, the individual algal colonies will be moving towards the best algal colony.

2.5 SUMMARY

This chapter provides methodologies for solving the job scheduling problem in the grid environment. It describes the shortcomings of conventional methods for solving a grid scheduling problem. Popular conventional techniques and some prominent bio-inspired approaches, as well as their mapping in the grid environment to solve the job scheduling problem and perform resource management, are devised in this chapter. This chapter consists of the research methodologies proposed and implemented to solve the problem of grid scheduling. The reason for choosing a metaheuristic over conventional scheduling algorithms is studied in this chapter. Standard metaheuristics such as ACO, PSO, and genetic algorithm (GA), along with their mapping to the grid scheduling problem, are discussed.

KEYWORDS

- **Ant colony optimization**
- **artificial algae algorithm**
- **cat swarm optimization**
- **chicken swarm optimization algorithm**
- **genetic algorithm**
- **metaheuristics**
- **particle swarm optimization**
- **resource management**
- **whale optimization algorithm**
- **wolf optimization algorithm.**

CHAPTER 3

Work Done Using Conventional and Bio-Inspired Algorithms

3.1 INTRODUCTION

Grid scheduling is an intrinsic component of grid computing infrastructure. This chapter collectively brings out work done using different scheduling approaches applied in the grid environment. Different works on scheduling and resource management have been discussed in this chapter. These problems are called multiobjective optimization problems because they involve more than one objective function to be optimized simultaneously. This is the case when an optimal decision is required to be made between two or more mutually dependent objective functions. In order to deal with the conflicting objectives and satisfy other constraints, an efficient algorithm is needed to find an optimal solution. The last decade has seen substantial contributions of bio-inspired algorithms in solving multiobjective optimization problems. These algorithms have attracted researchers from all over the world to solve static as well as dynamic optimization problems. They have been motivated by natural phenomena and biological evolution. In the very beginning, we had stand-alone algorithms, but later, hybrid algorithms were developed to produce more efficient results. Though hybrid algorithms are a little more complex compared to individual algorithms, they are more powerful and have the advantages of one or more candidate (hybridized) algorithms. In this chapter, we have studied different bioinspired as well as conventional algorithms implemented in the grid environment to schedule jobs and manage resources efficiently. Additionally, several research works have been included that incorporate conventional

Mastering Grid Computing: Scheduling and Resource Management.
Ankita & Sudip Kumar Sahana (Authors)

as well as non-conventional (bio-inspired) approaches to solve the grid scheduling problem and manage resources in the grid environment.

Scheduling, in simplest terms, is defined as the assignment of jobs over the resources in a computing environment. There are different forms of scheduling discussed below:

1. **Centralized and Decentralized Scheduling:** The process of centralized scheduling consists of a single scheduler that manages a set of resources belonging to a single organization. In decentralized scheduling, there are several entities, such as GridWay, Grid Resource Broker, and Metaschedulers, that manage a set of resources that may belong to several organizations. Decentralized scheduling follows part of a hierarchical model where scheduling decisions are made separately at different levels and require coordination among the levels for an effective solution.

2. **Optimal and Suboptimal Scheduling:** Optimal scheduling is achieved when the resource requirements of a job and the grid system state are known in advance under certain optimal conditions. The feasibility of such scheduling is not possible in a dynamic environment like the grid. A suboptimal type of scheduling is feasible in a grid environment, and hence suboptimal solutions are obtained because there is no possible method to draw information about the actual state of the grid.

3. **Static and Dynamic Scheduling:** A scheduling method that requires detailed information about the state of the grid is called static scheduling. A grid computing framework does not support static scheduling because it requires the state of the grid to remain unchanged before and after the completion of the scheduling process. Dynamic scheduling, or online scheduling, is a better option as it can handle jobs and resources that appear and disappear at any time in a dynamic grid environment.

4. **Immediate Mode Scheduling:** This is a simple scheduling approach where jobs are allocated to resources immediately as soon as the jobs arrive in the grid system.

5. **Preemptive and Non-Preemptive Scheduling:** The scheduling mode is said to be non-preemptive if the job completes its

execution on the resource and never leaves it before its completion. The scheduling mode is said to be preemptive if the execution of the current job is suspended from the resource and transferred to another resource when a higher-priority job enters the grid system.

6. **Adaptive Scheduling:** The scheduling methods must be adapted to incorporate the changing behavior of the grid environment. This method of scheduling stores information about the current resource status and also makes predictions about the future resource status in order to nullify the chances of performance degradation of the grid environment.
7. **Batch Mode Scheduling:** The jobs are organized into several groups called batches. These batches are sent to the appropriate resources by the scheduler, and the result of the execution of the entire batch comes after some time interval. The next batch of jobs is sent as soon as the processing result of the previous batch comes to the user.

3.1.1 SCHEDULER

A scheduler places a job over a resource based on the job's requirements and tracks the job and resource status until it finishes its execution. There are different types of schedulers listed below:

1. **The Grid Scheduler:** It is the most important entity in a grid system. It is responsible for selecting and allocating a resource from a set of resources for a particular job under given constraints.
2. **Local Schedulers:** These, sometimes called cluster schedulers, are responsible for assigning jobs to the resources in the same regional or local network.
3. **Meta-Schedulers:** The meta-brokers are used for the management of jobs/applications that are scheduled at multiple resources across various grid systems. These schedulers also help maintain a uniform load across different systems.
4. **Super-Schedulers:** These perform a centralized scheduling approach where the scheduler manages the selection of resources

and the execution of jobs over the chosen resources. The jobs are assigned to a single computing resource during their execution.

5. **Enterprise Schedulers:** These schedulers are viable in an enterprise that depends on local schedulers of the enterprise for job-resource management.
6. **Resource-Oriented Schedulers:** The goal of these schedulers is to escalate resource utilization (RU) in a computing network.
7. **High-Efficiency Schedulers:** These aim to achieve maximum efficiency of the system, and hence they are focused on elevating job performance, which eventually enhances the efficiency of the grid environment.

3.1.2 STAGES OF GRID SCHEDULING

The scheduling process of the grid primarily consists of four steps:

1. **A Collection of Information:** This is the first step of grid scheduling, sometimes called resource discovery. Complete and updated information about the status of available resources and jobs is made available to the grid scheduler for crucial decisions regarding job scheduling in the grid environment.
2. **Selection of Appropriate Resources:** The process of resource selection is based on the needs of the job and the characteristics of the resource. The scheduling algorithm decides the selection of resources based on some optimization criteria.
3. **Allocation of Job:** The job is allocated to the selected resource for execution.
4. **Job Execution and Monitoring of Performance:** The execution of the job is tracked by the grid scheduler. Additionally, the scheduler keeps monitoring the status of the resource for possible failures.

3.2 RESOURCE MANAGEMENT

In general, resource management is the efficient utilization of resources in the best possible manner. It involves deep planning and analysis of the job requirements as well as resource availability to make appropriate job-resource assignments in any working environment. Resource management consists of several approaches that can be used for handling resources.

A resource can be anything—human skills, information technology (IT), time, inventory, and many more depending on the type of organization. Resource management is focused on the optimization and performance of the resources.

3.2.1 STAGES IN RESOURCE MANAGEMENT

Resource management is accomplished through several stages stated below:

1. **Estimation:** This is the first stage where the resource management team decides the necessary resources required for the success of a project and the cost of running the project. The team members of the project communicate with the client side to discuss the requirements before the beginning of the project.
2. **Planning:** As soon as the requirements are stated from the client side, the project manager starts looking into the available resource pool. If the available resources are sufficient for fulfilling the project requirements, the project execution can begin in the next moment, or other measures are taken to set constraints on the available resource pool.
3. **Execution:** This is the phase when resources are scheduled over different jobs by analyzing the job requirements. The jobs are scheduled over the available resources, followed by the job execution.
4. **Analysis:** This phase allows the project manager to set measures to analyze the performance of the project once it is completed.
5. **Optimization:** In this phase, the project manager makes effective decisions in real-time to modify the approaches in order to minimize costs and optimize other resources. Proper resource management is necessary to optimize resources and improve efficiency.

There are some techniques that can be used to perform effective resource management:

1. **Resource Allocation:** It makes use of the available resources in the resource repository in the most efficient manner. The resource manager must have a complete report of available resources to make effective resource allocation.
2. **Resource Leveling:** This technique helps to uncover the under-used resources whose potential has not been fully realized in the organization.
3. **Resource Forecasting:** This technique allows the resource manager to predict future resource requirements before the actual start of the project. It also unveils the potential risks and unexpected costs that may be incurred after the completion of the project.

Resource management has been a critical issue for the research community in different domains. Natural resources, computing resources, and human resources all require efficient and effective management techniques to utilize the true potential of these resources.

3.3 GRID RESOURCE MANAGEMENT (GRM)

Grid computing is becoming a popular platform for user applications that require more computing power than a single resource can provide to solve scheduling problems at a reasonable cost and time. The resources of the grid, for example, clusters, supercomputers, sensors, and storage devices, are scattered around various regions across the territories. The availability of the internet and grid computing technology has made substantial advancements in the modern way of computing.

The goal of grid resource management (GRM) is to allocate jobs over different grid resources with the objective of:

- Reduce execution time of job;
- Minimize waiting time for the job;
- Optimize resource utilization;
- Distribute workload among the resources uniformly.

The GRM involves job scheduling and focuses on all aspects of a resource such as its allocation, utilization, and load, and also monitors the status of the resource. There are several elements or components of GRM (Figure 3.1).

1. **Resource Allocation:** It is accompanied by resource discovery and resource selection. The resources are stored in a central server, which contains complete information about the processing capabilities and current status of the resources. The resources are selected from the repository based on their current availability and suitability for a particular job. Once a resource is selected, it is allocated to the job for its execution.

2. **Resource Utilization (RU):** It is an important factor that affects the performance of the grid environment. Resource management enables the resources to the users, which considers both user and resource provider satisfaction. Optimal RU helps in achieving improved system performance.

3. **Load Balancing:** The workload distribution among the resources of the grid must be done in a uniform manner so that neither of the resources in the grid becomes overutilized nor underutilized. The utilization of all the resources in the grid should be uniform for effective RU.

4. **Resource Monitoring:** It is important to keep track of the status of the resources in a dynamic grid environment. It is possible that a new resource can be added to an existing grid infrastructure, or an existing resource may become unavailable at any point in time.

5. **Grid Scheduling:** Scheduling is a central part of a grid computing environment. The jobs of the grid are scheduled over appropriate resources according to the priority of the job and resource. A scheduling technique is adopted that finds the right matching of job to resource with the objective of reducing the TCT of jobs, which eventually elevates the performance of the job and the grid.

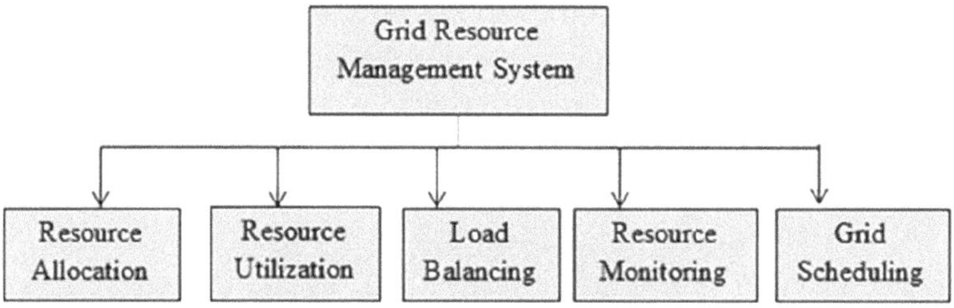

FIGURE 3.1 Elements of grid resource management (GRM).

A number of scheduling algorithms have been developed to schedule jobs over the resources in the grid environment. The conventional algorithms are deterministic approaches that have been applied to grid scheduling problems for many years. In a grid computing environment, resource management is an application that controls the way resources are used to enhance RU and job performance. The taxonomy of GRM shows a literature report on different scheduling algorithms applied in the grid computing environment (Table 3.1).

3.3.1 GRID RESOURCE MANAGEMENT (GRM): CONVENTIONAL ALGORITHMS

In the early period, scheduling techniques like FCFS, max-min, min-min, round robin, and SJF were used to schedule jobs over resources in a distributed environment. These techniques are no longer suitable for scheduling jobs because of the changing grid environment and the increased number of jobs. The job size and its heterogeneity, as well as resource heterogeneity, add more complexities to the grid scheduling problem. The number of jobs and resources changes continuously in the grid environment over time. This requires an efficient scheduling mechanism to allocate resources to jobs and handle the challenges of the grid environment. There are many well-known works in the area of grid scheduling and resource management using conventional algorithms at both national and international levels.

3.3.1.1 NATIONAL WORK ON GRID RESOURCE MANAGEMENT (GRM) USING CONVENTIONAL ALGORITHMS

Many researchers have applied different scheduling algorithms to the Grid Scheduling Problem to find an optimal solution. The efficiency of grid computing depends heavily on the way its resources are scheduled. Kokilavani and Amalarethinam (2010) provided a report on the application of conventional techniques to the grid scheduling problem. Mishra et al. (2014) have presented several challenges of scheduling in the grid environment. They have introduced a new way of classifying the scheduling algorithms and the performance metrics to determine their efficiency. Prajapati and Shah (2014) have discussed important concepts of resource and application scheduling in the grid environment. It also includes different scheduling systems, algorithms, and methodologies to measure the efficiency of these algorithms.

TABLE 3.1 Taxonomy on Grid Resource Management (GRM)

Author	Topic	Concept	Findings
Menasce and Casalicchio (2004)	A framework for resource allocation in grid computing.	In this chapter, the resource allocation problem is formalized for an enterprise application which consists of a set of SLA (service level agreement) constraints and has different requisites for resources and services in a grid environment.	Optimal resource allocation with minimum cost and time.
Buyya and Abramson (2000)	Grid resource management, scheduling, and computational economy.	This chapter presents various problems encountered in scheduling and resource management and highlights a few scheduling techniques using the concepts of computational economy.	In the future, a generic structure called GRACE (grid architecture for computational economy) can be developed for grid computational economy.
Balaton and Gombás (2003)	Resource and job monitoring in the grid.	This chapter studies the problems in resource monitoring and introduces a monitoring system based on GMA (grid monitoring architecture), which is flexible and efficient in providing the status of resources and running jobs.	The monitoring system has been implemented and is currently being operated in the GridLab project.
Buyya and Chapin (2000)	Architectural models for resource management in the grid.	This chapter discusses three architectural models (hierarchical, abstract owner, and computational) for grid resource management.	All three models are presented here in high-level form and can be used to implement future grid systems.
Buyya et al. (2002)	Economic models for resource management and scheduling in grid computing.	The author proposes a framework based on the computational economy (Nimrod/G) for the assignment of resources. The scheduling controls the resource request and delivery in the grid environment.	Optimal and effective resource utilization. It provides different ways to trade-off between cost and deadline of an application which makes Grid a basis for standard computing.
Kandagatla (2003)	Survey and taxonomy of grid resource management systems.	This chapter presents a survey report on existing grid resource management architectures and classification schemes for resource management architectures.	Different issues in resource management systems (RMS) and a survey report containing RMS architecture in different grid systems are discussed.

TABLE 3.1 *(Continued)*

Author	Topic	Concept	Findings
Qureshi et al. (2014)	Survey on grid resource allocation mechanisms.	This chapter provides a comprehensive survey report on various resource allocation techniques used in different grid architectures.	Comparison of resource allocation schemes based on their complexity, optimality, objective function, and searching technique. It helps in selecting the most relevant allocation mechanism for a particular grid system.
Sahana and Ankita (2019)	A comprehensive survey on computational grid resource management.	The author has classified resource allocation strategies into four categories – analytical, progressive, local search, and swarm-based.	The algorithms and their implementation in solving real-world problems are discussed in detail.
Czajkowski et al. (1999)	Resource co-allocation in computational grids.	In this chapter, the problems of co-allocation are discussed, and mechanisms that facilitate the co-allocation of resources in the grid environment are provided.	The author has introduced two different techniques – the atomic transaction approach and the innovative interactive approach, to solve the problem resource of co-allocation.
Cao et al. (2002)	Agent-based resource management for grid computing.	The author has discussed about the issues in resource management and introduces an agent-based mechanism called A4 (agile architecture and autonomous agents) for grid resource management.	A4 methodology is modeled, and simulation is carried out using PMA (performance monitor and advisor).
Yousif et al. (2015)	Job scheduling algorithms on grid computing: state-of-the-art.	In this chapter, the author has presented an extensive survey report on scheduling and various scheduling approaches in a grid computing environment.	The survey covers the basic approaches, such as max-min and min-min, as well as the swarm intelligence techniques.
Fatos Xhafa and Abraham (2008)	Meta-heuristics for grid scheduling problems.	In this chapter, the author presents an analysis of grid scheduling and also states the importance of heuristic and meta-heuristic approaches for solving grid scheduling problems.	The author deeply investigates the complexities of scheduling in computational grids and justifies the use of heuristic and meta-heuristic approaches for scheduling.

TABLE 3.1 *(Continued)*

Author	Topic	Concept	Findings
Prajapati and Shah (2014)	Scheduling in a grid computing environment.	This chapter presents a detailed overview of grid computing systems and scheduling (resource and application scheduling) in a grid environment.	It provides a classification of scheduling algorithms applied in the grid environment.
Mishra et al. (2014)	A survey on scheduling heuristics in a grid computing environment.	The chapter presents a comprehensive study of grid computing and scheduling mechanisms. It also proposes a new classification approach for classifying scheduling algorithms.	A detailed assessment of the scheduling techniques has been done on the basis of the parameters used in scheduling.
Flórez et al. (2015)	Methods for job scheduling on computational grids: review and comparison.	This chapter uses an ETC model (expected time to compute) to present a study report on heuristics and meta-heuristics for solving grid scheduling problems.	This chapter provides a deep analysis and comparison of scheduling algorithms that can assist aspiring researchers in studying the available scheduling techniques for performing future research.

Panda et al. (2013) have given semi-interquartile scheduling based on Min-Min and Max-Min heuristics for allocating resources to jobs. The experimental results have shown that their method has better scheduling results in terms of makespan and RU in comparison to other conventional methods. Kfatheen and Marimuthu (2017) have developed an efficient task-scheduling algorithm using the ETC matrix (expected time to compute) to solve the scheduling problem in the grid environment. The experimental analysis has been carried out using the GridSim simulation toolkit. The results show that the algorithm is able to manage workload among the resources and minimize the makespan of jobs. Kokilavani and Amalarethinam (2011) have proposed a modification to the conventional Min-Min algorithm. The conventional Min-Min algorithm fails to balance the load among the resources. The proposed algorithm schedules the jobs, minimizes makespan, and also balances the load among the resources in the grid environment. Ghosh et al. (2012) have proposed a load-balanced Max-Min scheduling heuristic, which initially schedules the jobs using the conventional Max-Min and then reschedules the tasks to utilize the idle resources. The experimental results show improved RU and a load-balanced schedule. Kfatheen and Banu (2015) have proposed a scheduling approach that is a combination of two conventional scheduling techniques, namely Min-Min and Max-Min. The results show that the proposed algorithm reduces the makespan in comparison to the parent algorithms.

Shanthini et al. (2015) have proposed a scheduling approach that combines features of two algorithms – the best gap search (BGS) and apparent tardiness cost (ATC) algorithm. The said algorithm reduces the total weighted tardiness of the jobs. Goswami and Das (2015) have modified the nearest deadline first scheduled (NDFS) algorithm. The authors have added the average load to the active load of the resource to find a solution for load distribution among the resources of the grid. The experimental results show that the efficiency of their algorithm has been improved by incorporating more parallelism in the computation.

3.3.1.2 INTERNATIONAL WORK ON GRID RESOURCE MANAGEMENT (GRM) USING CONVENTIONAL ALGORITHMS

In a grid network, there can be thousands of systems, and hence it is not possible to manually assign jobs to these systems. An effective scheduling algorithm is extremely needed to fully utilize the services provided by the grid environment. The classification helped in unveiling mechanisms that are being followed in the application of resource management systems (RMS) for computational grids. Fibich et al. (2005) have presented a model that contains important definitions, constraints, and terminologies regarding the grid scheduling problem.

The authors have also studied the properties of jobs and the resources in the grid network. Dong and Akl (2006) have analyzed the scheduling problem in the grid network and discussed the major challenges of the grid environment. Jiang et al. (2007) have given a report on various aspects of job scheduling and simulation strategies in the grid environment. It includes fault tolerance, and security, and also covers the limitations of scheduling in the grid environment. Gharehchopogh et al. (2013) have discussed several conventional algorithms such as min-min, minimum completion time (MCT), max-min, and XSuffrage. Amiri et al. (2014) have explained the resource allocation mechanism in the grid environment, as well as prominent algorithms for resource allocation in the grid environment. (Maipan-Uku et al. (2016) have introduced a scheduling approach called Max-Average, based on a popular conventional technique, that is, Max-Min, to solve the problem of scheduling in the grid environment. The experimental results show that the said algorithm gives better results in terms of RU and completion time of jobs in comparison to other scheduling algorithms such as MCT, minimum execution time (MET), max-min, and min-min algorithms.

Hamscher et al. (2000) have discussed structures of scheduling that can be found in the computational grid environment. The performance of the scheduling algorithms is dependent on these structures. For example, in the case of a central job pool, FCFS gives better results than the Backfill algorithm. Menasce and Casalicchio (2004) have presented a framework for allocation in the grid computing environment. This framework aims at minimizing the execution time at the minimum cost of the resources.

Jiang and Ni (2009) have presented a scheduling algorithm that contains the features of FCFS and Backfill scheduling algorithms. The scheduling results show improvements in the throughput of the grid system and also an efficient RU rate. Although conventional algorithms have been successful in obtaining solutions to a small set of problems, they are ineffective in finding solutions to complex problems and dealing with the constantly changing grid environment. This has led to the need for new scheduling algorithms that can deal with the dynamic grid environment as well as complex data sets. Research groups have found that algorithms inspired by nature and natural phenomena are potentially efficient in dealing with real-time complex problems in science and engineering. A lot of notable work has been done in this field by the research community at both national and international levels.

3.3.2 GRID RESOURCE MANAGEMENT (GRM): BIO-INSPIRED ALGORITHMS

The grid computing infrastructure consists of numerous homogeneous or heterogeneous resources, which require proper resource management (Sahana and Ankita, 2019) for efficient and effective RU. The conventional algorithms are unsuitable for larger problem sets and cannot meet the demands of a dynamically changing environment like Grid. In modern times, there are many applications in different streams of science and engineering where complexities arise due to various conflicting objective functions that require optimization simultaneously under certain constraints. These complex problems are termed multiobjective optimization problems. A good number of scheduling methods have evolved in the last decade, which have shown exemplary scheduling results. Metaheuristics are considered a good means of solving multiobjective problems under many constraints. Some of the potential reasons for applying a metaheuristic to Grid scheduling problems are listed below:

1. **Implied Metaheuristics:** Until now, researchers have applied metaheuristics to many multiobjective and complex problems. Therefore, it becomes quite easy to develop new metaheuristics for solving grid scheduling problems using past data and facts about the metaheuristics.
2. **No Obligation for an Exact Solution:** An exact solution is not required for an NP-complete problem. It is even difficult to reach an optimum solution in a dynamic grid environment, and hence a proper outlining of jobs over the resources will be quite sufficient.
3. **Competent Results in Less Time:** Metaheuristics take less time compared to other conventional approaches. This is one of the biggest reasons for opting for metaheuristics to solve

multiobjective problems. These methods provide features to adjust the convergence speed and obtain solutions in relatively less time.

4. **Suitability for Multiobjective Problems:** The research trend shows that metaheuristics have provided potential solutions when applied to both single-objective and multiobjective problems.
5. **Suitability for Periodic Scheduling:** Sometimes, user requests are submitted to the grid system in a periodic manner. Metaheuristics support resource provisioning in the grid environment and hence can run for higher completion times, which will enhance the planning of resource allocation to jobs.
6. **Support for a Decentralized Model of Resource Allocation:** The growing size of the grid system has led to the popularity of decentralized methods of resource allocation. Metaheuristics can easily work in such an environment where one scheduler is regulated by another scheduler.
7. **Support for Hybridization:** Metaheuristics can easily combine with other heuristic and metaheuristic approaches to provide feasible solutions for more concrete Grid applications. The research trend shows that the hybridized approaches have demonstrated better results compared to single approaches in solving complex multiobjective problems.
8. **Robustness:** A dynamic environment like a grid keeps changing over time in terms of its resources, networks, and job heterogeneity. Hence, a robust scheduler is an extreme need to maintain the performance of the grid environment. The literature study of metaheuristics shows that they are robust.

Those metaheuristics inspired by nature are called nature-inspired or swarm-based metaheuristics (Abraham et al., 2000; Krause et al., 2013; Yang, 2010). The metaheuristics inspired by natural processes or biological processes are called evolutionary-based metaheuristics (Phelps and Köksalan, 2003; Yu and Gen, 2010). These algorithms are fast and provide satisfactory results in a reasonable time. Bio-inspired mechanisms are divided into two groups: swarm-based mechanisms and evolutionary-based mechanisms.

The field of computer science that is driven by the behavior of swarms of living organisms is known as swarm intelligence. Swarm-based algorithms such as ACO (Blum, 2005), artificial bee colony (ABC) (Karaboga et al., 2014), PSO (Marini and Walczak, 2015), Cuckoo Search algorithm (Mareli and Twala, 2018), and many more draw their inspiration from nature. ACO and PSO are the prominent members of the swarm family. The underlying principle behind the working of ACO is influenced by the behavior of ants in the real world. The distinct way of exploring and exploiting food sources by the ants has provided several ideas for finding solutions to complex real-life problems. The behavior of bird flocking has motivated the design of the PSO algorithm. Apart from swarm-based algorithms, evolutionary algorithms like the genetic algorithm (GA) have also been very popular, as they are inspired by the biological phenomenon of evolution described by Charles Darwin.

3.3.2.1 NATIONAL WORK ON GRID RESOURCE MANAGEMENT (GRM) USING BIO-INSPIRED ALGORITHMS

A grid can be defined as an infrastructure that constitutes a large number of resources such as compute resources, storage devices, and network devices distributed at different locations. Grid computing aims at wide-scale resource sharing and utilization of idle resources for distributed applications. A good scheduling mechanism (Prajapati and Shah, 2014) is required, which can spontaneously adjust its policies with incoming jobs and the dynamic grid environment. Singh et al. (2014) have studied the grid scheduling problem and resource management in the grid. It also surveys different scheduling algorithms along with their applications in the grid system. There have been many notable works in the field of developing bio-inspired optimization algorithms (Binitha and Sathya, 2012; Grover and Chabbra, 2016; Pazhaniraja et al., 2017) for managing resources and scheduling jobs over appropriate resources in a legitimate time.

The striking features of ACO, such as parallelism, scalability, and dynamic behavior, make it a convincing approach for solving NP-complete problems like grid scheduling in the grid environment. Kant et al. (2010) have introduced the theory of red ants and black ants in ACO. They have applied a two-level optimization to improve RU in the grid environment. Mathiyalagan et al. (2010a) have modified the conventional ACO by changing the pheromone update rule. The simulation results show improvement in RU and system efficiency.

Tiwari and Vidyarthi (2016) have introduced the notion of lazy ants for exploring the search space around the best ant for solving the grid scheduling problem. The algorithm is an auto-controlled technique that dynamically adapts to changes in the grid environment. The simulation results show that their algorithm is efficient in terms of computational time and produces better scheduling results when compared to other bio-inspired algorithms such as ACO, PSO, and GA for solving the grid scheduling problem. Mathiyalagan et al. (2010b) have used PSO in the grid environment for scheduling and resource management. They modified the inertia parameter of PSO to improve its convergence rate. Singh et al. (2013) have provided a resource management technique based on a popular evolutionary algorithm, that is, GA. They have defined a new algorithm for the selection of the initial population and mutation operator to comply with the resource broker framework. The simulation results show that the TCT of jobs is minimized in the grid environment. Patel (2014) has applied GA to create multiobjective schedulers. They have considered several objectives like RU rate, makespan, and flow time. The simulation results show that the said algorithm enhances RU and minimizes makespan. Panwar et al. (2016) have represented the scheduling problem using direct acyclic graphs (DAG). The results show that the said algorithm minimizes the completion time of the jobs.

3.3.2.2 INTERNATIONAL WORK ON GRID RESOURCE MANAGEMENT (GRM) USING BIO-INSPIRED ALGORITHMS

Finding an optimal solution for NP-complete problems has always been an interesting field of research and development (R&D) for researchers all over the world. The problem of job scheduling in the computational grid environment is one such problem. Bio-inspired mechanisms are popular in solving NP category problems. The use of bio-inspired principles in computing has led to the development of many interesting and useful multiobjective optimization algorithms. Chen et al. (2006) have encoded the scheduling problem of the grid into a task-resource assignment graph problem. They have developed a PSO-based scheduling method to solve the grid scheduling problem and consider the longest path in the graph as the fitness value. The experimental results show that the said algorithm is effective in reducing the makespan of the jobs. Zhang et al. (2008) and Izakian et al. (2009) have developed a discrete PSO that minimizes the makespan and flow time of the jobs. PSO (Ambursa and Latip, 2013) is a randomized, global optimization algorithm that represents a swarm of particles as candidate solutions. Alyaseri and Ku-Mahamud (2013) have used foraging behavior techniques of bees for solving the grid scheduling problem. Karaboga et al. (2014) have presented a comprehensive survey on the ABC algorithm, which is driven by the foraging behavior of real bees for solving complex optimization problems.

Dorigo et al. (1996) have come up with a new population-based and robust approach called the ant system (AS), which can solve a set of NP-complete combinatorial optimization problems. Merkle et al. (2002) have used ACO for solving resource-constrained problems of scheduling. The experimental results show that the said algorithm is flexible and able to change the intensity of heuristic influence. It also changes the pheromone evaporation rate over the ant constructions. Fidanova and Durchova (2005) have used an ACO algorithm with the objective of minimizing the number of idle processors and decreasing makespan time during the execution of the jobs. Yan et al. (2005) have given a new scheduling method based on ACO. The algorithm schedules the jobs and performs load distribution. Chang et al. (2009) have applied the pheromone update rule for appropriate resource selection and uniform load distribution.

Wei et al. (2012) have modified the basic ACO by adding a new pheromone type and a rule for node (resource) redistribution in the case of node failure. The simulation results have shown that the introduced modification shortens the completion time of jobs and improves the robustness of the algorithm. Molaiy and Effatparvar (2014) have used ACO for scheduling jobs in the grid environment with the aim of increasing RU and optimizing total execution time. Yu and Buyya (2006) have proposed a GA-based scheduling approach that takes the budget constraints of users into account and reduces the job completion time. Xhafa et al. (2007) have developed schedulers based on GA for job-resource assignment in the grid system. The experimental analysis has shown that the developed schedulers have improved efficiency compared to other GA implementations in the grid environment. The flow time and makespan are minimized using the aforementioned GA-based schedulers. Younis and Yang (2017) have modified the mutation step of GA and applied it to the scheduling problem in the grid environment. The algorithm minimizes makespan and provides better scheduling results when compared to other algorithms.

We have proposed hybrid bio-inspired algorithms that differ from previous works in several ways:

- We have used a standard data set to test the effectiveness of our proposed scheduling algorithms. In most of the aforementioned papers, the data set is not a standard one. We have used real workload traces provided by a grid computing center, *MetaCentrum*.
- We have worked with important performance parameters such as total completion and wait time of jobs, RU, load balancing, and scalability to evaluate the efficiency of the proposed scheduling algorithms in the simulation environment. Most of the papers mentioned above have focused on a single or a few objectives.
- Previously, the authors have used task-resource assignment graphs that are unable to visualize the CPU state in real-time. Our results output a CPU state graph to show various states of the CPU, providing clear insight into the varying CPU states in real-time.

3.4 SUMMARY

The growing world of the internet, high-speed networks, and supercomputers has paved the way for the development of large-scale computing infrastructures called grid computing. The performance of a grid computing environment depends on several criteria, such as the least completion time of jobs, high RU, the least waiting time of jobs, and load balancing among the resources. A good and efficient scheduling algorithm is able to schedule jobs on appropriate resources while simultaneously satisfying all the above-mentioned criteria.

This chapter collectively presents different scheduling approaches that can be applied in the grid computing environment. Various works on scheduling and resource management have been discussed in this chapter. The last decade has seen substantial contributions from bio-inspired algorithms in solving multiobjective optimization problems. Grid scheduling belongs to the class of multiobjective optimization problems where multiple factors drive the performance of the grid environment. These algorithms have attracted researchers from all over the world to solve both static and dynamic optimization problems. This chapter briefly discusses the potential reasons for switching to metaheuristics from conventional scheduling algorithms. Some of the bioinspired as well as conventional algorithms and their implementation in the grid environment to schedule jobs and manage resources efficiently have been discussed. Additionally, several research works have been included that incorporate both conventional and non-conventional (bio-inspired) approaches to solve the grid scheduling problem and manage resources in the grid environment. These works showcase the performance of the grid computing environment when different (conventional and bio-inspired) scheduling algorithms have been implemented in the grid environment.

KEYWORDS

- **Ant colony optimization**
- **bio-inspired algorithms**
- **genetic algorithm**
- **grid computing**
- **metaheuristics**
- **multiobjective optimization**
- **particle swarm optimization**
- **resource management.**

CHAPTER 4

Scheduling Algorithms: Modified and Hybrid Algorithms

4.1 INTRODUCTION

In the previous chapters, some of the conventional and bio-inspired algorithms, along with their mapping in the grid environment, have been discussed. In this chapter, a few modifications have been incorporated into the bio-inspired algorithm in order to improve the performance of the grid environment. Hybridization is another way of improving performance by merging two or more algorithms. Hybridization provides a way of combining the advantages of two or more algorithms to develop a strong algorithm that can be used in solving grid scheduling problems. In the upcoming chapters, an analysis will be carried out to compare the performance of the grid environment using hybridized and non-hybridized scheduling algorithms in terms of total completion time (TCT) of jobs, resource utilization (RU), load distribution, and scalability.

4.2 MODIFICATION TO THE BASIC ACO (THRESHOLD-CONSTRAINED ACO, ACO_{THRESH})

ACO is a strong metaheuristic that solves the scheduling problem in the grid environment (Fidanova and Durchova, 2005). To enhance the performance of grid scheduling, some modifications have been applied to the conventional ACO in the grid environment.

The modifications in the basic ACO are listed below:

1. **Inclusion of a New Parameter Called Threshold Probability for Better Selection of Resources:** The basic ACO algorithm in grid

Mastering Grid Computing: Scheduling and Resource Management.
Ankita & Sudip Kumar Sahana (Authors)

computing simply assigns the job to the resource using Equations 4.1 and 4.2. The probability of moving a job from one resource to another must be a good (high) value to process the incoming job request because a poor (low) value of transition probability indicates the selection of a resource with less processing capabilities. In such cases, the job may not be able to finish its execution if the jobs are independent and cannot be preempted by some other resource. So, the value of transition probability needs to be high enough for the appropriate selection of resources.

2. **Threshold Probability (p_0):** It is a minimum probability value set by the scheduler. Initially, the conventional ACO is run several times, and the value of transition probability is calculated using Equation 4.1 for every iteration. The value of threshold probability is randomly selected from a set of transition probability values using conventional ACO. In the modified ACO algorithm, this value acts as a constraint in the selection of a resource such that the transition probability value must be greater than the value of the threshold probability. It will ensure that a resource is not selected below a minimal probability value. A high probability value helps in the selection of a resource with a high pheromone value (high processing capabilities), which minimizes the completion time of a job over the resource and eventually improves RU.

3. **Use of Hybridization for Better Scheduling Sequence, Which Also Eliminates the Initialization Problem of ACO:** The working of ACO starts with the random initialization of a population of solutions. These solutions are further improved iteratively to achieve a better solution. Therefore, it can be said that the performance of the ACO algorithm is affected by the population initialization (Chen and Liu, 2018). Out of the conventional scheduling techniques, shortest job first (SJF) is popular for its remarkable performance. The improved ACO is hybridized with the SJF algorithm, which removes the initialization problem of ACO and improves the performance of grid scheduling. ACO is an effective metaheuristic for finding good solutions in less time. Although the convergence rate of ACO is not certain, there is less chance of ACO falling into local optima in high-dimensional space. A new parameter, threshold probability, is added to the basic

ACO algorithm to improve the grid scheduling results. Threshold-constrained ACO is represented by ant colony optimization with threshold (ACO_{thresh}), and its flowchart is shown in Figure 4.1.

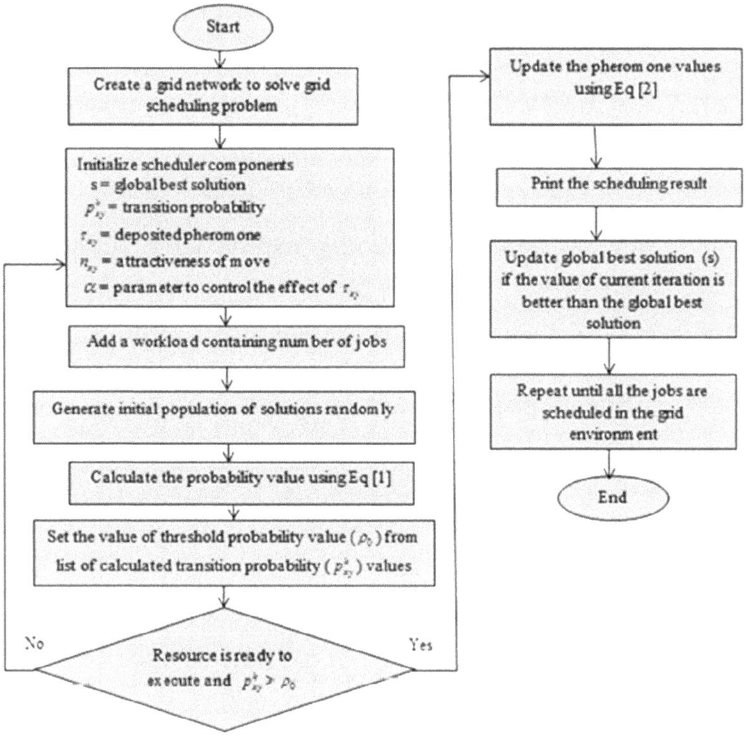

FIGURE 4.1 Flowchart of ACO_{thresh} algorithm.

The description of the proposed threshold-constrained ACO algorithm, ACO_{thresh} (Algorithm 1), to solve the grid scheduling problem is given below:

Algorithm 1: ACOthresh in Grid Environment

Input: Number of jobs and available resources.
Output: Allocation of each job to available resources.
begin

Initialize grid environment
Initialize scheduler components (p^k_{xy} $\Delta\tau_{xy}$ $\eta\rho\alpha\beta$)
Initialize global best solution = s

while the jobs of the workload are not scheduled **do**

- **Step 1:** Add a workload containing a number of jobs.
- **Step 2:** Generate the initial population of solutions in a random manner.
- **Step 3:** Calculate the probability value using Equation 4.1.
- **Step 4:** Set the value of the threshold probability ρ_0 from the list of calculated transition probability ρ^k_{xy} values.
- **Step 5:** Check the availability and suitability of the resource (quality of food source).
- **Step 6:** if the resource is suitable for the job and available to execute and the value of $\rho^k_{xy} > \rho_0$ then
  update the pheromone values using Equation 4.2.

else

go to Step 1

end if

- **Step 7:** Job is scheduled over the selected resource.
- **Step 8:**

  if the value obtained in the current iteration is better than the global best solution **then**

  Set s = current solution

end if

end while

- **Step 9:** Repeat the above steps till all the jobs are scheduled over available resources.

end

The description of the proposed threshold-constrained ACO algorithm, ACO_{thresh} (Algorithm 1) to solve the grid scheduling problem is given below:

- For each resource, a Resourcelnfo object is created, which keeps the updated information about the current status of the resource.
- A Resource list containing available resources, a job list of unscheduled jobs of the Zewura workload, and a global best solution is initialized.
- The initial population of solutions is generated randomly.
- The conventional ACO is modified by adding a new parameter called threshold probability ρ_0, which ensures that a resource is not selected below a minimal probability value.
- The transition probability value ρ_xy^k, with which an ant moves from one position to another, is calculated using Equation 4.1.
- An ant moves from one position to another only when the value of transition probability ρ_xy^k is greater than the value of threshold probability ρ_0, and the selected resource is available and suitable for the job.
- The value of pheromone is updated using Equation 4.2.
- The value obtained in the current iteration is compared with the global best solution(s).
- The value of the global best solution(s) is updated with the value obtained in the current iteration if the obtained value is better than the value of the previous global best solution.
- The steps are repeated until all the jobs are scheduled.

4.3 HYBRIDIZATION OF SJF WITH ACO_{THRESH}

Hybridization offers a method to combine the strengths of two or more algorithms, creating a robust solution for addressing grid scheduling problems. The modified ACO, that is, ACO_{thresh} is combined with SJF for better performance of grid scheduling. The flow diagram of the proposed hybrid SJF-ACO_{thresh} (shortest job first with ant colony optimization and threshold) algorithm is given in Figure 4.2.

The algorithm for SJF-ACO_{thresh} is given in Algorithm 2.

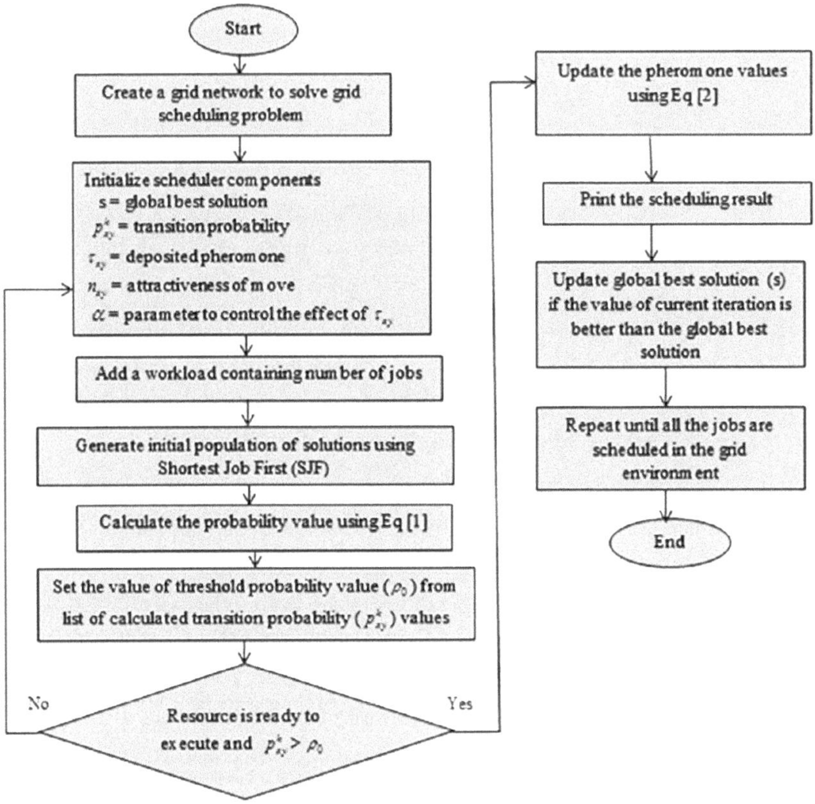

FIGURE 4.2 Flowchart of hybrid SJF-ACO$_{thresh}$ algorithm.

Algorithm 2: Swarm-based Hybrid SJF-ACOthresh Algorithm in Grid Environment

Input: Number of jobs and available resources.
Output: Allocation of each job to available resources.
begin

Initialize grid environment
Initialize scheduler components $(p^k_{xy} \Delta\tau_{xy} \eta\, \rho\, a\, \beta)$
Initialize global best solution = s

while the queue of unscheduled jobs is not empty **do**

- **Step 1:** Add a workload containing a number of jobs.

- **Step 2:** Generate the initial population of solutions using shortest job first (SJF).
- **Step 3:** Calculate the probability value using Equation 4.1.
- **Step 4:** Set the value of threshold probability ρ_0 from the list of calculated transition probability ρ^k_{xy} values.
- **Step 5:** Check the availability and suitability of the resource (quality of food source).
- **Step 6:** **if** the resource is suitable for the job and available to execute and the value of $\rho^k_{xy} > \rho_0$ **then**
  update the pheromone values using Equation 4.2.

else
  go to Step 1
end if

- **Step 7:** Job is scheduled over the selected resource.
- **Step 8:**

  if the value obtained in the current iteration is better than the global best solution **then**

  Set s = current solution

end if
end while

- **Step 9:** Repeat the above steps till all the jobs are scheduled over available resources.

end

The scheduling parameters of ACO are given in Table 4.1. The values of and are taken from (Chang et al., 2009). A promising range of parameter values of ACO has been tested and tuned using an automated parameter tuning approach (Sahana and Ankita, 2019). It is observed that the value of deposited pheromone 〚Δτ〛_xy ranges from 0.1465 to 0.1473, and the value of threshold probability ρ_0 ranges from 0.00155 to 0.00161 (Sahana and Ankita, 2019), providing a better schedule in less time for job scheduling in the grid environment.

TABLE 4.1 Scheduling Parameters of ACO

Parameters	Values
α	0.5
β	0.5
$\Delta\tau_{xy}$	0.1467
ρ_u	0.0016
ρ	0.99

The description of the proposed swarm-based hybrid algorithm (Algorithm 2) to solve the grid scheduling problem is given below:

1. For each resource, a Resource Info object is created, which keeps updated information about the current status of the resource.
2. A resource list containing available resources, a job list of unscheduled jobs of the Zewura workload, and a global best solution is initialized.
3. The initial population of solutions is generated using a conventional algorithm, that is, SJF.
4. The conventional ACO is modified by adding a new parameter called threshold probability ρ_0, which ensures that a resource is not selected below a minimal probability value.
5. The transition probability value ρ_xy^k, with which an ant moves from one position to another, is calculated using Equation 4.1.
6. An ant moves from one position to another only when the value of transition probability ρ_xy^k is greater than the value of threshold probability ρ_0, and the selected resource is available and suitable for the job.
7. The value of pheromone is updated using Equation 4.2.
8. The value obtained in the current iteration is compared with the global best solution(s).
9. The value of the global best solution(s) is updated with the value obtained in the current iteration if the obtained value is better than the value of the previous global best solution.
10. The steps are repeated until all the jobs are scheduled.

4.4 HYBRIDIZATION OF SJF WITH GA

GA is the most popular evolutionary optimization algorithm. The success rate of GA greatly depends on the selection of the fitness function of the problem to be solved. During the generation of the initial population of solutions, the conventional GA assigns the resources to the jobs in a random manner. This random selection may form an inadequate search space. However, the proposed hybrid GA makes significant changes in the initialization step of GA, which improves the grid scheduling results. One solution in the population of solutions is generated using SJF, and other solutions are generated randomly, which helps in finding optimum solutions in a reasonable time.

The flow diagram of the proposed hybrid GA-SJF algorithm is given in Figure 4.3. In general, the initial population of solutions in GA is constructed randomly. However, various studies in the literature (Younis et al., 2017) have shown that the construction of the initial population of solutions using some conventional or non-conventional methods can lead to better solutions. The hybridization of a strong conventional scheduling approach with a popular evolutionary technique is performed to utilize the benefits of both algorithms. The hybridization of SJF with GA improves the performance of grid scheduling. Instead of random initialization, the SJF algorithm is used for generating the initial population of solutions. The working of GA starts with the generation of the initial population of solutions. Hence, the performance of GA greatly depends on the initial population of solutions.

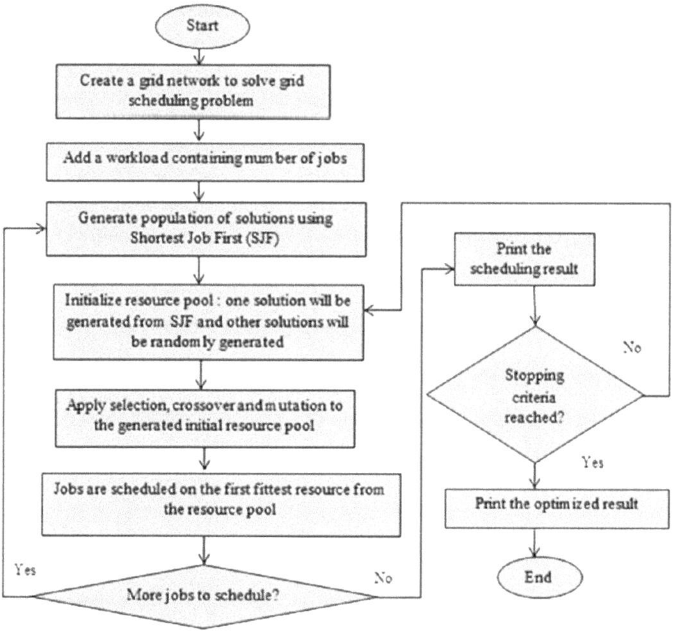

FIGURE 4.3 Flowchart of SJF-GA algorithm.

The initial population is treated by three operators – selection, crossover, and mutation to find an optimal solution for the problem. The parameters of GA are discussed in Table 4.2.

TABLE 4.2 Scheduling Parameters of GA

Parameters	Values
Probability of crossover	0.8
Probability of mutation	0.2
Size of the initial population of solutions	4
Size of the population	17,256
Number of generations	100
Selection operator	Binary tournament selection
Crossover operator	One point crossover

The hybrid algorithm (SJF-GA (shortest job first-genetic algorithm)) to solve the job scheduling problem in GA is given in Algorithm 3.

Algorithm 3: Evolutionary-based Hybrid (SJF-GA) in Grid Environment

Input: Number of jobs and available resources.
Output: Allocation of each job to available resources.
begin

Initialize grid environment
Initialize scheduler components
Probability of Crossover = p_c
Probability of Mutation = p_m
Number of generations = m

- **Step 1:** Add a workload containing a number of jobs.
- **Step 2:** Initialize the population of solutions (R_y); one solution will be generated from SJF and other solutions will be randomly generated.

repeat

- **Step 3:** Selection operator ()
- **Step 4:** Crossover operator ()
- **Step 5:** Mutation operator ()

- **Step 6:** $R_{y'}$ is created containing chromosomes (job-resource assignment) with the best fitness values.
- **Step 7:** The jobs are scheduled over the first best-selected resource from $R_{y'}$ according to the fitness function.
- **Step 8:** Repeat until all the jobs are scheduled over the available resources.
- **Step 9:** Print the scheduling result.
- **Step 10:** Repeat until the number of generations

Return the best solution
end

The description of the proposed evolutionary-based hybrid algorithm (Algorithm 3) to solve the grid scheduling problem is given below:

1. For each resource, a Resource Info object is created, which keeps updated information about the current status of the resource.
2. A resource list containing available resources, a job list of unscheduled jobs of the workload, and a global best solution is initialized.
3. The solution representation: A permutation-based representation is used for representing chromosomes in GA for the grid scheduling problem. It is a list representation where the size of the list is equal to the number of resources.
4. A population of solutions is generated using SJF.
5. The initial generation: The initial population of solutions Ry is initialized with one solution generated from SJF, and other solutions are generated randomly. There are seven cluster resources (CRs), so an optimum solution pool of four resources is taken, as shown in Table 4.2.
6. The fitness function: The fitness function of the proposed SJF-GA is defined below:

$$fitness = min \sum_{n=1}^{N} (TCT_{jobs}) + max \sum_{r=1}^{R} (RU_{resources}) \tag{4.1}$$

where; N is a set of jobs and $n \in N$; TCT is the total completion time of the jobs; R is a set of resources and $r \in R$; and RU is the RU.

7. In this step a new generation is created by using three GA operators given below:
   i. **Selection:** The binary tournament selection approach has been applied to selecting two individuals from the initial population of solutions. It randomly selects two individuals and calculates their fitness scores. The individual with a high fitness score gets selected for the next step of the GA.
   ii. **Crossover:** The one-point crossover method is used to generate a new solution. The crossover probability is randomly selected between [0.5 and 1].
   iii. **Mutation:** It is performed by randomly changing the assignment of one job from one resource to another. The mutation probability is randomly selected between [0.5 and 1].
8. The steps are repeated until all the jobs are scheduled to the available resources.
9. The steps are repeated for a specified number of generations.

4.5 COMPLEXITY ANALYSIS OF ALGORITHMS

In a grid environment, the number of iterations required to allocate a job to a resource will be $O(uv)$. If u number of jobs are scheduled over v resources, then the number of required iterations in the case of the ACO algorithm will be $O(uv^2)$. In our implementation, the population size (PS) is fixed, hence the time complexity of ACO is given as *(*uv^2 *x generations x population size)*. For PSO, the time complexity of the fitness function evaluation will be $O(v)$. Hence, the time complexity will be given as *(*uv^2 *x generations x population size)*.

In the case of GA, the time complexity of selection, crossover, and mutation function for each iteration will be $O(v^2)$. Hence, the time complexity of the genetic algorithm (GA) for allocating a job to a resource will be $O(uv^2$ *x generations x* $f)$, where f is the time complexity of fitness function evaluation.

The complexity of the proposed ACO_{thresh} will be similar to that of the ACO algorithm. The time complexity of the SJF algorithm is $O(ulogu)$, where u is the number of jobs in the grid system. Hence, the time complexity of the proposed SJF-ACO_{thresh} scheduling algorithm will be

O(ulogu) + *O(uv^2 x generations x population size)*. In the case of SJF-GA, the time complexity will be *O(ulogu)* + *O(uv^2 x generations x f)*.

4.6 SIMULATION TOOLKIT FOR GRID RESOURCE MANAGEMENT (GRM)

A grid is a dynamic environment with a varying number of jobs and resources. Therefore, it becomes essential to illustrate the efficiencies of the scheduling algorithms under different constraints, such as varying job requests and varying job requirements of users. It is very hard and not feasible to perform these tests in real-time in a real grid environment under different constraints because of factors such as the cost of setting up a grid, the changing load on the resources, and the reliability of the resources.

There are several other simulation toolkits and technologies that have been developed over the years to provide simulation functionalities for clusters and grid environments. Some of them are discussed below:

1. **Microgrid:** It is an emulator designed using the Globus toolkit. It uses the API (application programming interface) of Globus for the execution of its applications. Since microgrid (Liu et al., 2004) is an emulator, it takes more time to run applications on emulated resources. Though the output of the emulator is explicit, the design of the application and scheduling environment is also time-consuming. It can be used as a verification tool for checking the simulation results with other real applications.

2. **Bricks Simulation System:** It is designed to facilitate the simulation of the client-server computing model, where remote access is provided to libraries and packages executing on supercomputers (Takefusa et al., 1999). It has a centralized scheduling mechanism, developed at the Tokyo Institute of Technology in Japan.

3. **GridSim:** It is a Java-based and platform-independent simulation toolkit that provides support for designing and simulating various scheduling models in the grid environment (Buyya and Murshed, 2002). This toolkit was developed by Rajkumar Buyya and his team at the Grid Computing and Distributed Systems (GRIDS) lab. New scheduling methods can be easily integrated into GridSim. The framework of GridSim facilitates reservation and includes

multiple functionalities such as Data Grid functionalities and network traffic functionalities. This simulator has the capability to test scheduling algorithms by reading workload traces from large systems and supercomputers to simulate a real Grid environment.

4. **SimGrid:** It is designed for modeling distributed applications and testing them in a distributed environment with real-life scenarios (Legrand et al., 2003). It is a C-based simulator that consists of various tools such as MSG, GRAS, and SMPI. The MSG tool of SimGrid supports the testing of scheduling algorithms in the simulation environment. The other two tools, GRAS and SMPI, are used in the development and analysis of real applications.

5. **BeoSim:** It is designed for analyzing job scheduling algorithms running in parallel at different scheduling sites for a multi-cluster computational grid (Jones et al., 2005). It can work with synthetic or real workload traces. It also provides visualization tools based on Java.

6. **Simbatch:** It is designed for batch schedulers and provides simulation for scheduling (Caniou and Gay, 2009). The design of Simbatch is based on the MSG tool of SimGrid.

7. **SimBOINC:** The design of SimBOINC (Berkeley Open Infrastructure for Network Computing) is also based on the SimGrid simulator. SimBOINC (Kondo, 2007) supports the simulation of heterogeneous and volatile computing systems. It follows a client-server model where many clients make requests to the central server. The client request contains simulation inputs such as speed and workload availability.

8. **Monarc 2:** It aims to provide a modeling as well as optimization tool for large, distributed computing systems (Dobre et al., 2008). It is mainly designed to support data processing architectures and provide a flexible environment for evaluating their performance. Monarc 2 is an extension of the Monarc Simulator. Monarc 2 is developed by enhancing the flexibility and performance of Monarc.

9. **GSSIM:** Grid scheduling simulator (GSSIM) is a GridSim-based simulator that came into operation in 2009. GSSIM (Kurowski

et al., 2007) aims to provide a simple scheduling framework for simulating and testing scheduling algorithms in the Grid environment. The slow rate of execution and poor visualization outputs are the problems encountered in GSSIM.

4.6.1 OVERVIEW OF ALEA

The simulation is a good alternative to perform the test of the scheduling algorithms in a controllable manner under different constraints (or scenarios). Alea (Klusáček and Rudová, 2010) is a GSSIM developed by Dalibor Klusáček and Hana Rudová to evaluate different scheduling algorithms in the grid environment. This software is the result of the research intent no. 0021622419 (Ministry of Education, Youth and Sports of the Czech Republic) and the grant no. 201/07/0205 (Grant Agency of the Czech Republic).

The Alea simulator used here is Alea 3.0, which is an improved version of Alea 2.1, based on a popular grid simulation toolkit called the GridSim toolkit (Buyya and Murshed, 2002; Murshed and Buyya, 2002). This simulator is able to handle common problems of scheduling in the grid environment, like resource and job heterogeneity, resource failure, and dynamic job arrival. The simulator uses two interfaces called Scheduling Policy and Optimization Algorithm in order to add a new scheduling algorithm into the simulator. The first interface handles job arrival and job selection for execution. The latter interface is implemented when the users create their method.

4.6.2 ELEMENTS OF ALEA

Alea is an event-based standard simulator, which is made up of several independent elements having their simulation functionalities. The entities of the simulator with their respective functionalities are discussed below:

1. **The Centralized Scheduler:** The central scheduler is the most non-trivial element of Alea 3.0. It makes scheduling decisions based on the selected scheduling algorithm. Communication between the scheduler and the other entities is carried out using events and corresponding messages. It communicates with three entities of the simulator: Job Loader, Grid Resources, and Result Collector. The first part of the scheduler keeps dynamic information

about the resources and maintains updated information about the current state of the resources. The Job Loader sends new jobs to the scheduler. The scheduler processes the incoming jobs based on the selected scheduling algorithm. The simulation is completed when all the jobs have finished their execution, and no new job appears for the scheduler. The output files are used to store the results.

2. **The Job Loader:** It is responsible for reading the file that contains the description of the job, and job instances are created dynamically over time. Different workload formats are supported by the Job Loader, such as standard workload format (SWF) and Grid Workload Format (GWF). Only one job can be read by the Job Loader at a time.
3. **The Failure Loader:** This, as the name suggests, reads the file that contains the description of the failed machines or systems.
4. **The Machine Loader:** It is responsible for initializing the components of the simulation environment. It reads a file that contains the description of the machines and creates the resources of the Grid accordingly.
5. **Allocation Policy:** The simulation system supports the Advanced SpaceShared policy, which is based on the SpaceShared policy of GridSim. It supports several features, such as the execution of parallel as well as sequential jobs. This policy has improved the speed of simulation and also provides simulation for the failed machines.
6. **Visualization and Simulator Output Generation:** A graphical output of the simulator is generated using the Visualizator class. Different types of objectives are supported and can be visualized through these graphs. The Result Collector stores the output during simulation.
7. **Additional Classes:** There are classes that help the simulator in setting up the scheduling environment. Some of these classes are discussed below:

   i. **ExperimentSetup.java:** The new scheduling algorithm is added to the ExperimentSetup.java class for proper loading during simulation.

ii. **GridletInfo.java:** It contains job-related information that is ready for processing in the simulation environment.

iii. **JobLoader.java:** It is responsible for translating the workload. The workload is in SWF, which is parsed by SWFLoader.java.

iv. **Scheduler.java:** It manages the events associated with the scheduling, arrival, and completion of jobs.

v. **ResourceInfo.java:** It stores updated information about the resources in the instances of the class.

vi. **ComplexGridResource.java:** This class manages the distribution of jobs to the resources after being selected by the appropriate scheduling algorithm. The simulator follows the AdvancedSpaceSharing policy, where a job is assured to get the required resources.

4.6.3 STANDARD WORKLOAD

The workload plays a crucial part in evaluating the performance of new scheduling algorithms. A standard workload is considered for the implementation of the proposed algorithms in order to set up a benchmark result for future research directions.

4.6.3.1 ZEWURA WORKLOAD

MetaCentrum, the Czech national grid infrastructure (NGI), has provided the workload called Zewura Workload for testing new algorithms and comparing their performance with other reference algorithms. The workload traces are produced from TORQUE traces, which contain 17,256 jobs. These jobs were gathered together between January and May 2012. The workload is in SWF. The workload requires two files, namely, a Job Description File and a Machine Description File.

1. **Job Description File:** The job description file has 18 data fields which are given below:

   i. **Job Number:** It is a counter field that starts from 0 or 1.

   ii. **Submit Time (In Seconds):** It is the time at which the job is submitted to the system. It is arranged in increasing order in the workload log.

iii. **Wait Time (In Seconds):** The difference between the submission time of the job and the actual start of the job execution is called wait time.

iv. **Run Time (In Seconds):** The difference between the finish time and actual start time (AST) of the jobs is called run time.

v. **Number of Allocated Processors:** It is an integer value that indicates the number of processors utilized by the job.

vi. **Average CPU Time Used (in Seconds):** The average CPU time can be calculated by taking the average of the CPU time taken by all the processors.

vii. **Used Memory (In Kilobytes):** It is the average memory used by all the processors.

viii. **Requested Number of Processors:** It is the total number of processors requested by the job.

ix. **Requested Time (In Seconds):** This field can be either a runtime estimates for the user or an average CPU time for each processor.

x. **Requested Memory (In Kilobytes):** It is the memory requested per processor.

xi. **Status:** It is an integer value which can be 0, 1, or 5. The status value is 1 if the job is completed, and the status value is 0 if the job fails to complete its execution. The canceled jobs are indicated by 5.

xii. **User ID:** It is a natural number that lies between one and the total number of users.

xiii. **Group ID:** It is a natural number that lies between one and the total number of different groups.

xiv. **Executable Number:** It is a natural number that lies between one and the total number of applications arriving in the workload.

xv. **Queue Number:** It is a natural number that lies between one and the total number of queues in the computing system.

xvi. **Partition Number:** It is a natural number that lies between one and the total number of different partitions in the computing system. Partition numbers can be used to locate a utilized processor within a CR.

xvii. **Preceding Job Number:** It is a number that indicates the previous job in the computing system such that a new job can only start its execution if the preceding job has been terminated.

xviii. **Think Time from Preceding Job (In Seconds):** It is a number that indicates the time elapsed between the submission of a new job and completion of the previous job.

2. **Machine Description File:** There are seven clusters of resources called Zewura clusters. Each Zewura cluster consists of 20 shared memory machines. Each machine has 80 CPUs and 512 GB of RAM.

4.6.3.2 CONSTRAINTS

We have considered the various constraints under the job scheduling model:

- The jobs are independent and belong to a standard data set.
- The jobs are non-preemptive.
- A unique job ID is assigned to each job of the workload. There are 17,256 jobs in the Zewura workload.
- A job can have single (sequential) or multiple (parallel) processor requirements.
- One CR is composed of various machines.
- The processors within a cluster follow the Advanced Space Sharing processor allocation policy. This policy facilitates the parallel execution of jobs at the cluster when the requested number of processors is equal to or less than the processors of the cluster.
- The machines belonging to one cluster can combine to execute parallel jobs. The machines of two different clusters can never co-allocate together to execute the same parallel job.

4.7 SUMMARY

In this chapter, the process of hybridization is carried out between a conventional and a modified bio-inspired algorithm, and a more powerful hybridized algorithm has been developed containing the benefits of stand-alone algorithms. The process of hybridization increases the capacity of individual algorithms to perform well in the case of complex computational problems. Alea is a powerful simulator that handles common problems of scheduling in the grid environment, such as resource and job heterogeneity, resource failure, and dynamic job arrival. In the next chapter, we will witness the execution of the proposed modified and hybrid scheduling algorithms in the grid environment using Alea and a standard workload to understand the behavior of the proposed and other reference algorithms.

KEYWORDS

- **Alea simulator**
- **allocation policy**
- **centralized scheduler**
- **cluster resources**
- **hybridization**
- **standard workload**
- **visualization**
- **Zewura workload**

PART II

IMPLEMENTATION OF SCHEDULING ALGORITHMS

CHAPTER 5

Research-Based Case Study to Solve Grid Scheduling Problem Using FCFS, SJF, ACO, PSO, and GA

5.1 INTRODUCTION

In this chapter, the implementation of FCFS, SJF, ACO, PSO, and GA is carried out in a grid environment. In order to perform this implementation, a grid simulator called Alea is used to virtually set up the grid environment and execute the above-mentioned algorithms. An overview of the Alea simulator used for scheduling jobs and managing resources in a large, distributed computing environment like a grid has been discussed. Alea presents a setup of the simulation environment for scheduling jobs in the grid environment. The description of the workload used for testing the performances of the conventional as well as bio-inspired algorithms in the grid environment has been included in this chapter. The workload used for scheduling the algorithms in the grid environment is called the Zewura workload. It is a standard workload for testing the performance of scheduling algorithms provided by a Czech national grid infrastructure (NGI) called MetaCentrum. The workload traces are produced from TORQUE traces, which contain 17,256 jobs. The workload is in standard workload format (SWF). The workload requires two files, namely, the job description file and the machine description file. The criteria for the performance evaluation of scheduling algorithms are four-fold: Total completion time (TCT), resource utilization (RU), load balancing, and scalability. These parameters are evaluated for each scheduling algorithm in the grid environment.

Mastering Grid Computing: Scheduling and Resource Management.
Ankita & Sudip Kumar Sahana (Authors)

5.2 PARAMETERS FOR PERFORMANCE EVALUATION OF SCHEDULING ALGORITHMS

In order to evaluate the performance of traditional and bio-inspired scheduling algorithms, four parameters have been taken into consideration. These parameters are explained below:

1. **Total Completion Time (TCT):** The TCT of the jobs is defined as the total of the time taken by all the jobs in the grid environment. Minimization of the TCT of the jobs is one of the central objectives of a good scheduling algorithm. In order to assign the jobs to cluster resources (CRs), the actual start time (AST) of the processors in a CR is calculated using Equation 5.1 (Xu et al., 2014).

$$AST(J_i, CR_k) = \max(EST(J_i, CR_k), Avail(CR_k)) \quad (5.1)$$

where; *EST* is the earliest start time (EST) of the processor of a CR, and $Avail(CR_k)$ is the earliest time at which the processor of a CR is available and ready to execute a job.

The EST of the processors is calculated using Equation 5.2:

$$EST(J_i, CR_k) = 0, \text{ if } J_i = J_{entry}$$

$$= max\ (J_k, AFT(J_k, CR_l), \text{ if } P_k = P_l)$$

$$= max\ (J_k, AFT(J_k, CR_l) + C(J_k, J_l)) \text{ if } P_k \neq P_l \quad (5.2)$$

where; *AFT* is the actual finish time.

The AFT of a job on the processor is the time at which the job finishes its execution on that processor and can be calculated using Equation 5.3:

$$AFT(J_i, CR_k) = AST(J_i, CR_k) + C(J_i, CR_k) \quad (5.3)$$

where; $C(J_i, CR_k)$ is the average computation cost of a job on the processor (CR).

The TCT of jobs can be calculated using Equation 5.4:

$$Total\ Completion\ Time = \sum_{i=1}^{n} AFT(J_i, P_k) \quad (5.4)$$

2. **Cluster Resource Utilization (CRU):** The CRU of the clusters denotes the utilization of individual clusters in the grid environment. The utilization of CRs should be high for better performance of grid scheduling. The utilization of a CR can be calculated using Equation 5.5:

$$CU_{rate}(CR_k) = \sum_{i=1}^{t} \frac{AFT(J_i, CR_k) = AST(J_i, CR_k)}{\min(EST(J_i, CR_k) - Avail(CR_k))} \tag{5.5}$$

If t number of jobs are scheduled using the cluster resource CR_k.

3. **Load Distribution:** The level of the workload over a CR is dependent on two factors:

- The assignment of the jobs to the nodes or CRs by the scheduler.
- The processing capabilities of the CR (number of processing elements on a CR).

It is notable here that a scheduling algorithm aims at minimizing the deviations in the workloads on all the resources. A small value of the standard deviation (SD) indicates that the scheduling algorithm is more efficient. The formula for SD is given in Equations 5.6 and 5.7, respectively.

$$SD = \sqrt{variance} \tag{5.6}$$

$$\sigma^2 = \Sigma \frac{(x_i - \mu)^2}{n} \tag{5.7}$$

where; $\sigma^2 = Variance$; x_i is the ith element; n is the sample size; μ is the mean of the sample.

4. **Scalability:** It is used to investigate the performance of the algorithms with an increasing number of jobs in the grid environment. The algorithm should be able to find solutions for both small and large data sets. We have tested the performance of the scheduling algorithms with a smaller number of jobs as well as a larger number of jobs to evaluate the variation in the behavior of the scheduling algorithms with changing job counts.

5.3 CASE STUDY REPORT: A COMPARISON OF PERFORMANCE RESULTS OF FCFS, SJF, ACO, PSO, AND GA

5.3.1 TOTAL COMPLETION TIME (TCT) OF JOBS

The TCT of jobs is defined as the time taken by all the jobs of the workload to complete their execution. The Zewura workload has been randomly divided into several groups (3000, 6000, 11,000, 17,256) to study the change in the behavior of the scheduling algorithms.

5.3.1.1 FCFS

The TCT of jobs in the case of FCFS for different sets of workloads is given below:

1. **For 3000 Jobs and 6000 Jobs:** The red line indicates the total number of CPUs, that is, 560. The green curve indicates the number of used CPUs, while the blue curve shows the number of requested CPUs. The TCT of 3000 jobs and 6000 jobs of the Zewura workload using FCFS is 68 days and 110 days, respectively (Figures 5.1 and 5.2).
2. **For 11,000 Jobs and 17,256 Jobs:** The TCT of 11,000 jobs and 17,256 jobs of Zewura workload using FCFS is 142 days and 245 days, respectively (Figures 5.3 and 5.4).

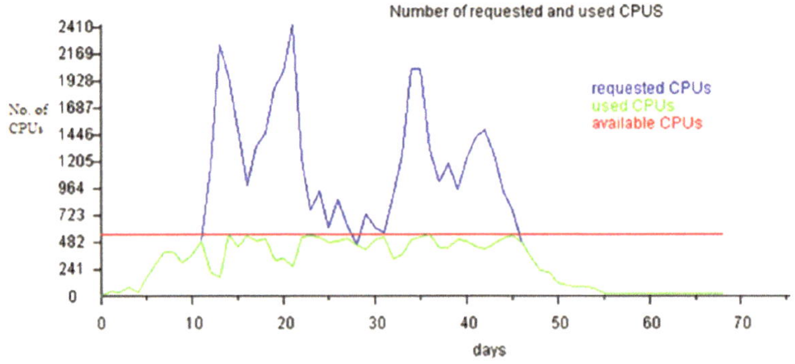

FIGURE 5.1 $TCT_{3000jobs}$ using FCFS.

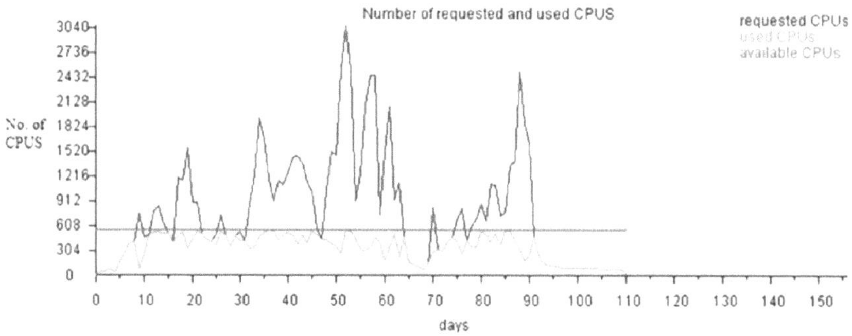

FIGURE 5.2 TCT$_{6000jobs}$ using FCFS.

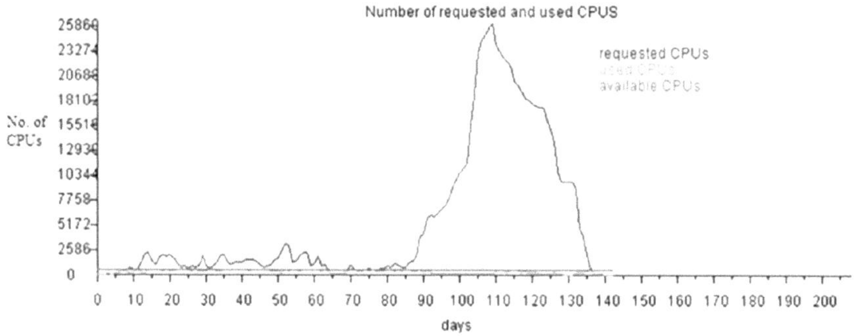

FIGURE 5.3 TCT$_{11000jobs}$ using FCFS.

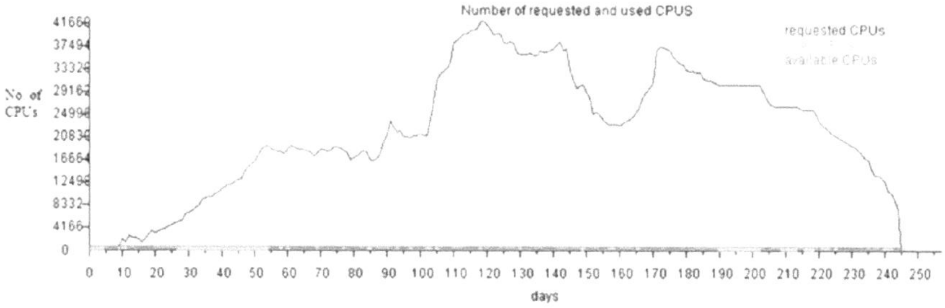

FIGURE 5.4 TCT$_{17256jobs}$ using FCFS.

5.3.1.2 SJF

The TCT of jobs in the case of SJF for different sets of workloads is given below:

1. **For 3000 Jobs 6000 Jobs:** The TCT of 3000 jobs and 6000 jobs of zewura workload using SJF is 71 days and 104 days, respectively (Figures 5.5 and 5.6).
2. **For 11,000 Jobs and 17,256 Jobs:** The TCT of 11,000 jobs and 17,256 jobs of zewura workload using SJF is 122 days and 204 days, respectively (Figures 5.7 and 5.8).

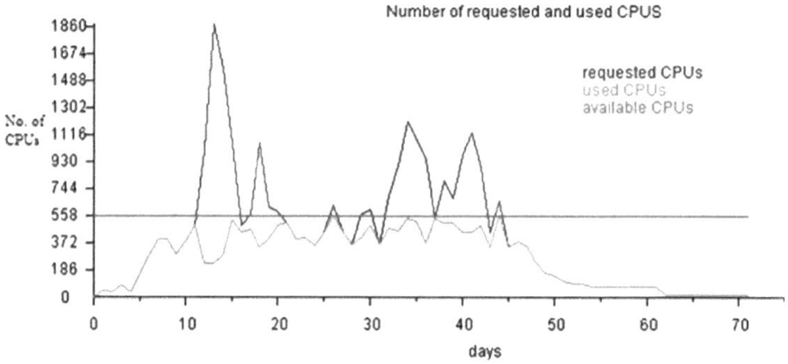

FIGURE 5.5 $TCT_{3000Jobs}$ using SJF.

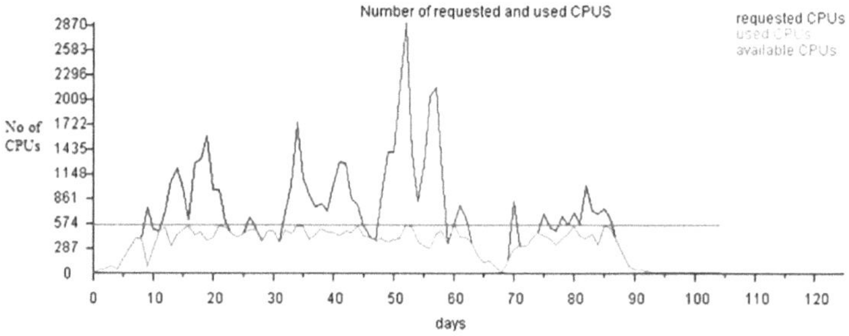

FIGURE 5.6 $TCT_{6000jobs}$ using SJF.

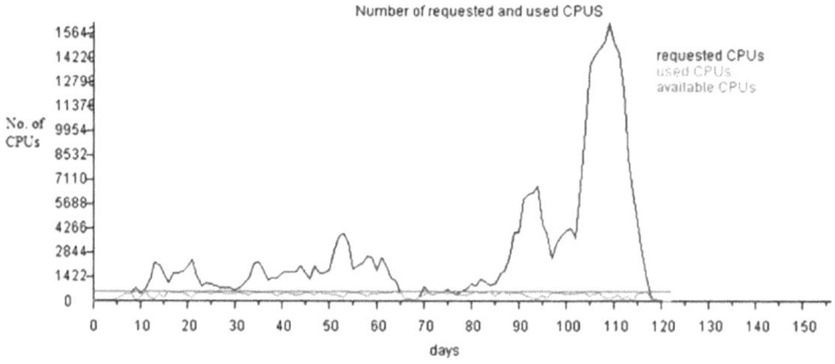

FIGURE 5.7 $TCT_{11000jobs}$ using SJF.

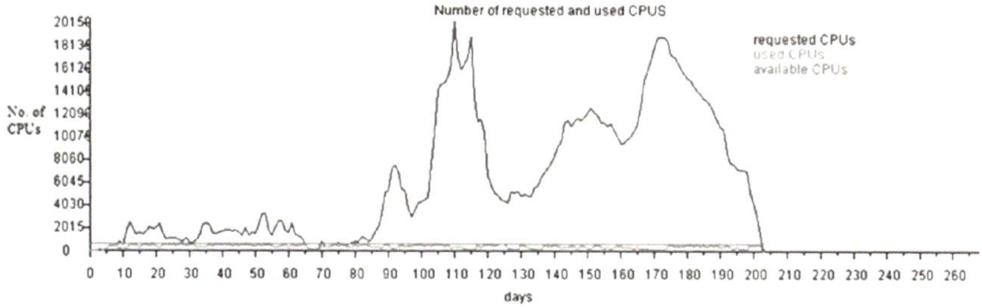

FIGURE 5.8 $\text{TCT}_{17256\text{jobs}}$ using SJF.

5.3.1.3 ACO

The TCT of jobs in the case of ACO for different sets of workloads is given below:

1. **For 3000 Jobs and 6000 Jobs:** The TCT of 3000 jobs and 6000 jobs of zewura workload using ACO is 69 days and 92 days, respectively (Figures 5.9 and 5.10).
2. **For 11,000 Jobs and 17,256 Jobs:** The TCT of 11,000 jobs and 17,256 jobs of zewura workload using ACO is 114 days and 196 days, respectively (Figures 5.11 and 5.12).

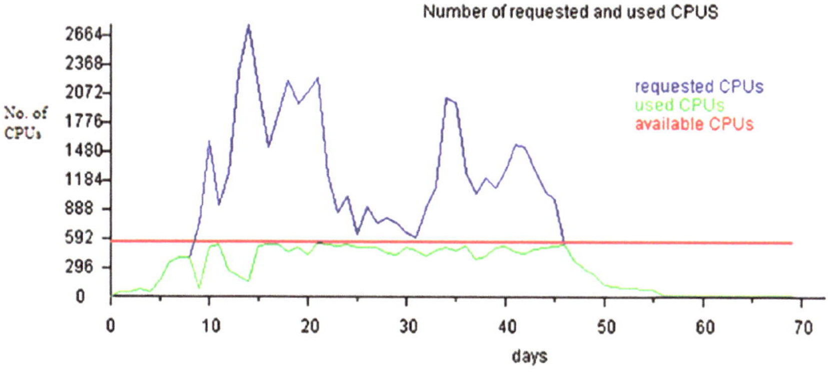

FIGURE 5.9 $\text{TCT}_{3000\text{jobs}}$ using ACO.

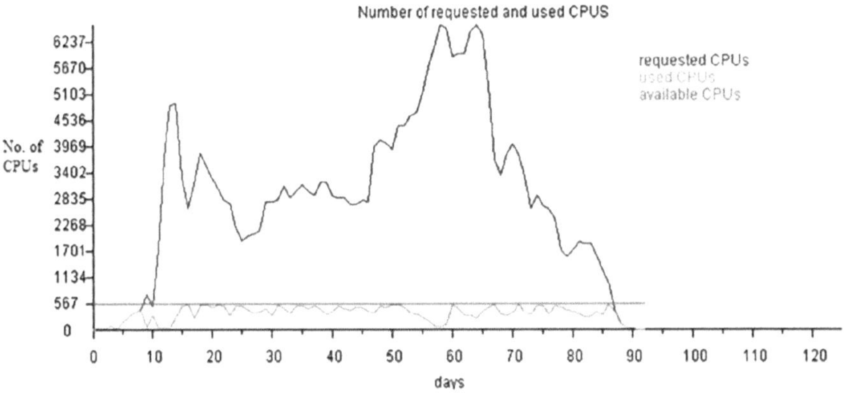

FIGURE 5.10 $TCT_{6000jobs}$ using ACO.

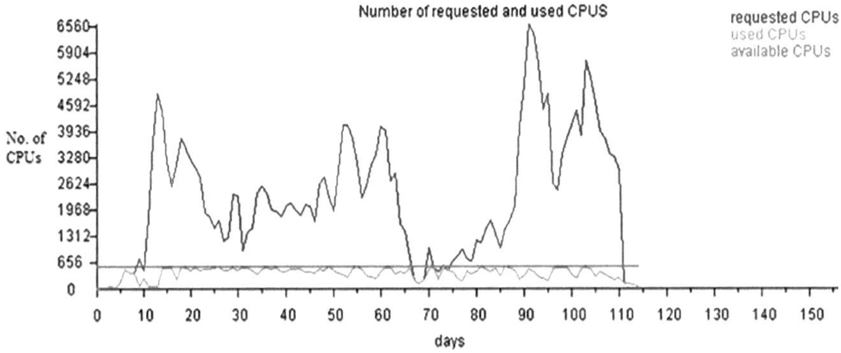

FIGURE 5.11 $TCT_{11000jobs}$ using ACO.

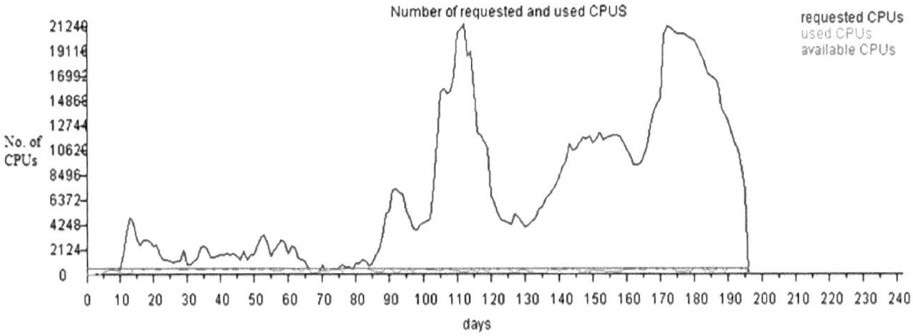

FIGURE 5.12 $TCT_{17256jobs}$ using ACO.

5.3.1.4 PSO

The TCT of jobs in the case of PSO for different sets of workloads is given below:

i. **For 3000 Jobs and 6000 Jobs:** The TCT of 3000 jobs and 6000 jobs of zewura workload using PSO is 67 days and 93 days, respectively (Figures 5.13 and 5.14).

ii. **For 11,000 Jobs and 17,256 Jobs:** The TCT of 11,000 jobs and 17,256 jobs of zewura workload using PSO is 120 days and 197 days, respectively (Figures 5.15 and 5.16).

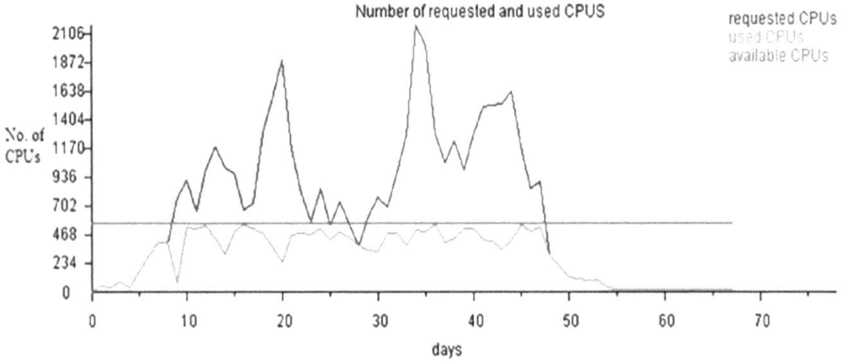

FIGURE 5.13 $TCT_{3000jobs}$ using PSO.

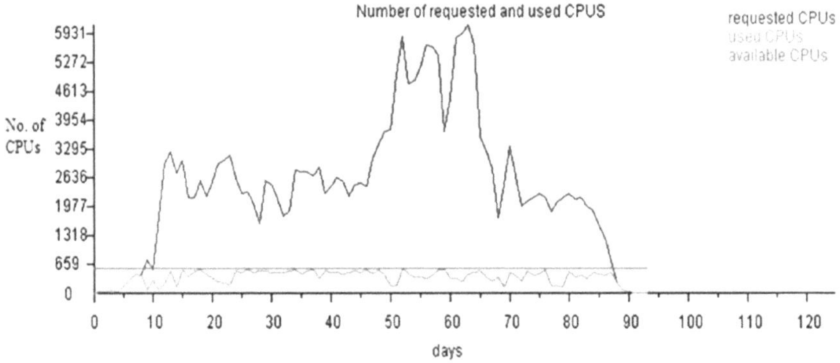

FIGURE 5.14 $TCT_{6000jobs}$ using PSO.

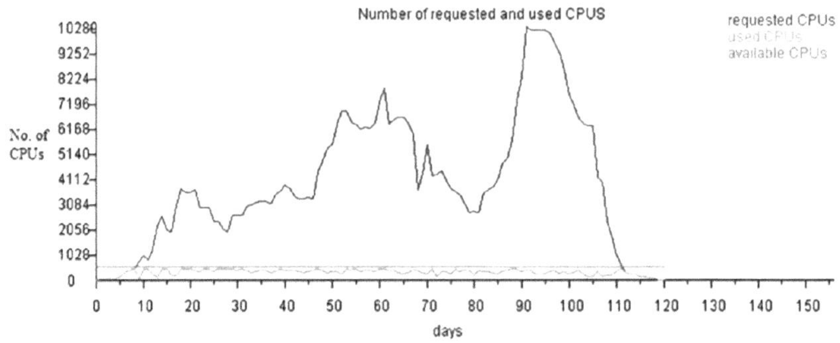

FIGURE 5.15 $TCT_{11000jobs}$ using PSO.

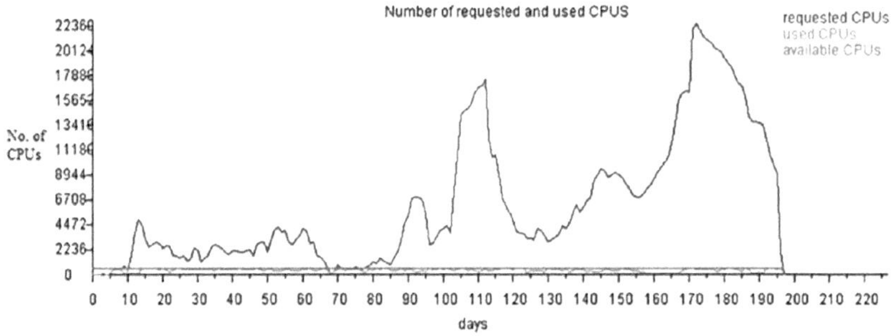

FIGURE 5.16 $TCT_{17256jobs}$ using PSO.

5.3.1.5 GA

i. **For 3000 Jobs and 6000 Jobs:** The TCT of 3000 jobs and 6000 jobs of zewura workload using GA is 67 days and 90 days, respectively (Figures 5.17 and 5.18).

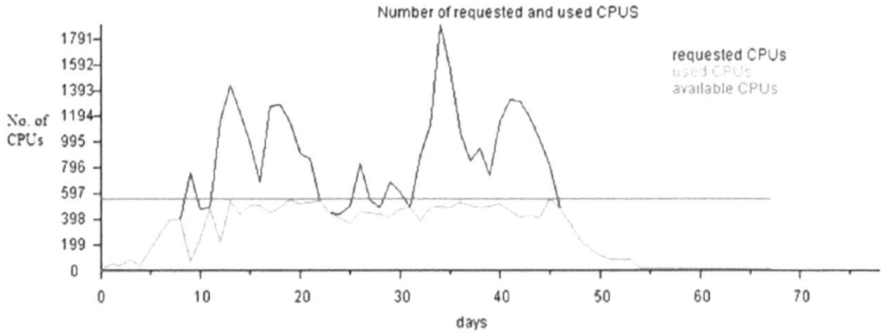

FIGURE 5.17 $TCT_{3000jobs}$ using GA.

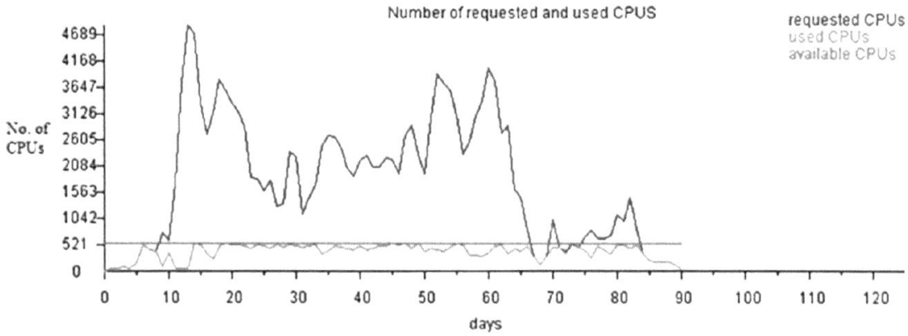

FIGURE 5.18 $TCT_{6000jobs}$ using GA.

ii. **For 11,000 Jobs and 17,256 Jobs:** The TCT of 11,000 jobs and 17,256 jobs of Zewura workload using GA is 111 days and 193 days, respectively (Figures 5.19 and 5.20).

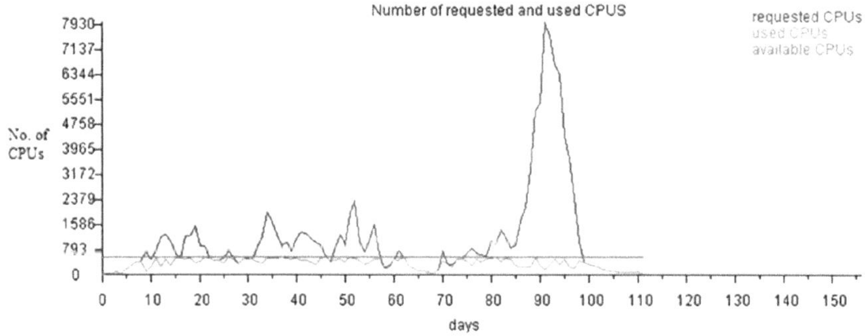

FIGURE 5.19 $TCT_{11000jobs}$ using GA.

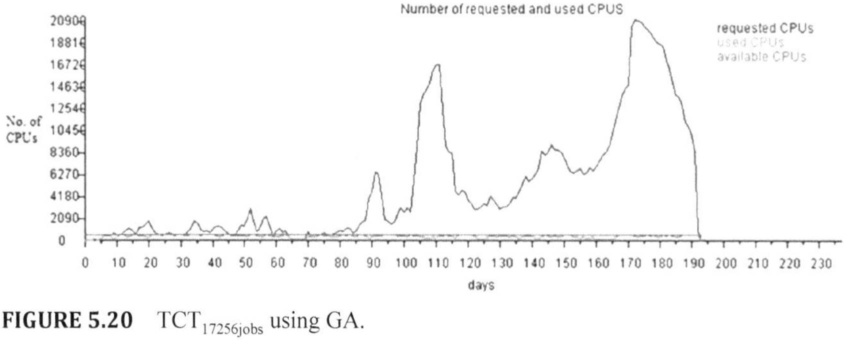

FIGURE 5.20 $TCT_{17256jobs}$ using GA.

5.3.1.6 COMPARATIVE ANALYSIS OF ALGORITHMS (FCFS, SJF, ACO, PSO, AND GA) ON THE BASIS OF TCT

In the case of a low job count (say 3000), FCFS shows good performance compared to SJF and ACO. With the increase in job counts, the performance graph of FCFS started to decline, and the TCT of jobs increased compared to other algorithms. SJF, being a conventional algorithm, has better performance than FCFS in terms of TCT for the same workload. Out of the bio-inspired algorithms, it is evident (Figures 5.9–5.20) that GA has outperformed ACO and PSO for both small and large sets of jobs (Table 5.1).

TABLE 5.1 TCT of Zewura Workload for FCFS, SJF, ACO, PSO, and GA

Scheduling Algorithms	TCT of Zewura Workload (In Days)			
	3000	6000	11,000	17,256
FCFS	68	110	142	240
SJF	71	104	122	204
ACO	69	92	114	196
PSO	67	93	120	197
GA	67	90	111	193

5.3.2 CLUSTER RESOURCE UTILIZATION (CRU)

The utilization of all seven cluster resources (CRs) (zewura1, zewura2, zewura3, zewura4, zewura5, zewura6, and zewura7) for different job counts (3000, 6000, 11,000, 17,256) of the zewura workload is given in subsections using individual algorithms.

5.3.2.1 FCFS: FOR 3000, 6000, 11,000, AND 17,256 JOBS

The red color indicates a high rate of cluster utilization. The rate of CR utilization should be high for better performance of grid scheduling and resource management. The green color indicates the least utilization or idleness of the CPU during that time period (Figures 5.21–5.24). The individual utilization of all seven CRs for a given workload using the FCFS scheduling algorithm has been calculated (Table 5.2).

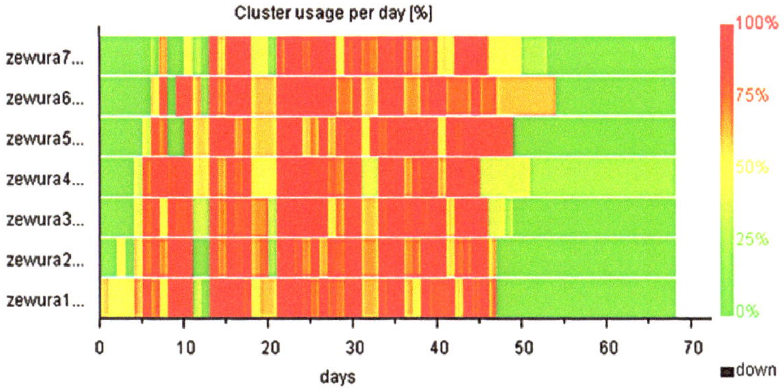

FIGURE 5.21 $CRU_{3000jobs}$ using FCFS.

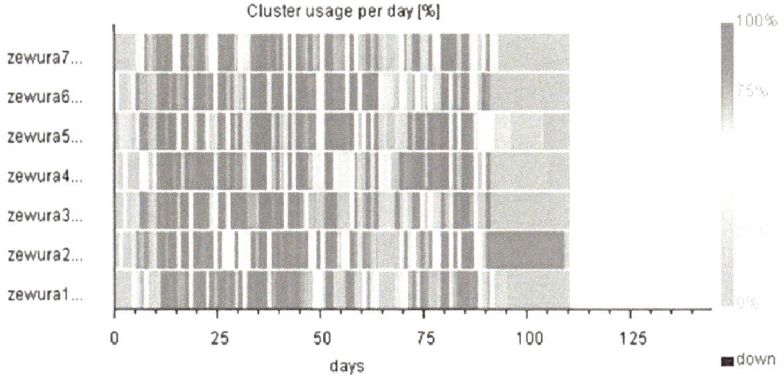

FIGURE 5.22 $CRU_{6000jobs}$ using FCFS.

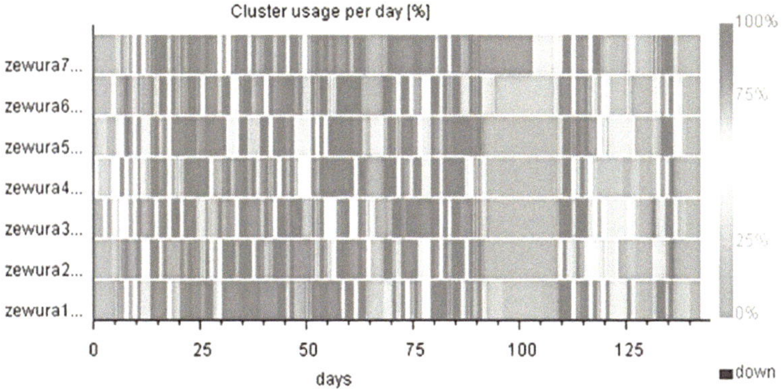

FIGURE 5.23 $CRU_{11000jobs}$ using FCFS.

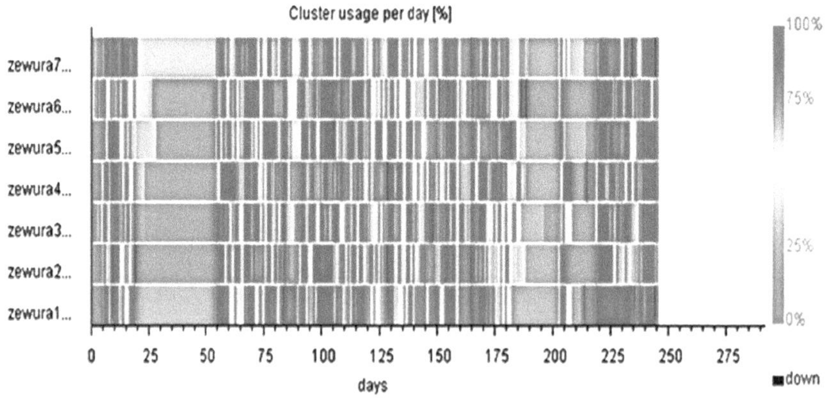

FIGURE 5.24 $CRU_{17256jobs}$ using FCFS.

TABLE 5.2 CRU of Zewura Clusters (in Percentage) Using FCFS Scheduling Algorithm

Zewura Clusters	Cluster Resource Utilization of Zewura Clusters for Given Set of Jobs (in Percentage)			
	3000 Jobs	**6000 Jobs**	**11,000 Jobs**	**17,256 Jobs**
Zewura 1	55.15	61.18	60.38	57.40
Zewura 2	51.76	72.41	54.82	49.94
Zewura 3	51.65	56.23	55.93	52.45
Zewura 4	58.62	62.21	54.04	53.03
Zewura 5	50.82	62.94	59.83	52.11
Zewura 6	54.76	60.21	57.76	52.62
Zewura 7	45.74	57.13	66.66	63.50
Average utilization	54.64	61.75	58.48	54.35

5.3.2.2 SJF: FOR 3000, 6000, 11,000, AND 17,256 JOBS

The rate of utilization of seven clusters using SJF for different sets of jobs is given (Figures 5.25–5.28). The individual utilization of all seven CRs for a given workload using the SJF scheduling algorithm has been calculated (Table 5.3).

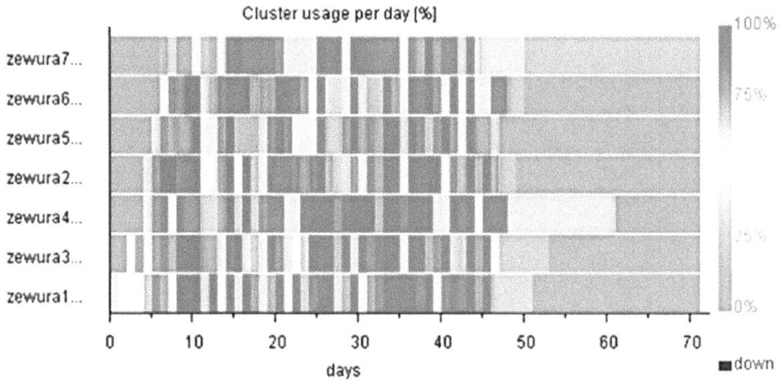

FIGURE 5.25 $CRU_{3000jobs}$ using SJF.

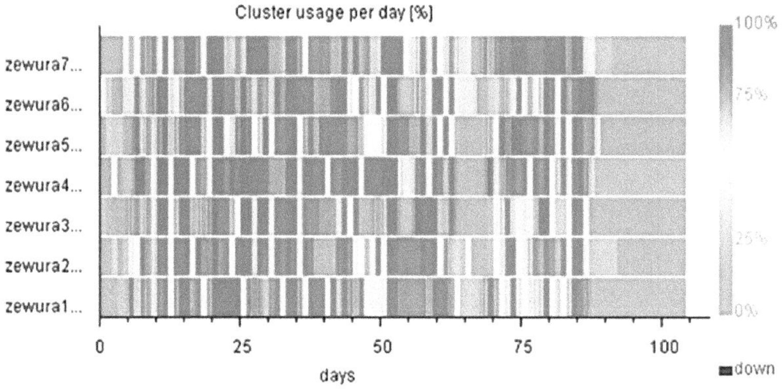

FIGURE 5.26 $CRU_{6000jobs}$ using SJF.

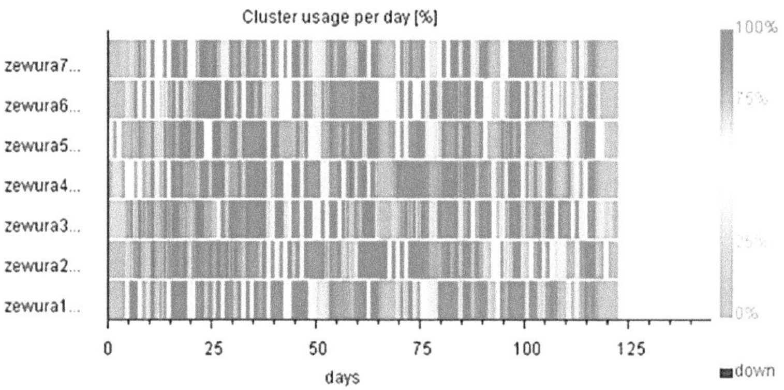

FIGURE 5.27 $CRU_{11000jobs}$ using SJF.

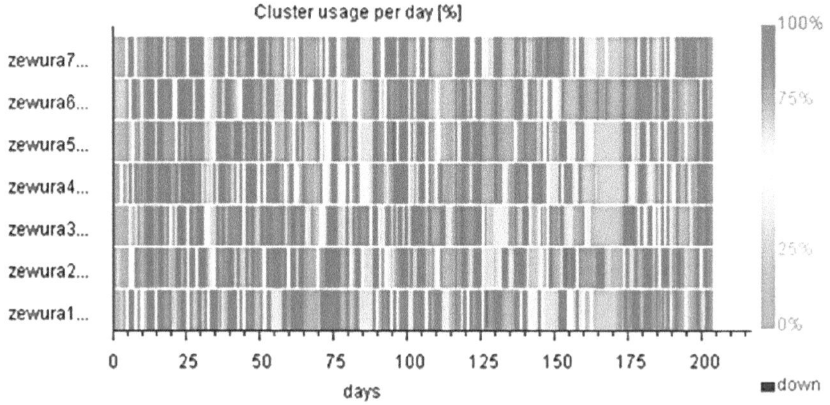

FIGURE 5.28 $CRU_{17256jobs}$ using SJF.

TABLE 5.3 CRU of Zewura Clusters (in Percentage) Using SJF Scheduling Algorithm

Zewura Clusters	Cluster Resource Utilization of Zewura Clusters for Given Set of Jobs (in Percentage)			
	3000 Jobs	**6000 Jobs**	**11000 Jobs**	**17256 Jobs**
Zewura 1	52.74	59.60	62.49	66.49
Zewura 2	53.56	61.63	59.76	66.76
Zewura 3	51.10	55.58	60.82	66.82
Zewura 4	60.22	65.53	61.23	65.23
Zewura 5	56.76	59.98	63.76	62.07
Zewura 6	52.63	62.80	62.23	64.87
Zewura 7	51.11	63.55	60.98	66.32
Average utilization	54.02	61.29	61.61	65.51

5.3.2.3 ACO: FOR 3000, 6000, 11,000, AND 17,256 JOBS

The rate of utilization of seven clusters using ACO for different sets of jobs is given (Figures 5.29–5.32). The individual utilization of all seven CRs for a given workload using the ACO scheduling algorithm has been calculated (Table 5.4).

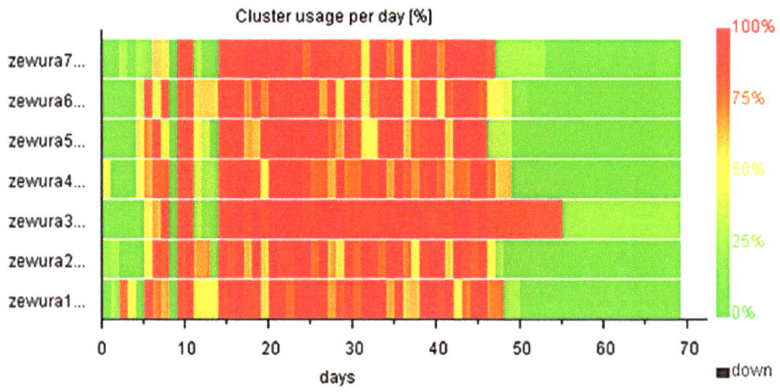

FIGURE 5.29 $CRU_{3000jobs}$ using ACO.

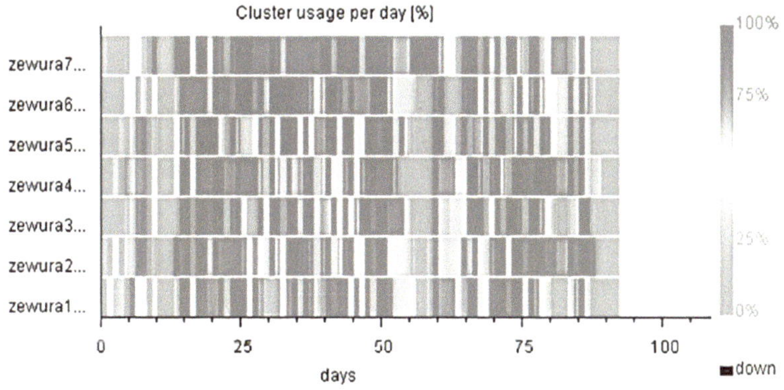

FIGURE 5.30 $CRU_{6000jobs}$ using ACO.

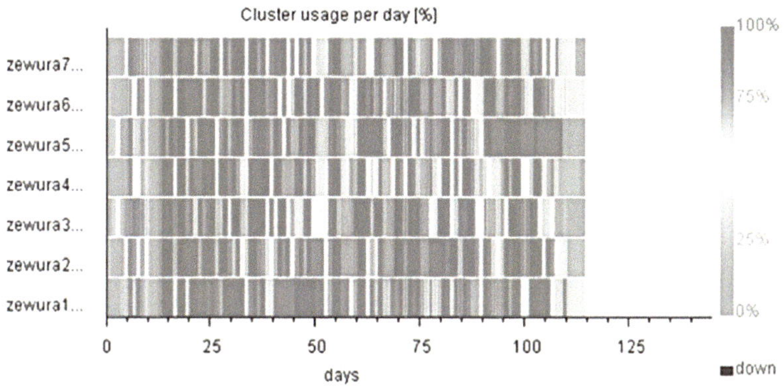

FIGURE 5.31 $CRU_{11000jobs}$ using ACO.

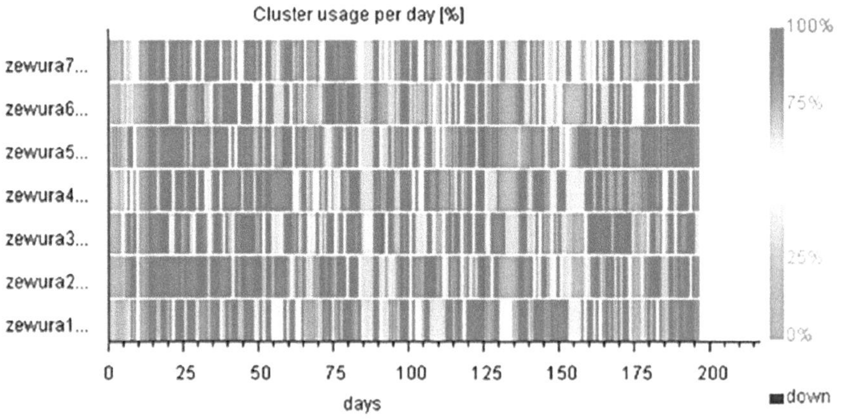

FIGURE 5.32 $CRU_{17256jobs}$ using ACO.

TABLE 5.4 CRU of Zewura Clusters (in Percentage) Using ACO Scheduling Algorithm

Zewura Clusters	Cluster Resource Utilization of Zewura Clusters for Given Set of Jobs (in Percentage)			
	3000 Jobs	**6000 Jobs**	**11,000 Jobs**	**17,256 Jobs**
Zewura 1	59.03	60.03	70.05	67.84
Zewura 2	51.87	65.66	69.94	68.92
Zewura 3	49.63	58.34	64.01	70.34
Zewura 4	51.55	66.46	66.14	70.33
Zewura 5	57.22	60.17	67.81	67.84
Zewura 6	54.23	63.89	68.82	62.80
Zewura 7	54.83	67.58	64.54	68.36
Average utilization	54.05	63.16	67.33	68.06

5.3.2.4 PSO: FOR 3000, 6000, 11,000, AND 17,256 JOBS

The rate of utilization of seven clusters using PSO for different sets of jobs is given (Figures 5.33–5.36). The individual utilization of all seven CRs for a given workload using the PSO scheduling algorithm has been calculated (Table 5.5).

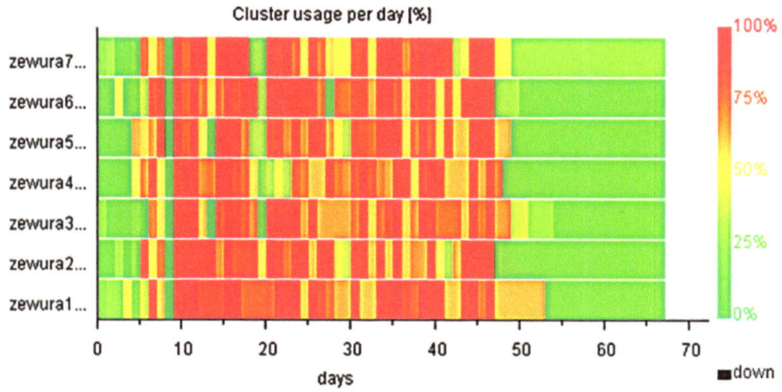

FIGURE 5.33 $CRU_{3000jobs}$ using PSO.

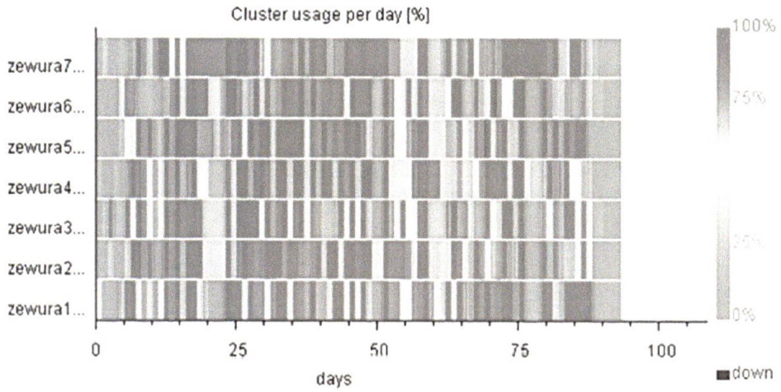

FIGURE 5.34 $CRU_{6000jobs}$ using PSO.

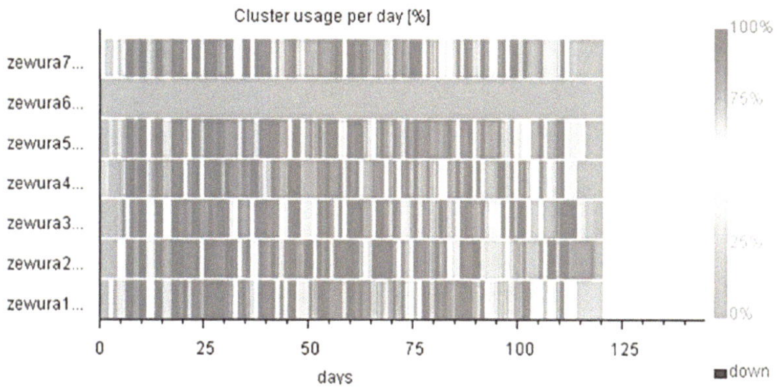

FIGURE 5.35 $CRU_{11000jobs}$ using PSO.

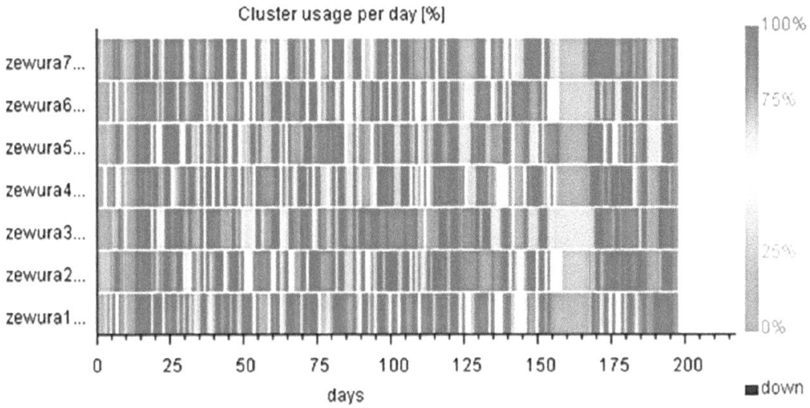

FIGURE 5.36 $CRU_{17256jobs}$ using PSO.

TABLE 5.5 CRU of Zewura Clusters (in Percentage) Using PSO Scheduling Algorithm

Zewura Clusters	Cluster Resource Utilization of Zewura Clusters for Given Set of Jobs (in Percentage)			
	3000 Jobs	**6000 Jobs**	**11,000 Jobs**	**17,256 Jobs**
Zewura 1	51.56	62.45	61.15	68.99
Zewura 2	54.40	64.19	63.29	67.76
Zewura 3	48.85	61.66	60.18	68.62
Zewura 4	51.19	61.77	62.85	65.76
Zewura 5	58.17	62.99	63.39	67.41
Zewura 6	59.65	59.42	61.42	67.84
Zewura 7	52.43	70.80	61.80	67.93
Average CRU	53.75	63.32	62.01	67.75

5.3.2.5 GA: FOR 3000, 6000, 11,000, AND 17,256 JOBS

The rate of utilization of seven clusters using GA for different sets of jobs is given (Figures 5.37–5.40). The individual utilization of all seven CRs for a given workload using the GA scheduling algorithm has been calculated (Table 5.6).

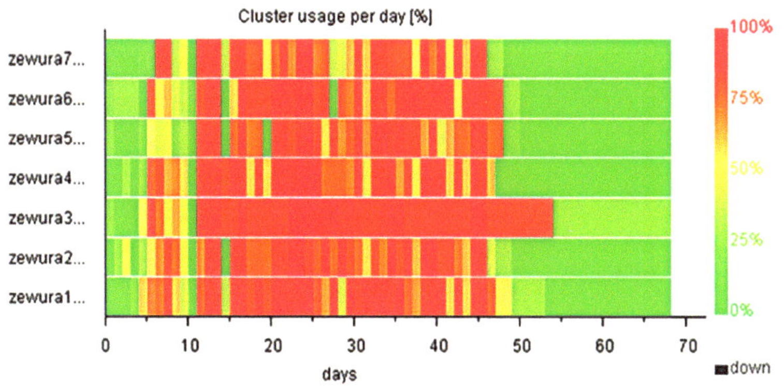

FIGURE 5.37 $CRU_{3000jobs}$ using GA.

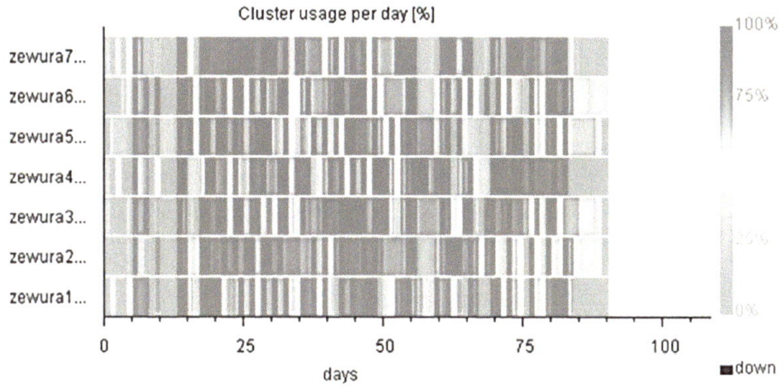

FIGURE 5.38 $CRU_{6000jobs}$ using GA.

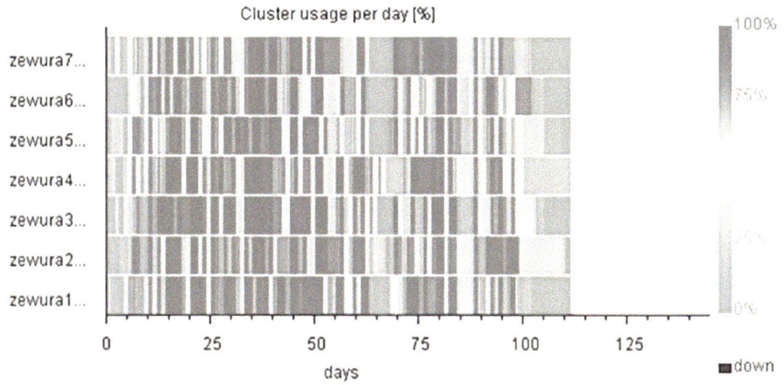

FIGURE 5.39 $CRU_{11000jobs}$ using GA.

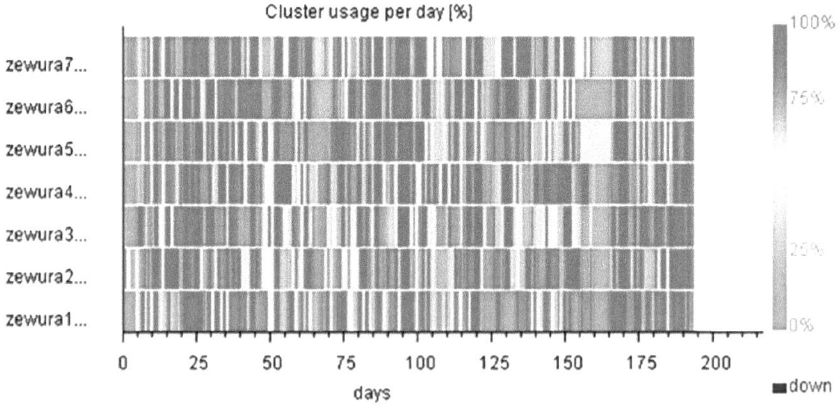

FIGURE 5.40 $CRU_{17256jobs}$ using GA.

TABLE 5.6 CRU of Zewura Clusters (in Percentage) Using GA Scheduling Algorithm

Zewura Clusters	Cluster Resource Utilization of Zewura Clusters for Given Set of Jobs (in Percentage)			
	3000 Jobs	**6000 Jobs**	**11,000 Jobs**	**17,256 Jobs**
Zewura 1	51.80	63.54	65.78	65.07
Zewura 2	51.73	64.08	69.52	68.88
Zewura 3	58.36	63.76	65.97	67.33
Zewura 4	54.89	65.67	67.82	70.79
Zewura 5	52.36	65.44	66.54	71.40
Zewura 6	57.05	63.82	67.87	68.52
Zewura 7	53.53	62.67	62.71	72.87
Average CRU	54.24	64.14	66.60	69.26

5.3.3 AVERAGE MACHINE UTILIZATION (AMU)

The average machine utilization (AMU) (zewura1, zewura2, zewura3, zewura4, zewura5, zewura6 and zewura7) for different job counts (3000, 6000, 11,000, 17,256) of zewura workload are given in subsections using individual algorithms.

5.3.3.1 FCFS

The peak in the graphs indicates a high rate of machine utilization on a particular day. With the increase in the number of jobs, the graph becomes denser (Figures 5.41–5.44) due to the increase in machine utilization.

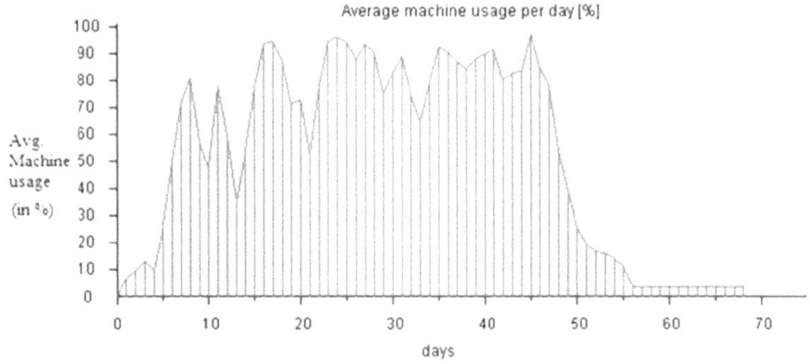

FIGURE 5.41 AMU for 3000 jobs using FCFS.

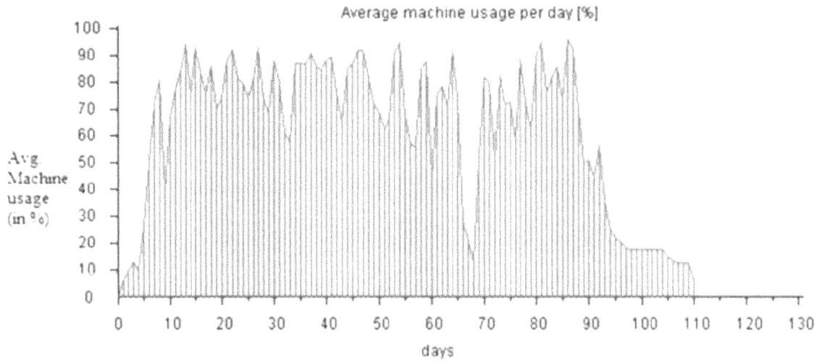

FIGURE 5.42 AMU for 6000 jobs using FCFS.

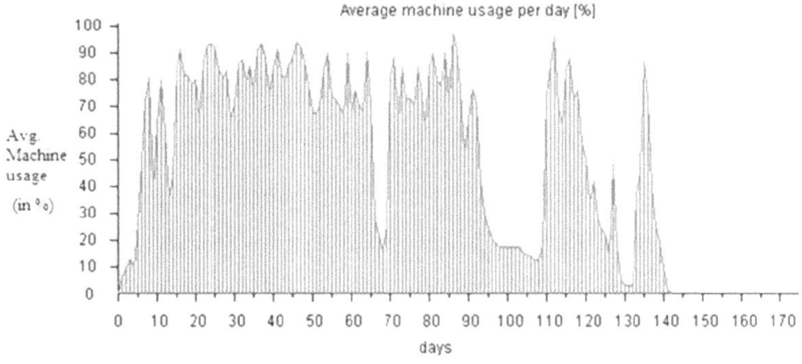

FIGURE 5.43 AMU for 11,000 jobs using FCFS.

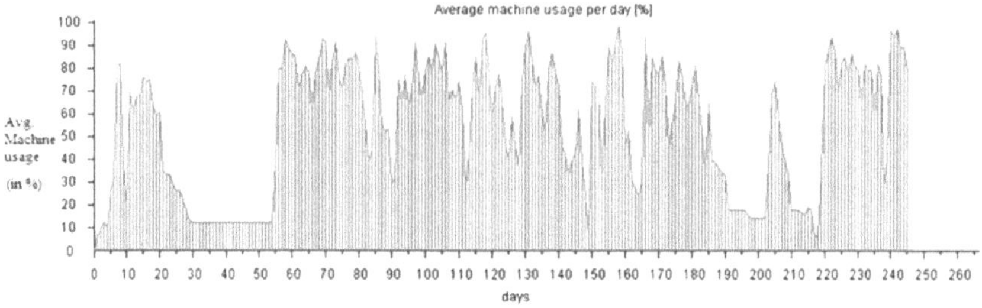

FIGURE 5.44 AMU for 17,256 jobs using FCFS.

5.3.3.2 SJF

The graphs (Figures 5.45–5.48) show the AMU in the case of the SJF scheduling algorithm for different sets of Zewura workloads.

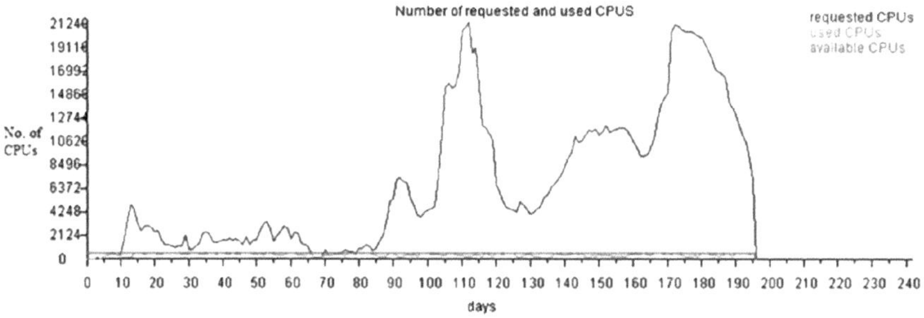

FIGURE 5.45 AMU for 3000 jobs using SJF.

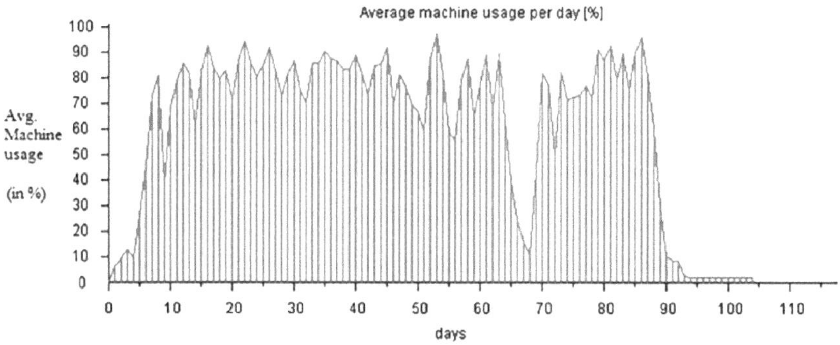

FIGURE 5.46 AMU for 6000 jobs using SJF.

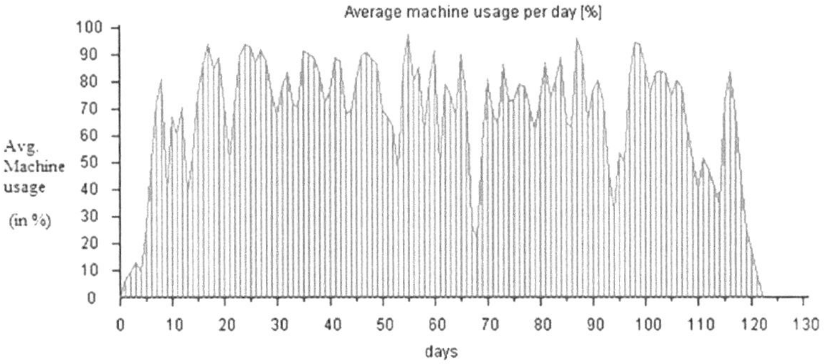

FIGURE 5.47 AMU for 11,000 jobs using SJF.

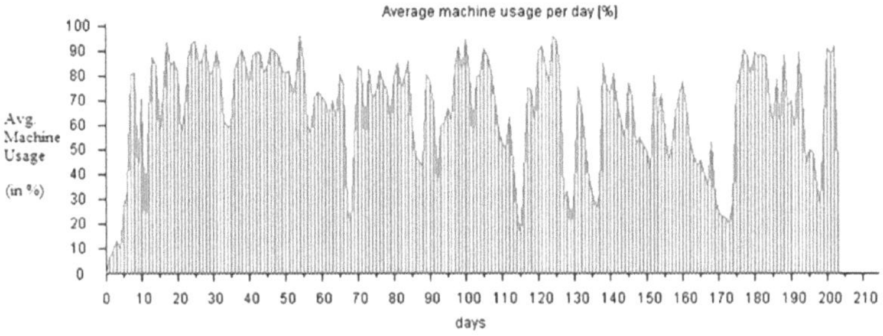

FIGURE 5.48 AMU for 17,256 jobs using SJF.

5.3.3.3 ACO

The graphs (Figures 5.49–5.52) show the AMU in the case of the ACO scheduling algorithm for different sets of Zewura workloads.

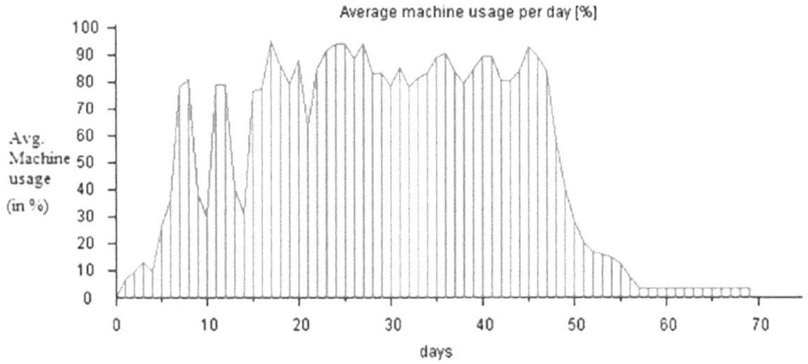

FIGURE 5.49 AMU for 3000 jobs using ACO.

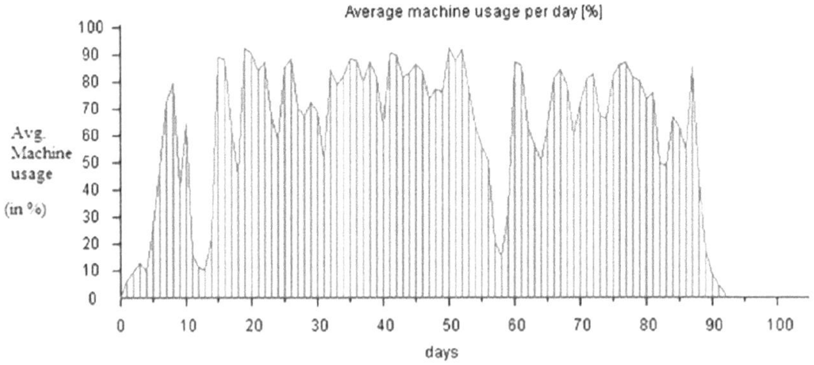

FIGURE 5.50 AMU for 6000 jobs using ACO.

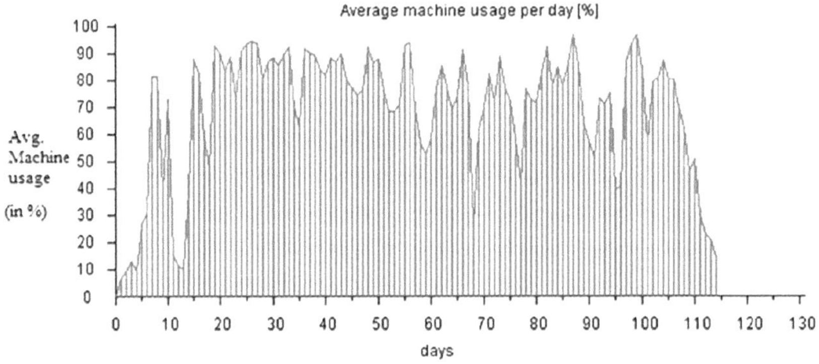

FIGURE 5.51 AMU for 11,000 jobs using ACO.

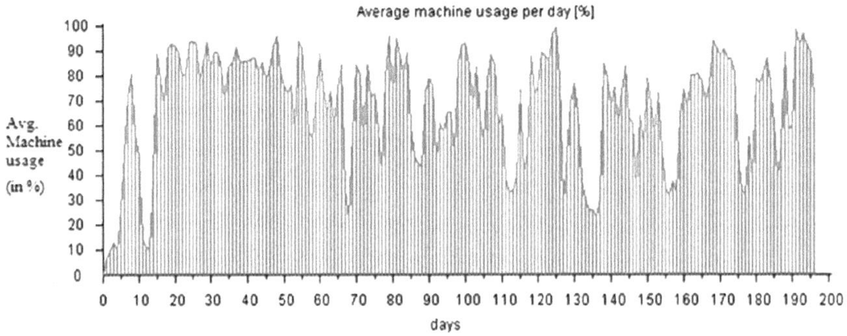

FIGURE 5.52 AMU for 17,256 jobs using ACO.

5.3.3.4 PSO

The graphs (Figures 5.53–5.56) show the AMU in the case of the PSO scheduling algorithm for different sets of Zewura workloads.

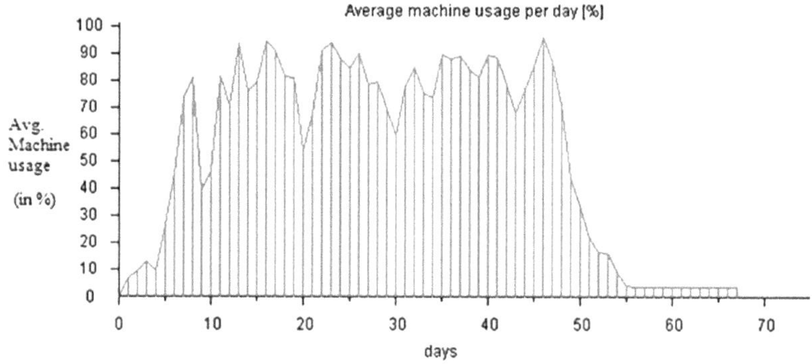

FIGURE 5.53 AMU for 3000 jobs using PSO.

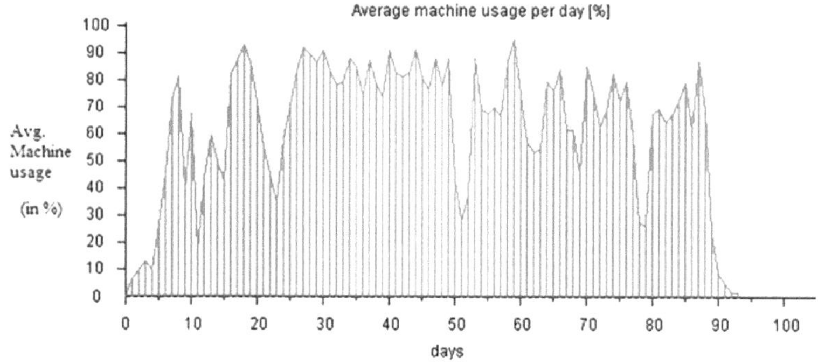

FIGURE 5.54 AMU for 6000 jobs using PSO.

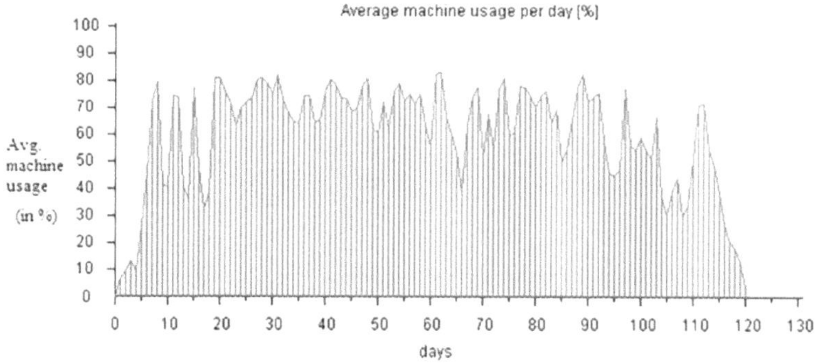

FIGURE 5.55 AMU for 11,000 jobs using PSO.

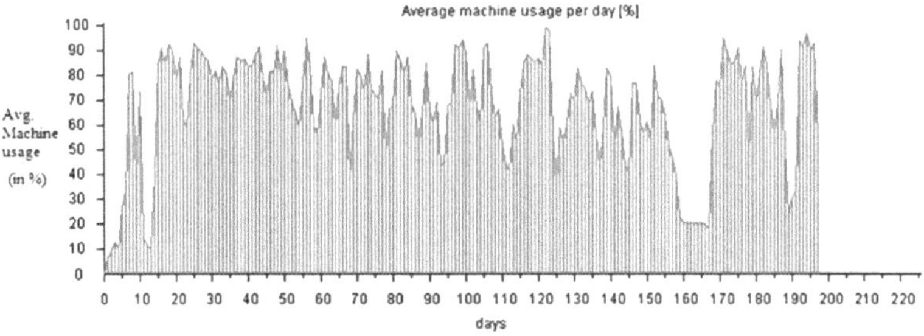

FIGURE 5.56 AMU for 17,256 jobs using PSO.

5.3.3.5 GA

The graphs (Figures 5.57–5.60) show the AMU in the case of the GA scheduling algorithm for different sets of Zewura workloads.

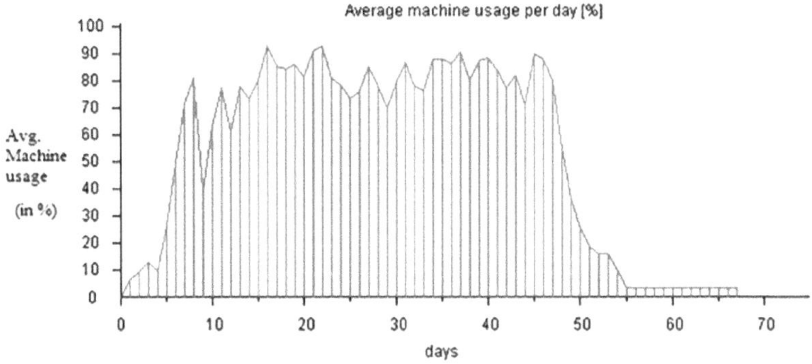

FIGURE 5.57 AMU for 3000 jobs using GA.

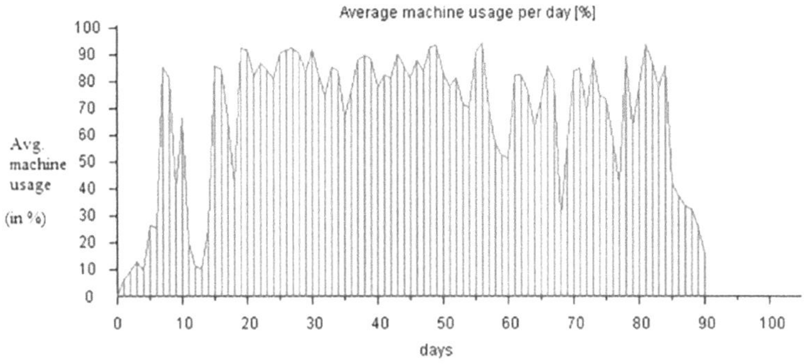

FIGURE 5.58 AMU for 6000 jobs using GA.

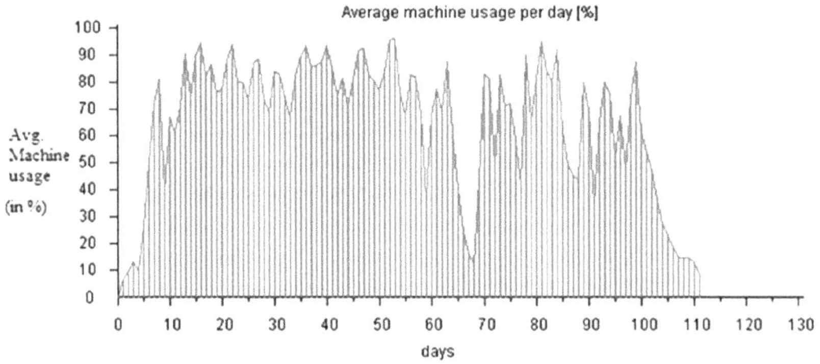

FIGURE 5.59 AMU for 11,000 jobs using GA.

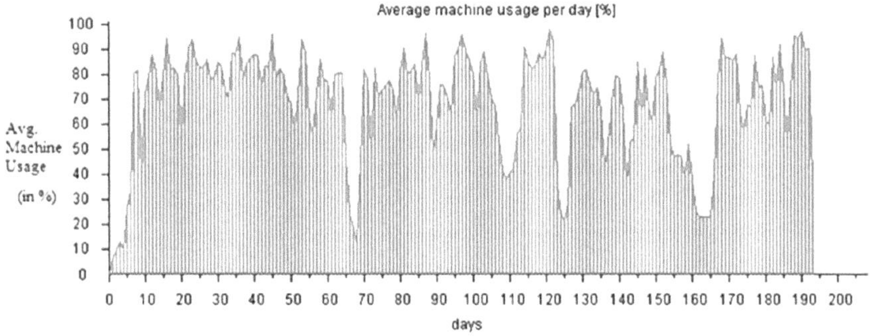

FIGURE 5.60 AMU for 17,256 jobs using GA.

5.3.4 LOAD DISTRIBUTION

Standard deviation (SD) has been used to measure the uniformity in the distribution of load among the CRs. A low value of SD indicates less variation in the load distribution. Using the data (Tables 5.2–5.6), the value of SD for FCFS, SJF, ACO, PSO, and GA using the Zewura workload is calculated (Table 5.7). The value of SD is lowest in PSO for a smaller set of jobs, while it is highest for a larger set of jobs. The value of SD is low in GA in both cases of job sets, which shows the diversity of GA to work with both smaller and larger workloads. The value of SD in the utilization of CRs for FCFS using 3000 jobs is calculated below:

Average utilization of FCFS for 3000 jobs = 54.64 (Table 5.2)

$$\text{Variance} = 16.54$$

$$\text{SD} = \sqrt{\textit{variance}} = 4.07$$

The value of SD in the utilization of CRs for SJF using 3000 jobs is calculated below:

Average utilization of SJF for 3000 jobs = 54.02 (using Table 5.3)

$$\text{Variance} = 11.12$$

$$\text{`SD} = \sqrt{11.12} = 3.33$$

Similarly, the value of SD in the utilization of CRs for FCFS, SJF, ACO, PSO, and GA is calculated for different sets of jobs of the Zewura workload (Table 5.7). The value of SD is lowest in PSO for smaller sets of jobs, while it is highest for larger sets of jobs. The value of SD is low in GA in both cases of job sets, which shows the diversity of GA to work with both smaller and larger workloads.

TABLE 5.7 Standard Deviation for FCFS, SJF, ACO, PSO, and GA

Scheduling Algorithms	**SD in the Utilization of Cluster Resources of Zewura Clusters for a Given Set of Jobs (in Percentage)**			
	3000 Jobs	**6000 Jobs**	**11,000 Jobs**	**17,256 Jobs**
FCFS	4.07	4.92	4.00	4.32
SJF	3.33	2.99	1.21	1.56
ACO	3.07	3.36	2.29	2.35
PSO	3.62	3.33	1.11	0.95
GA	2.43	0.98	1.99	2.44

5.4 SUMMARY

In this chapter, we have taken five parameters to calculate the efficiency of scheduling algorithms. These parameters are TCT, cluster resource utilization (CRU), average utilization (AU), load distribution, and scalability. All these parameters have been evaluated for traditional as well as bio-inspired algorithms using a standard workload, that is, the Zewura workload. The diversified workload helps in evaluating the algorithm's performance on both small and large sets of jobs. Out of all scheduling algorithms, it is evident from the evaluated results that the genetic algorithm (GA) has better performance in terms of the above-stated parameters for both small and large sets of jobs. GA is a powerful metaheuristic that belongs to the set of evolutionary algorithms. These algorithms are well-suited to NP-complete and optimization problems such as the Grid Scheduling Problem.

KEYWORDS

- **Ant colony optimization**
- **average machine utilization**
- **cluster resource utilization**
- **genetic algorithm**
- **particle swarm optimization**
- **shortest job first**
- **standard deviation**
- **total completion time**

CHAPTER 6

Research-Based Case Study to Solve Grid Scheduling Problem Using Modified and Hybrid Algorithms: ACOTHRESH, SJF-ACOTHRESH, and SJF-GA

6.1 PARAMETERS FOR PERFORMANCE EVALUATION

ACO has emerged as a powerful metaheuristic in solving different problems in computer science and related areas. The literature survey report shows the popularity of the ACO algorithm in solving various NP-complete problems. In this chapter, the author has introduced an enhancement to the basic ACO algorithm by including a new parameter in the conventional ACO algorithm. The new parameter introduced to the basic ACO is called threshold probability and the developed algorithm is called ACO_{thresh}. A detailed explanation of the ACO_{thresh} algorithm has been given in Chapter 4. This chapter covers the implementation of the ACO_{thresh} algorithm in a simulation environment using a standard workload. The performance parameters such as completion time of jobs, workload distribution, cluster resource (CR) utilization, average machine utilization (AMU), and standard deviation (SD) of ACO_{thresh}, SJF-ACO_{thresh}, and SJF-GA are calculated using a standard workload.

Alea simulator (Alea 3.0) creates a setup of a simulation environment for scheduling jobs in the grid environment. ACO_{thresh} has been implemented in a simulation environment using the Zewura workload. In this chapter, in order to evaluate the performance of ACO_{thresh}, SJF-ACO_{thresh},

Mastering Grid Computing: Scheduling and Resource Management.
Ankita & Sudip Kumar Sahana (Authors)

and SJF-GA, four parameters have been taken into consideration. A detailed description of all these parameters has already been covered in Chapter 5. The behavior of ACO_{thresh}, SJF-ACO_{thresh}, and SJF-GA have been observed and studied in the case of varying workloads using the parameters given in subsections.

6.1.1 TOTAL COMPLETION TIME (TCT)

The Zewura workload contains 17,256 jobs, which are divided into four sets: 3000, 6000, 11,000, and 17,256 jobs. The random distribution of the zewura workload helps in studying the change in the behavior of the scheduling algorithms.

6.1.1.1 ACO_{THRESH}

The TCT of jobs in the case of ACO_{thresh} for different sets of workloads is given below:

i. **For 3000 and 6000 Jobs:** The red line indicates the total number of CPUs, that is, 560. The green curve indicates the number of used CPUs, while the blue curve shows the number of requested CPUs. The TCT of 3000 jobs and 6000 jobs of the zewura workload using ACO_{thresh} is 67 days and 89 days, respectively (Figures 6.1 and 6.2).

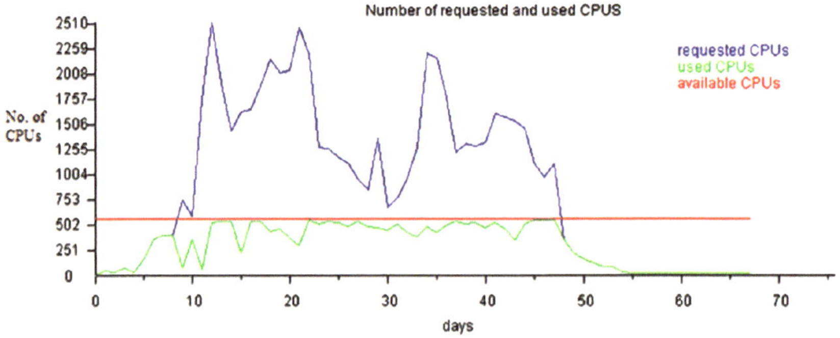

FIGURE 6.1 $TCT_{3000jobs}$ using ACO_{thresh}.

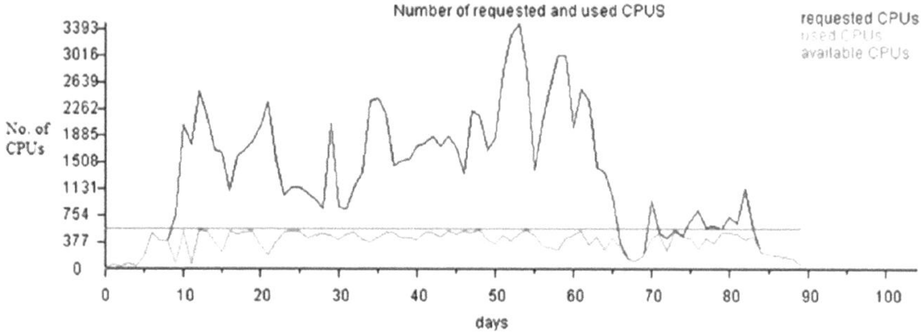

FIGURE 6.2 $TCT_{6000jobs}$ using ACO_{thresh}.

ii. **For 11,000 and 17,256 Jobs:** The TCT of 11,000 jobs and 17,256 jobs of zewura workload using ACO_{thresh} is 67 days and 89 days, respectively (Figures 6.3 and 6.4).

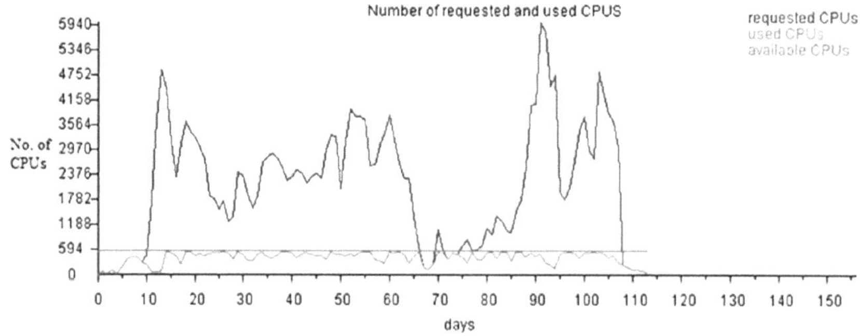

FIGURE 6.3 $TCT_{11000jobs}$ using ACO_{thresh}.

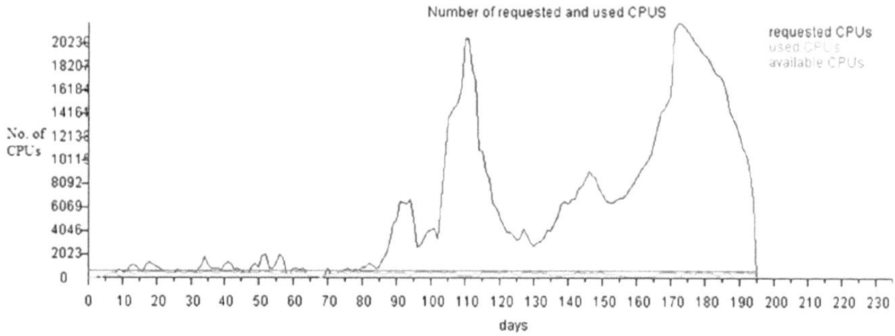

FIGURE 6.4 $TCT_{3000jobs}$ using ACO_{thresh}.

6.1.1.2 SJF-ACO$_{THRESH}$

The TCT of jobs in the case of SJF-ACO$_{thresh}$ for different sets of workloads is given below:

i. **For 3000 and 6000 Jobs:** The TCT of 11,000 jobs and 17,256 jobs of zewura workload using SJF-ACO$_{thresh}$ is 66 days and 88 days, respectively (Figures 6.5 and 6.6).

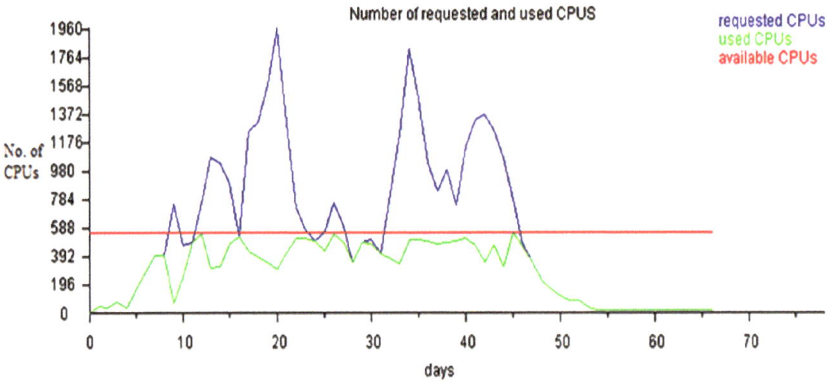

FIGURE 6.5 TCT$_{3000jobs}$ using SJF-ACO$_{thresh}$.

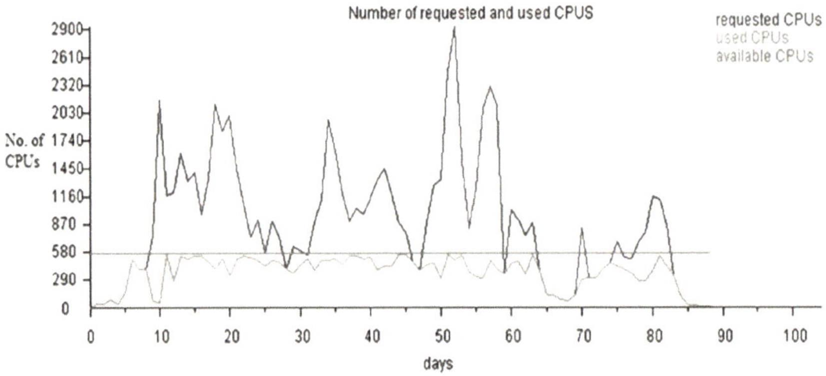

FIGURE 6.6 TCT$_{6000jobs}$ using SJF-ACO$_{thresh}$.

ii. **For 11,000 and 17,256 Jobs:** The TCT of 11,000 jobs and 17,256 jobs of zewura workload using SJF-ACO$_{thresh}$ is 109 days and 191 days, respectively (Figures 6.7 and 6.8).

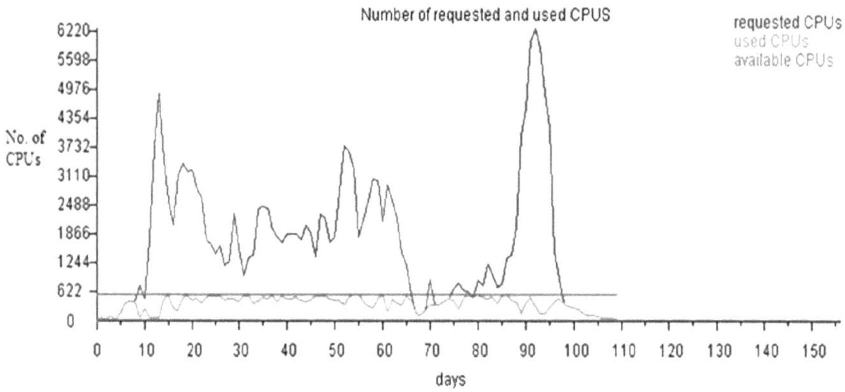

FIGURE 6.7 $TCT_{11000jobs}$ using SJF-ACO_{thresh}.

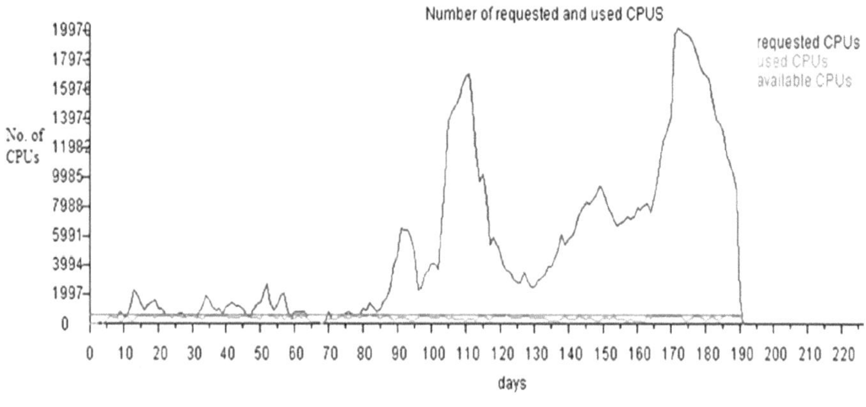

FIGURE 6.8 $TCT_{17256jobs}$ using SJF-ACO_{thresh}.

6.1.1.3 SJF-GA

The TCT of jobs in the case of SJF-GA for different sets of workloads is given below:

i. **For 3000 and 6000 Jobs:** The TCT of 11,000 jobs and 17,256 jobs of zewura workload using SJF-GA is 66 days and 86 days, respectively (Figures 6.9 and 6.10).

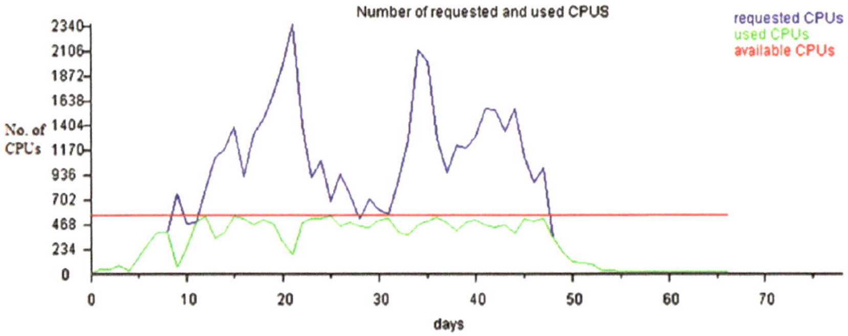

FIGURE 6.9 $TCT_{3000jobs}$ using SJF-GA.

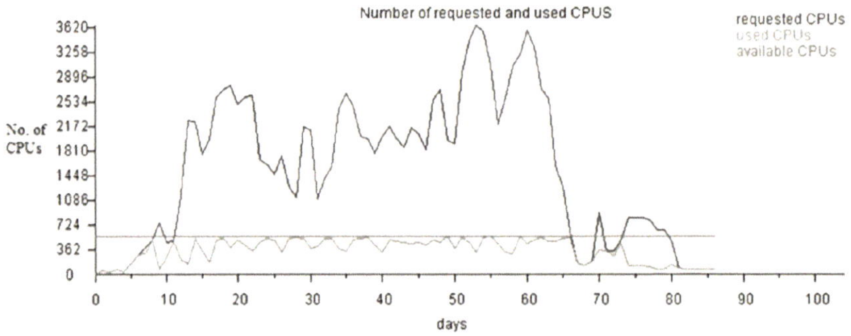

FIGURE 6.10 $TCT_{6000jobs}$ using SJF-GA.

iii. **For 11,000 and 17,256 Jobs:** The TCT of 11,000 jobs and 17,256 jobs of zewura workload using SJF-GA is 106 days and 190 days, respectively (Figures 6.11 and 6.12).

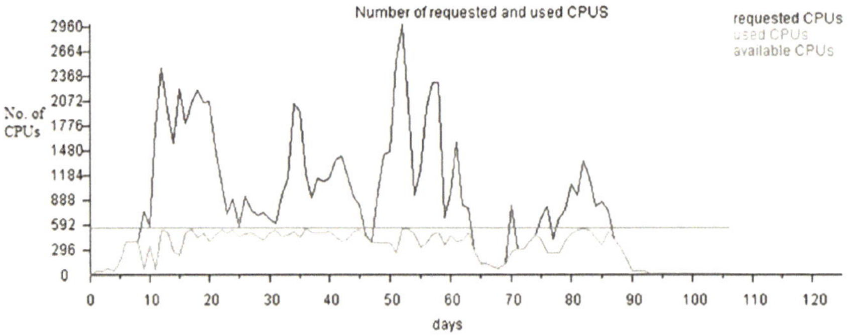

FIGURE 6.11 $TCT_{11000jobs}$ using SJF-GA.

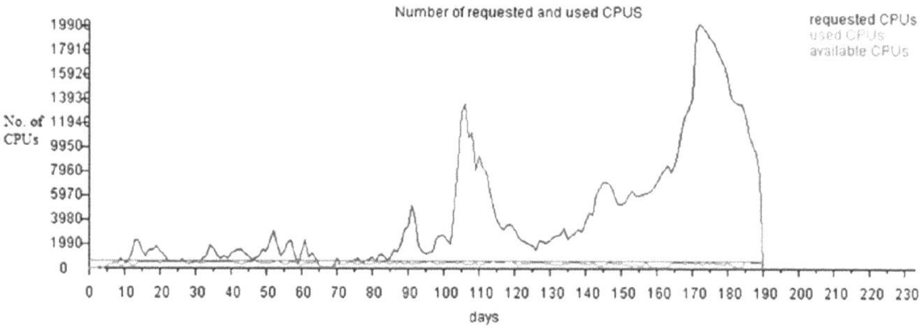

FIGURE 6.12 $TCT_{17256jobs}$ using SJF-GA.

6.1.1.4 COMPARATIVE ANALYSIS OF ALGORITHMS (ACO_{THRESH}, SJF-ACO_{THRESH}, SJF-GA) ON THE BASIS OF TCT

Out of all the hybrid algorithms, it is evident (Figures 6.1–6.12), that SJF-GA has outperformed ACO_{thresh} and SJF-ACO_{thresh} for small as well as large sets of jobs (Table 6.1).

TABLE 6.1 TCT of Zewura Workload for ACO_{thresh}, SJF-ACO_{thresh}, and SJF-GA

Scheduling Algorithms	TCT of Zewura Workload (In Days)			
	3000	6000	11,000	17,256
ACO_{thresh}	67	89	113	195
SJF-ACO_{thresh}	66	88	109	191
SJF-GA	66	86	106	190

6.1.2 CLUSTER RESOURCE UTILIZATION (CRU)

The utilization of all seven cluster resources (CRs) (zewura1, zewura2, zewura3, zewura4, zewura5, zewura6, and zewura7) for different job counts (3000, 6000, 11,000, 17,256) of the zewura workload is given in subsections using different modified and hybrid algorithms.

6.1.2.1 ACO_{THRESH}

For 3000, 6000, 11,000, and 17,256 Jobs: The red color indicates a high rate of cluster utilization. The rate of CR utilization should be high for better performance in grid scheduling and resource management. The green color indicates the least utilization or idleness of the CPU during that time period. The rate of utilization of seven clusters using ACO_{thresh} for different sets of jobs is given (Figures 6.13–6.16). The individual utilization of all seven CRs for a given workload using the ACO_{thresh} scheduling algorithm has been calculated (Table 6.2).

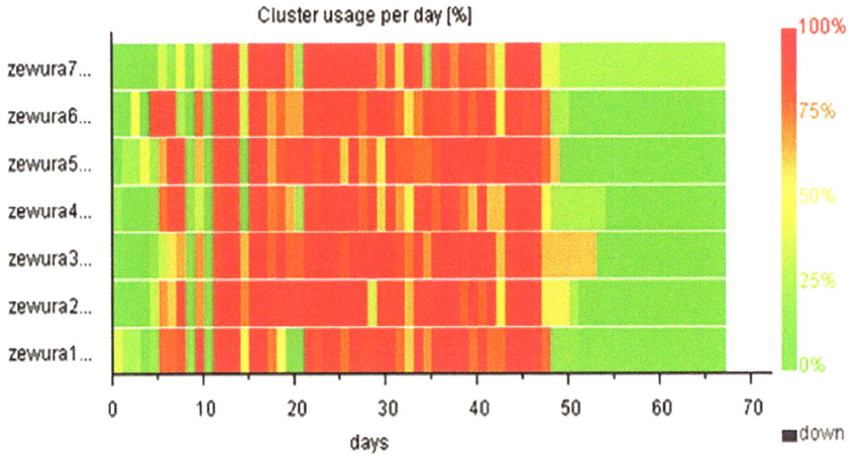

FIGURE 6.13 $CRU_{3000jobs}$ using ACO_{thresh}.

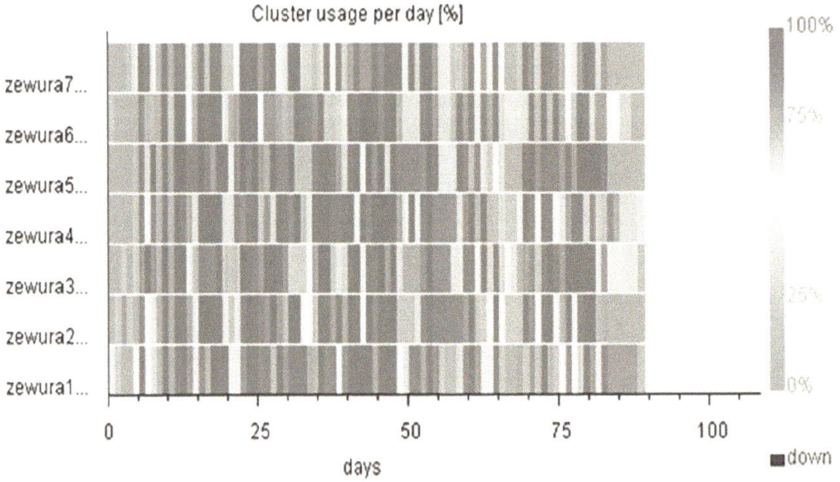

FIGURE 6.14 $CRU_{6000jobs}$ using ACO_{thresh}.

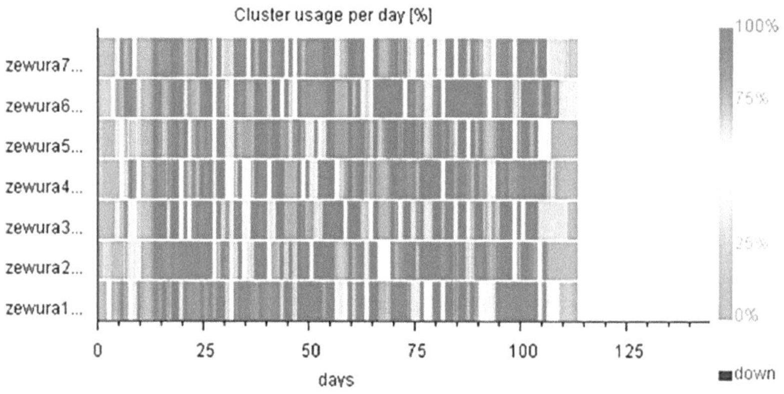

FIGURE 6.15 $CRU_{11000jobs}$ using ACO_{thresh}.

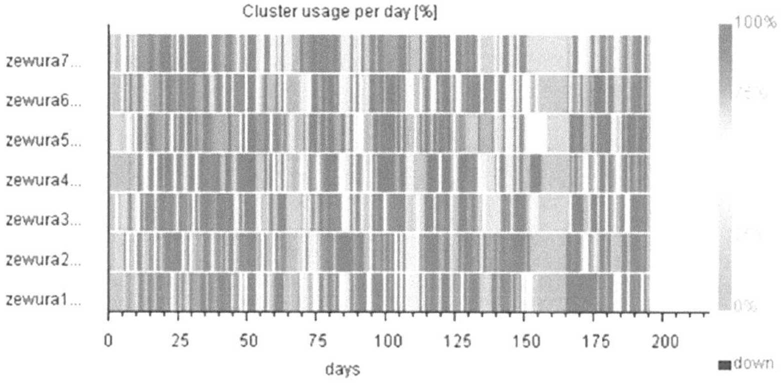

FIGURE 6.16 $CRU_{17256jobs}$ using ACO_{thresh}.

TABLE 6.2 CRU of Zewura Clusters (in Percentage) Using ACO_{thresh} Scheduling Algorithm

Zewura Clusters	Cluster Resource Utilization of Zewura Clusters for Given Set of Jobs (in Percentage)			
	3000 Jobs	**6000 Jobs**	**11,000 Jobs**	**17,256 Jobs**
Zewura 1	50.51	58.51	63.81	67.63
Zewura 2	54.80	53.89	64.82	68.18
Zewura 3	58.05	61.05	61.34	68.15
Zewura 4	51.01	59.11	63.29	68.08
Zewura 5	51.82	56.92	64.36	67.10
Zewura 6	52.82	61.02	59.18	69.71
Zewura 7	55.87	69.54	65.76	69.92
Average utilization	53.55	60.01	63.22	68.39

6.1.2.2 $SJF\text{-}ACO_{THRESH}$

For 3000, 6000, 11,000, and 17,256 Jobs: The rate of utilization of seven clusters using SJF-ACO_{thresh} for different sets of jobs is given (Figures 6.17–6.20). The individual utilization of all seven CRs for a given workload using the SJF-ACO_{thresh} scheduling algorithm has been calculated (Table 6.3).

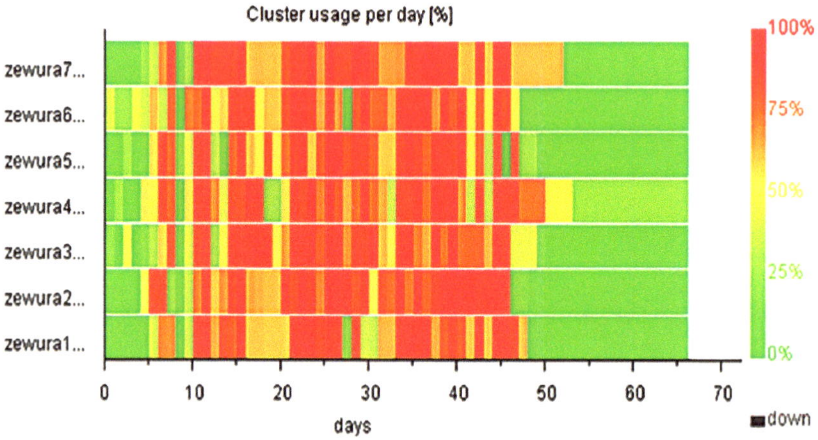

FIGURE 6.17 $CRU_{3000jobs}$ using SJF-ACO_{thresh}.

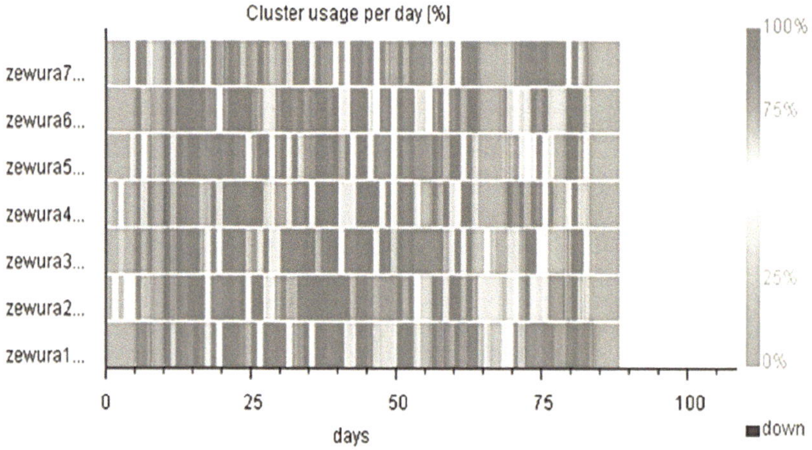

FIGURE 6.18 $CRU_{6000jobs}$ using SJF-ACO_{thresh}.

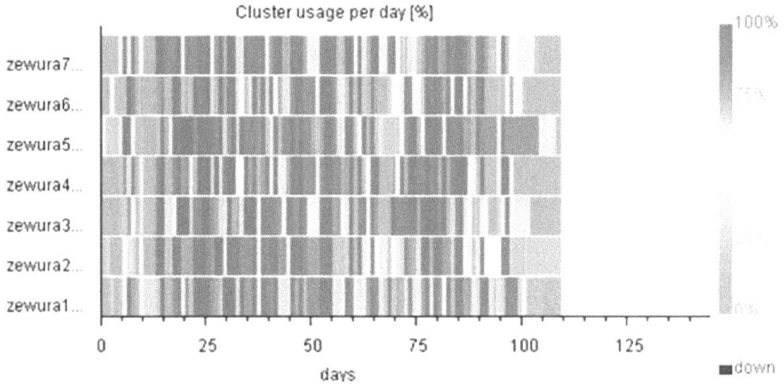

FIGURE 6.19 $CRU_{11000jobs}$ using SJF-ACO_{thresh}.

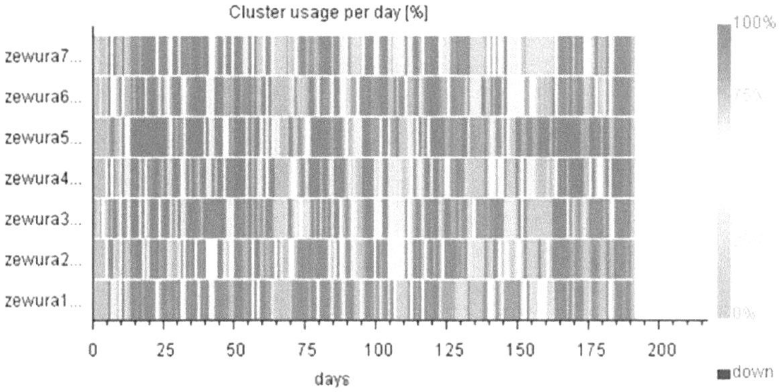

FIGURE 6.20 $CRU_{6000jobs}$ using SJF-ACO_{thresh}.

TABLE 6.3 CRU of Zewura Clusters (in Percentage) Using SJF-ACO_{thresh} Scheduling Algorithm

Zewura Clusters	Cluster Resource Utilization of Zewura Clusters for Given Set of Jobs (in Percentage)			
	3000 Jobs	6000 Jobs	11,000 Jobs	17,256 Jobs
Zewura 1	52.11	64.36	65.29	68.94
Zewura 2	52.55	66.96	64.11	68.93
Zewura 3	53.18	66.44	64.15	71.35
Zewura 4	60.82	61.17	63.11	66.84
Zewura 5	50.86	63.23	67.47	75.53
Zewura 6	52.59	60.02	62.83	69.00
Zewura 7	57.91	65.28	63.92	68.70
Average utilization	54.33	63.92	64.41	69.89

6.1.2.3 SJF-GA

For 3000, 6000, 11,000, and 17,256 Jobs: The rate of utilization of seven clusters using SJF-GA for different sets of jobs is given (Figures 6.21–6.24). The individual utilization of all seven CRs for a given workload using the $SJF\text{-}ACO_{thresh}$ scheduling algorithm has been calculated (Table 6.4).

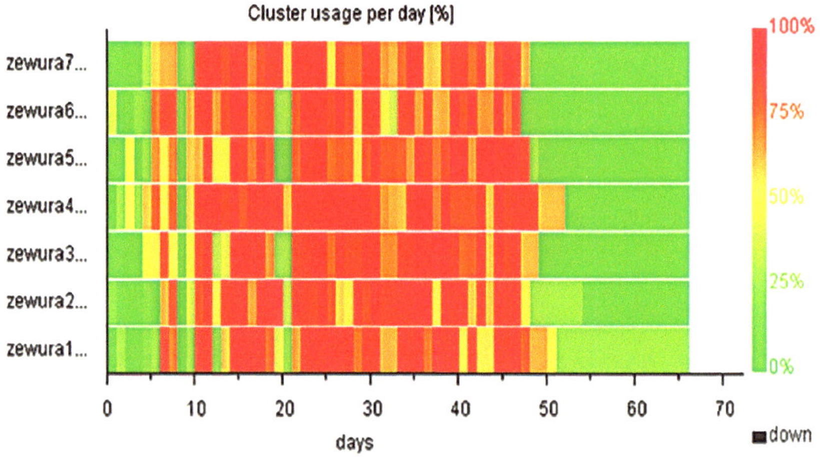

FIGURE 6.21 $CRU_{3000jobs}$ using SJF-GA.

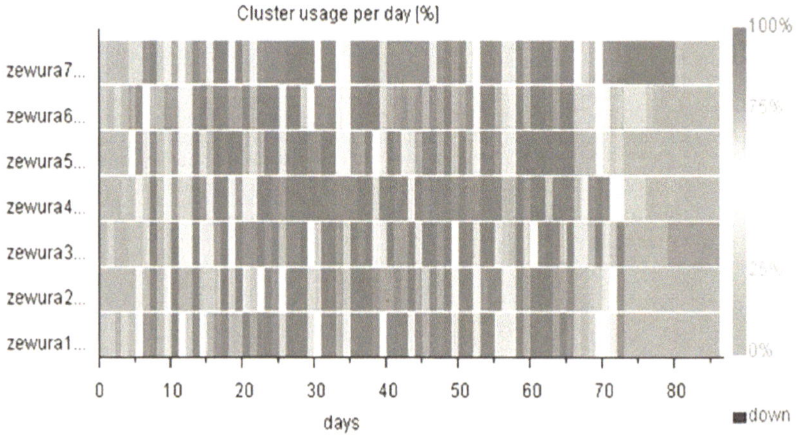

FIGURE 6.22 $CRU_{6000jobs}$ using SJF-GA.

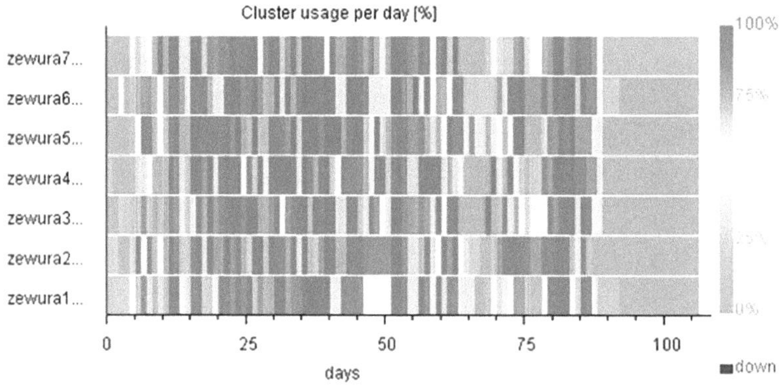

FIGURE 6.23 $CRU_{11000jobs}$ using SJF-GA.

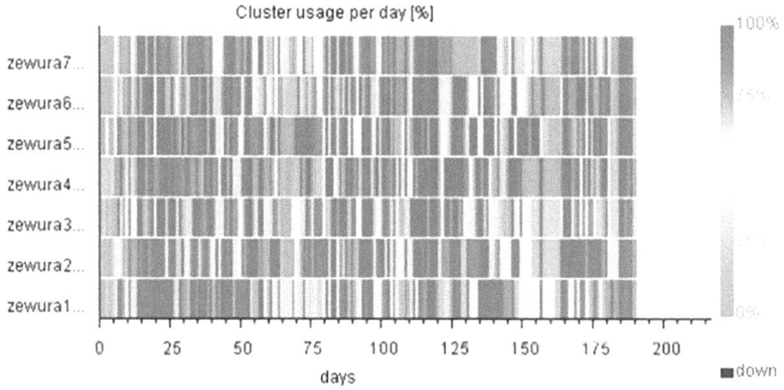

FIGURE 6.24 $CRU_{17256jobs}$ using SJF-GA.

TABLE 6.4 CRU of Zewura Clusters (in Percentage) Using SJF-GA Scheduling Algorithm

Zewura Clusters	Cluster Resource Utilization of Zewura Clusters for Given Set of Jobs (in Percentage)			
	3000 Jobs	**6000 Jobs**	**11,000 Jobs**	**17,256 Jobs**
Zewura 1	58.16	60.82	67.42	71.71
Zewura 2	54.13	58.07	65.24	71.22
Zewura 3	48.76	69.65	67.43	69.13
Zewura 4	50.74	65.76	68.83	69.63
Zewura 5	54.41	62.58	70.63	71.62
Zewura 6	59.13	63.74	64.23	70.15
Zewura 7	54.92	71.21	69.93	67.44
Average utilization	54.32	64.54	67.67	70.12

6.1.3 AVERAGE MACHINE UTILIZATION (AMU)

The average machine utilization (AMU) (zewura1, zewura2, zewura3, zewura4, zewura5, zewura6, and zewura7) for different job counts (3000, 6000, 11,000, 17,256) of the zewura workload is given in subsections using individual algorithms.

6.1.3.1 ACO_{THRESH}

The peak in the graphs indicates a high rate of machine utilization on a particular day. With the increase in the number of jobs, the graph becomes denser (Figures 6.25–6.28) because of the increase in machine utilization. The graphs (Figures 6.25–6.28) show the AMU in the case of the ACO_{thresh} scheduling algorithm for different sets of Zewura workloads.

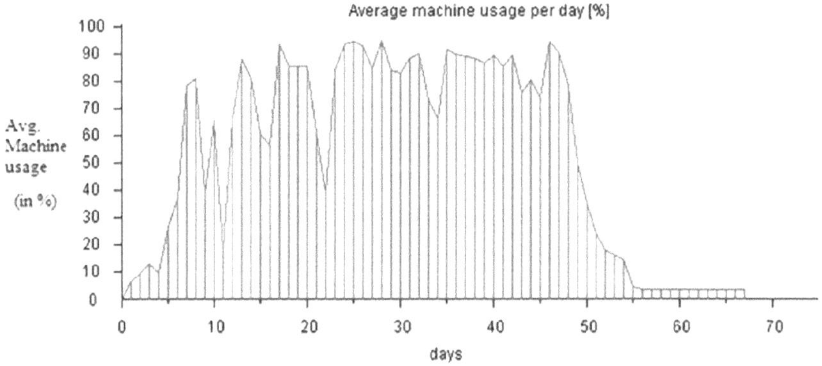

FIGURE 6.25 AMU for 3000 jobs using ACO_{thresh}.

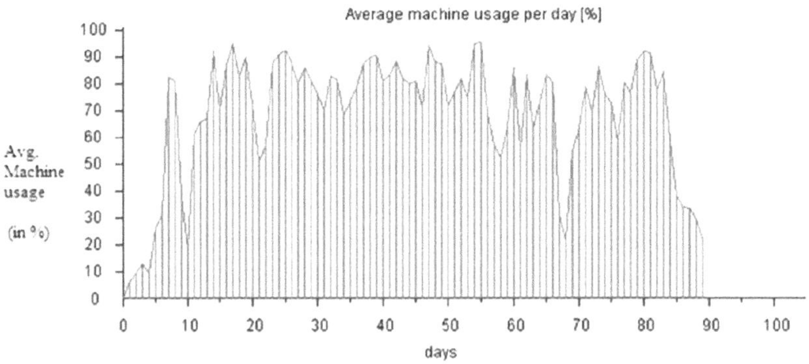

FIGURE 6.26 AMU for 3000 jobs using ACO_{thresh}.

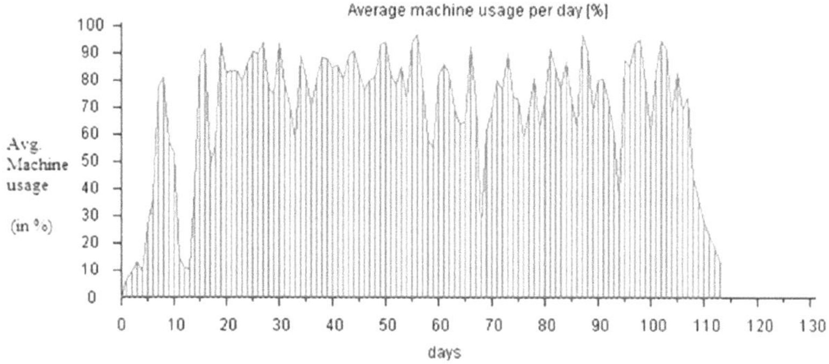

FIGURE 6.27 AMU for 11,000 jobs using ACO_{thresh}.

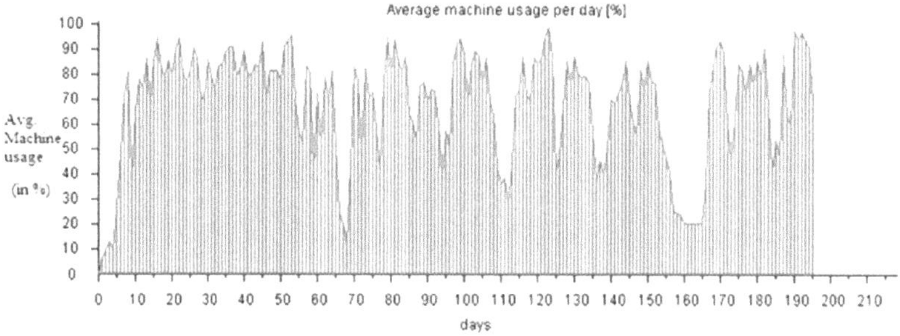

FIGURE 6.28 AMU for 17,256 jobs using ACO_{thresh}.

6.1.3.2 *SJF-ACO*$_{THRESH}$

The graphs (Figures 6.29–6.32) show the AMU in the case of the SJF-ACO_{thresh} scheduling algorithm for different sets of Zewura workloads.

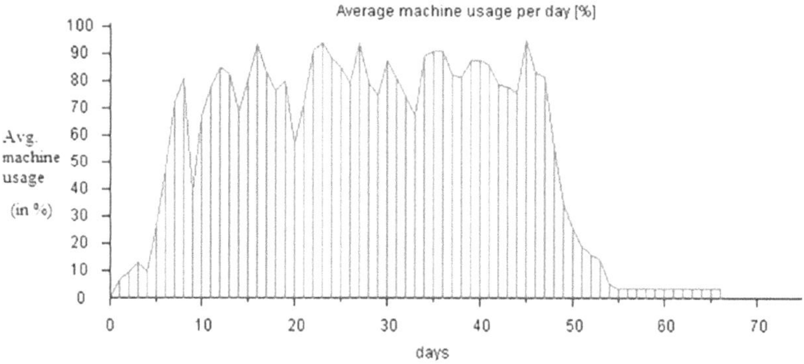

FIGURE 6.29 AMU for 3000 jobs using SJF-ACO_{thresh}.

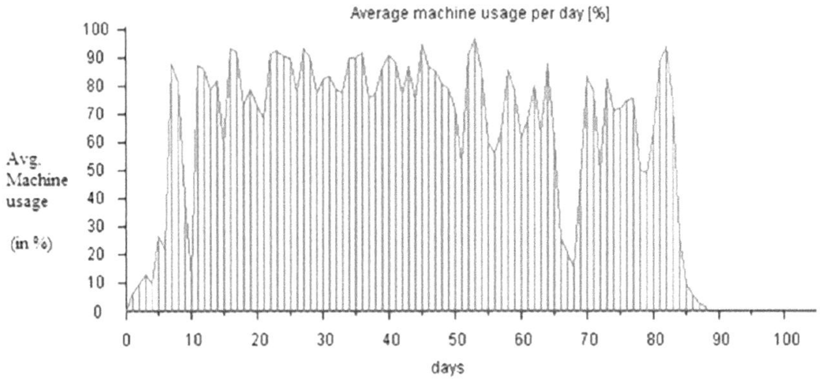

FIGURE 6.30 AMU for 6000 jobs using SJF-ACO_{thresh}.

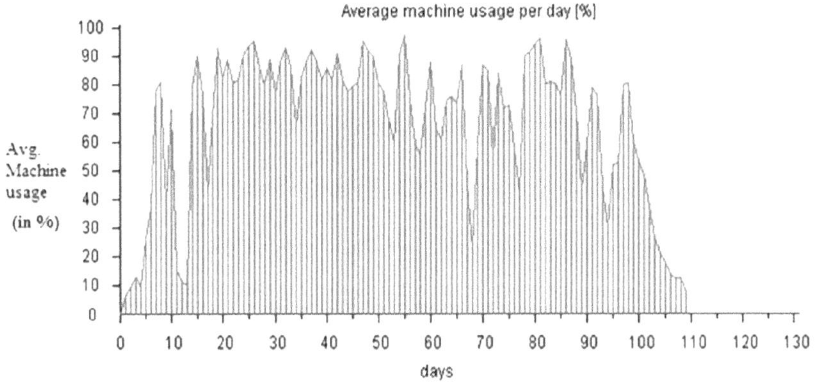

FIGURE 6.31 AMU for 11,000 jobs using SJF-ACO_{thresh}.

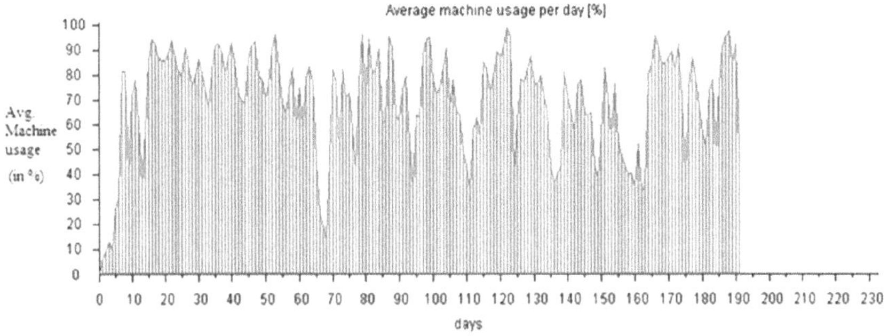

FIGURE 6.32 AMU for 17,256 jobs using SJF-ACO_{thresh}.

6.1.3.3 SJF-GA

The graphs (Figures 6.33–6.36) show the AMU in the case of the SJF-GA scheduling algorithm for different sets of Zewura workloads.

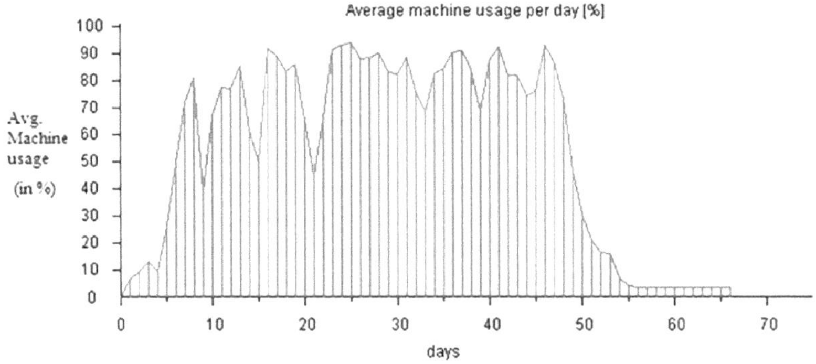

FIGURE 6.33 AMU for 3000 jobs using SJF-GA.

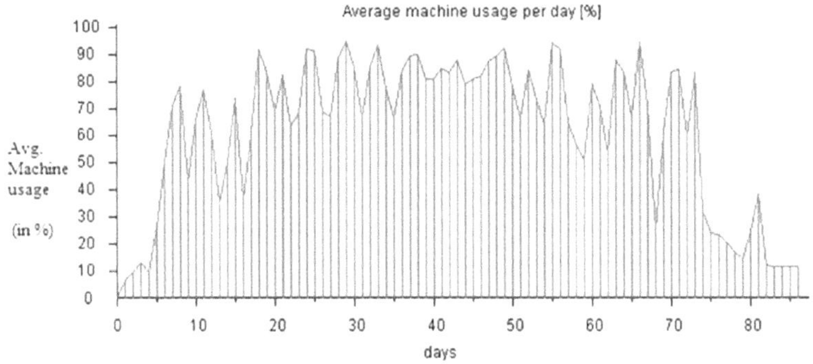

FIGURE 6.34 AMU for 6000 jobs using SJF-GA.

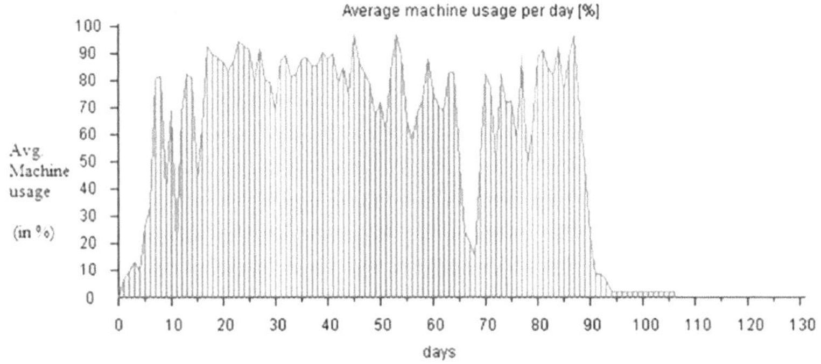

FIGURE 6.35 AMU for 11,000 jobs using SJF-GA.

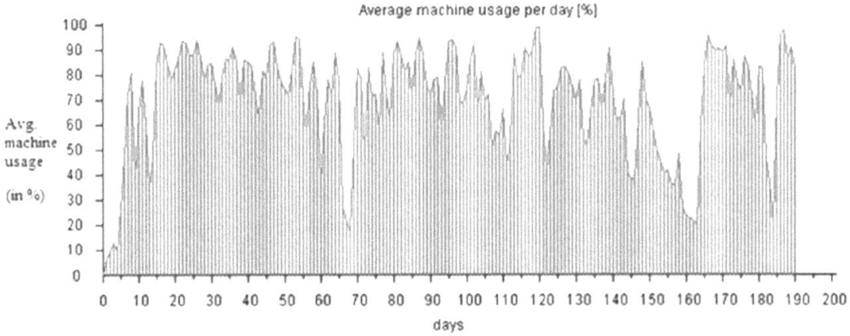

FIGURE 6.36 AMU for 17,256 jobs using SJF-GA.

6.1.4 LOAD DISTRIBUTION

As discussed in the previous chapter, we have used SD as the parameter to measure the evenness in workload distribution among different CRs. A low value of SD indicates less variation in the load distribution. The value of SD in the utilization of CRs for ACO_{thresh}, SJF-ACO_{thresh}, and SJF-GA is calculated for different sets of jobs of zewura workload (Table 6.5).

TABLE 6.5 Standard Deviation for ACO_{thresh}, SJF-ACO_{thresh}, and SJF-GA

Scheduling Algorithms	SD in the Utilization of Cluster Resources of Zewura Clusters for a Given Set of Jobs (in Percentage)			
	3000 Jobs	6000 Jobs	11,000 Jobs	17,256 Jobs
ACO_{thresh}	2.57	4.51	2.08	0.96
SJF-ACO_{thresh}	3.34	2.39	1.45	2.59
SJF-GA	3.42	4.34	2.17	1.43

6.2 SUMMARY

This chapter covers the execution of the proposed modified bio-inspired algorithm and a hybrid algorithm in a grid simulation environment for different numbers of jobs. Various parameters have been taken into consideration to analyze the behavior of the proposed scheduling algorithm. The grid environment is dynamic, and hence, it becomes a non-trivial task to schedule the jobs effectively with the least completion time and maximum resource utilization (RU). In the next chapter, we will perform a performance comparison of the execution results of the proposed modified and hybrid algorithms, as well as other reference algorithms.

KEYWORDS

- **algorithms**
- **average machine utilization**
- **cluster resource utilization**
- **grid simulation environment**
- **performance metrics standard deviation**
- **total completion time.**

PART III

PERFORMANCE COMPARISON OF ALGORITHMS

CHAPTER 7

Comparison of Conventional, Bio-Inspired, and Hybrid Algorithms: A Review

7.1 INTRODUCTION

In the last two chapters, we have witnessed several research-based case studies to solve the grid scheduling problem using conventional, bio-inspired, and hybrid algorithms. This chapter presents a review report on the performance of different scheduling algorithms based on some performance parameters such as total completion time (TCT) of jobs, cluster resource utilization (CRU), load distribution, average machine utilization (AMU), and scalability. The computations of scheduling algorithms have been carried out in a grid simulation environment using a standard workload. The workload contains 17,256 jobs and seven cluster resources (CRs) called Zewura clusters. The analysis report will help the readers understand the behavior of conventional (FCFS and SJF), bio-inspired (ACO, PSO), and hybrid (ACO_{thresh}, SJF-ACO, SJF-GA) algorithms under different scheduling conditions. It will eventually help the readers understand and apply these algorithms to complex problems.

7.2 ANALYSIS OF TOTAL COMPLETION TIME (TCT) OF JOBS

In the previous chapters, we have already seen various performance parameters to measure the effectiveness of scheduling algorithms. The TCT of jobs for conventional, bio-inspired, and hybrid scheduling algorithms has been calculated (Table 7.1). FCFS is a conventional

Mastering Grid Computing: Scheduling and Resource Management.
Ankita & Sudip Kumar Sahana (Authors)

scheduling algorithm that takes 68 days to complete 3000 jobs of the zewura workload. Compared to SJF, it is better since SJF takes 71 days to complete the same set of jobs. The bio-inspired and hybrid algorithms take less time compared to conventional scheduling algorithms for 3000 jobs of the zewura workload. As the job count increases, the number of days to complete the execution of jobs increases gradually. In the case of traditional algorithms, the performance of FCFS starts to decline as the job count increases, and SJF begins to show better performance than FCFS. Out of the bio-inspired algorithms, PSO and GA take 93 days and 90 days, respectively. The performance of hybrid algorithms is better than that of bio-inspired and conventional algorithms for both small and large sets of jobs. Out of the two hybrid algorithms, the performance of SJF-GA is more satisfying compared to SJF-ACO_{thresh} for both small and large sets of jobs.

TABLE 7.1 TCT of Zewura Workload for FCFS, SJF, ACO_{thresh}, SJF-ACO_{thresh}, and SJF-GA

Scheduling Algorithms	TCT of Zewura Workload (In Days)			
	3000 Jobs	**6000 Jobs**	**11,000 Jobs**	**17,256 Jobs**
FCFS	68	110	142	240
SJF	71	104	122	204
ACO	69	92	114	196
PSO	67	93	120	197
GA	67	90	111	193
ACO_{thresh}	67	89	113	195
SJF-ACO_{thresh}	66	88	109	191
SJF-GA	66	86	106	190

7.3 ANALYSIS OF CLUSTER RESOURCE UTILIZATION (CRU)

The utilization of clusters (in percentage) and their utilization graphs have been discussed in previous chapters. The average utilization of Zewura clusters for different scheduling algorithms has been calculated (Table 7.2). Among all the scheduling algorithms, the average CRU for 3000 jobs in the case of FCFS is the highest. However, the utilization decreases with an increase in the number of jobs. From Table 7.2, it is evident that SJF-GA has the best cluster utilization in comparison to other conventional, bio-inspired, and hybrid algorithms. Resource utilization (RU) is one of the non-trivial parameters used to measure the efficiency of a scheduling algorithm. High RU indicates that the resources have been allocated in an appropriate manner while maintaining fairness among the resources in terms of load distribution.

TABLE 7.2 Average Utilization of Zewura Clusters (in Percentage) for Different Workloads Using FCFS, SJF, ACO_{thresh}, $SJF\text{-}ACO_{thresh}$, and SJF-GA

Average Utilization of 7 Zewura Clusters	Cluster Resource Utilization of Zewura Clusters for Given Set of Jobs (in Percentage)			
	3000 Jobs	**6000 Jobs**	**11,000 Jobs**	**17,256 Jobs**
FCFS	54.64	61.75	58.48	54.35
SJF	54.02	61.29	61.61	65.51
ACO	54.05	63.16	67.33	68.06
PSO	53.75	63.32	62.01	67.75
GA	54.24	64.14	66.60	69.26
ACO_{thresh}	53.55	60.01	63.22	68.39
$SJF\text{-}ACO_{thresh}$	54.33	63.92	64.41	69.89
SJF-GA	54.32	64.54	67.67	70.12

7.4 LOAD DISTRIBUTION

Standard deviation (SD) indicates the amount of deviation in the distribution of workload among the CRs. A low value of SD indicates that the deviation is less, and hence, the distribution of load is uniform among the resources. A high value of SD shows that the deviation in the distribution of workload among the CRs is high. Therefore, a good scheduling algorithm must have a low value of SD, indicating minimum deviation of workload among the CRs. The SD of different scheduling algorithms using the Zewura workload has been calculated (Table 7.3), and it shows that the value of SD is highest for FCFS, which proves that the distribution of workload among the resources in FCFS has not been an optimal case. Among all the scheduling algorithms, GA has the lowest value of SD, indicating fairness in the distribution of workload among all the CRs.

TABLE 7.3 Standard Deviation for ACO_{thresh}, SJF-ACO_{thresh}, and SJF-GA

Scheduling Algorithms	SD in the Utilization of Cluster Resources of Zewura Clusters for a Given Set of Jobs (in Percentage)				Average SD
	3000 Jobs	6000 Jobs	11,000 Jobs	17,256 Jobs	
FCFS	4.07	4.92	4.00	4.32	4.32
SJF	3.33	2.99	1.21	1.56	2.27
ACO	3.07	3.36	2.29	2.35	2.76
PSO	3.62	3.33	1.11	0.95	2.25
GA	2.43	0.98	1.99	2.44	1.96
ACO_{thresh}	2.57	4.51	2.08	0.96	2.53
SJF-ACO_{thresh}	3.34	2.39	1.45	2.59	2.44
SJF-GA	3.42	4.34	2.17	1.43	2.84

7.5 SUMMARY

This chapter presents a comparative report of different conventional, bio-inspired, and hybrid algorithms to solve the problem of job scheduling in the grid environment. The performance comparison report showcases that the hybrid bio-inspired algorithms have better scheduling results in comparison to other reference algorithms in terms of TCT of jobs, RU, and load distribution. The analysis shows that the proposed hybrid SJF-GA scheduling algorithm has shown promising results compared to other reference algorithms in terms of various parameters taken into consideration to evaluate the performance of scheduling algorithms.

KEYWORDS

- **average machine utilization**
- **cluster resource utilization**
- **conventional algorithmsgrid scheduling problem**
- **hybrid algorithms**
- **load distribution uniformity**
- **resource utilization**
- **total completion time**

CHAPTER 8

New Computing Platforms for Solving Convoluted Engineering Problems: A Review

8.1 INTRODUCTION

In today's world of high-speed Internet, modern devices, and a growing number of users generating vast amounts of data, effective management and seamless service delivery are essential. The emergence of parallel and distributed computing has transformed the landscape of computing. A good number of computing platforms are available for users on a demand basis, and their service needs are being taken care of by the developers and the service providers. There is no need to buy technology or set up a computing environment to fulfill one's need for computing resources. One can easily request the desired resources and gain access in real-time at any location, hence breaking all the barriers and bringing the computing world closer than ever. The grid computing platform is one such platform that has changed the ideology of computing and enabled resource sharing among computational resources to meet the computing demands of its users, thereby providing immense computing power equivalent to supercomputers at a reasonable cost. In this chapter, we will study some of the latest trends in computing platforms that can serve users' requests according to their requirements. Also, we will identify issues or limitations of these computing models and possible solutions to those problems.

The commercialization of primitive services such as gas and water and their delivery to the doorstep of a customer is a very good example of service delivery. In this case, the customer utilizes the services provided

Mastering Grid Computing: Scheduling and Resource Management.
Ankita & Sudip Kumar Sahana (Authors)

by the gas owner or the electricity provider without being concerned about how and where the services are being generated. This is analogous to the computing world, where computing services will be provided to the users according to their requirements and the availability of computing resources. The location of users or computing resources does not affect the service delivery to the users.

The computing needs of the users have substantially increased in the past few years. Leonard Kleinrock (2005) was a great scientist in advanced research projects agency network (ARPANET) who forecasted the present computing scenario in one of his powerful writings. He said, "As of now, computer networks are still in their infancy, but as they grow up and become sophisticated, we will probably see the spread of "computer utilities" which, like present electric and telephone utilities, will service individual homes and offices across the country." Kleinrock's computing vision came into existence in the 21st century and revolutionized the computing industry.

The notable progress in the field of information and communication technology (ICT) escalated the need for a computing technology that can satisfy the requirements of the users. A good number of computing paradigms are available for users, such as cluster computing, grid computing, edge computing, fog computing, and cloud computing, which can be applied to complex science and engineering problems.

8.2 FORMS OF COMPUTING PLATFORMS

Computing can be defined as a systematic approach to learning algorithmic processes used to display and convert information. Nowadays, several computing platforms are widely used for a range of applications across the globe. In the next section, we will study some traditional computing platforms as well as the latest computing trends in the computational world.

8.2.1 DISTRIBUTED COMPUTING

Distributed computing (Attiya and Welch, 2004) involves the study of algorithms for the proper management of distributed systems. It refers to a mechanism where data processing and storage are distributed among several nodes or systems and not controlled by a single pivotal system. The nodes in a distributed computing network have their own computing or data processing capabilities and are capable of storing and managing their data. These nodes are entitled to work together to execute tasks and share resources without being controlled by a single central device.

Multiple programs run across several computing nodes over one network and fulfill the requirements for better performance in the scientific domain as well as general applications. Performance, fault tolerance, resource sharing, and resource availability are the important characteristics of distributed computing that have led to its success. It allows multiple nodes to combine and increase the computational power, memory, and bandwidth of the network. A number of approaches are available that can help to implement distributed computing in a network. An interconnection of desktop computers can be created using a high-speed network, which can provide computing power equivalent to supercomputers.

Autonomous computers (van Steen and Tanenbaum, 2016) are combined, creating a view of one intelligible system for its users in a distributed network. Distributed computing has been running in the computing world for more than five decades now. The aggregation of distributed computing resources and their consolidated usage (Belfiore et al., 2006) is an important characteristic of a distributed system. Communication is an important property because data and information exchange are highly required for computing nodes to interact and work together in a distributed computing network. Message passing is the mode of communication among the connected nodes in a distributed network.

There are several benefits of using a distributed computing environment. Some of them are given below:

1. **Resource Availability:** There are multiple systems or nodes running in a distributed computing framework; hence, an organization is not reliant on a single server. The distributed computing platform has greatly reduced the dependency on a central server because the failure of one server will not affect the functioning of the organization. It provides a property called fault tolerance, which enables the distributed network to deal with single or multiple system failures in the network.

2. **Availability of Data:** Multiple nodes or systems provide multiple storage points in the distributed network. The distributed network is not affected by the failure of one storage device, and data remains protected and stored at different locations.

3. **Least System Overloading:** This is one of the important characteristics of distributed computing. Instead of hitting a single machine, user requests can easily be redirected to various servers in a distributed computing platform.
4. **Scalable:** The distributed network is scalable in nature, such that its design can easily be updated by including new machines in the network.
5. **Parallel Computing:** The property of parallel computation allows complex simulations to break into various sub-parts and run them in parallel during scientific computation. This yields faster results in comparison to the entire computation performed in series mode.

   Limitations of distributed computing network:

   i. Since the data is stored in multiple places in a distributed computing network, a strong security mechanism is required to ensure the privacy and integrity of the data.
   ii. Synchronization becomes difficult and often results in possible errors when multiple systems simultaneously try to read or write the same data.

8.2.2 CLUSTER COMPUTING

In cluster computing, various machines are combined to execute an application or individual job. A typical illusion of one virtual machine (server) is presented before the user in such a manner that the user believes that they are interacting with a single system. A high-performance cluster (Buyya, 1999) contains a good number of computing machines called nodes. These nodes are further classified as general computing nodes and a master node.

Cluster models are classified into two categories: The high-availability cluster model (Gadir et al., 2005) and load balancing cluster model. The high availability cluster model utilizes implicit repetition to provide the availability of services and resources in a steady manner. The failure of one cluster node will not affect the functioning of the cluster computing network because other nodes are available to provide the required services to the users. In this way, the application is mitigated from one machine to another to continue the ongoing application. This process is called the failover of an application to another machine in a clustered computing network.

The binding of important missions, files, and servers is one of the prominent application areas of cluster computing networks. In this network, continual services are provided by high-availability clusters through extreme restructuring of hardware and software. Cluster load balancing (Werstein et al., 2006; Overeinder et al., 1996) is another model where computing nodes are combined to handle client requests in a balanced fashion. The scheduler and scheduling algorithm plays an important role in redirecting client requests to appropriate cluster nodes. This type of network is primarily used in real-time applications, such as handling cargo discrepancies from numerous input requests.

The advantages of working in a cluster computing environment are listed below:

- Like distributed computing, the cluster computing model is also scalable, allowing any new node (machine) to be added to the network in order to widen the network size.
- Fault tolerance is also provided in the case of single or multiple node failures in the clustered network. It has the capability to handle a sudden increase in job count and accordingly balances the load in the clustered network.

The drawbacks of the cluster computing model are given below:

- The cost of installation of workstations and other machines is quite high.
- The cluster computing network requires an appropriate monitoring and maintenance system to observe any possible malfunctioning of systems within the network. Also, proper checks are required before adding any new system to the existing network infrastructure.

8.2.3 GRID COMPUTING

Grid computing (Berman et al., 2003) has greatly transformed the computing approach of scientists and researchers around the world. The latest high-tech advancements in the field of computing and technology have allowed for the interlinking of a considerable number of computing and storage resources such as servers, mainframes, storage devices, and many more. The interconnected devices build a unified resource framework that can be regarded as a single resource to users. These resources are accessible to users in a coherent manner and enable the cooperative and pervasive use of computing resources for users to solve their complex problems.

The field of distributed computing networks has been widened with the growth of grid computing. The concept of grid computing (Buyya and Venugopal, 2005) came into existence in the early 1990s and emerged as a strong computing platform with phenomenal capabilities. Though grid computing is similar to cluster computing, both computing platforms have fundamental differences. The nodes in a cluster computing network are always homogeneous, but a grid computing network is not restricted to homogeneous nodes. It allows both homogeneous and heterogeneous nodes to form a grid computing network. The cluster computing nodes are closely placed to each other, whereas the grid computing nodes may be positioned at far locations from each other. The resources are managed centrally in a clustered network environment, whereas the grid resources have distributed resource management.

The enormous development of computing and communication technologies has led to the current modernization in the present age. The concept of ubiquitous computing (Lyytinen and Yoo, 2002) platform uses standardized protocols that allow universal access to resources and manage resource sharing. The global grid forum (GGF) provides the necessary protocols that allow accessing and discovering resources and also provides the necessary mechanisms for carrying out communication among the resources.

Grid computing is still evolving and can help scientists and engineers to implement real-time complex problems of science and engineering in the coming time.

Some of the benefits of the grid computing platform are listed below:

1. The deployment cost of a number of parallel machines has always been a matter of concern for infrastructure developers. Grid computing (Foster et al., 2001) is a collection of heterogeneous or homogeneous machines with enormous computational power at a very low cost in comparison to parallel machines.

2. Security in the grids is provided by the intergrids, which are similar to the type of security provided by the LAN (local area network).
3. Grid computing is a fault-tolerant computing platform (Foster, 2003; Foster and Kesselman, 2003a) where the grid system quickly identifies a single machine failure and immediately redirects the job to an operational (working) machine where the job finishes its execution. Thus, the grid computing platform provides a flexible and invulnerable computing framework.

There are a few imitations while working in a grid computing environment.

i. It is difficult to maintain synchronization among all the servers in a big and dynamic computing environment like a grid. A good number of small servers are distributed across several administrative sites.
ii. Political indifferences between countries may create hindrances or restrict resource sharing across geographical boundaries.
iii. The grid computing network is a huge network that encompasses a large number of machines connected, forming a ubiquitous computing network. A proper safety mechanism is required to ensure the integrity and privacy of users' data.

8.2.4 CLOUD COMPUTING

A cloud computing platform (Buyya et al., 2009; Weiss, 2007) is an amalgam of cluster and grid computing but also has inherent attributes that add to its popularity and utility. Cloud computing (Zhang et al., 2010; Varghese and Buyya, 2018) can be considered a next-generation computing technology whose nodes are virtualized through "hypervisor" technologies to meet explicit service-level agreements. The cloud environment can be accessed using web service technologies such as simple object access protocol (SOAP) and representational state transfer (REST). The service model's setup relies on user requirements that can be public, private, community, or hybrid. The cloud computing model provides three types of service models (Kavis, 2014). The first model is SaaS (Cusumano, 2010), which stands for software-as-a-service (SaaS). SaaS is an on-demand software delivery model where the applications are hosted by a third party for the available users over the Internet. Network-dependent access to a copy of an application is given to the customer. This is generated by the supplier for SaaS distribution.

The second model is PaaS (Pahl, 2015), which stands for the platform as a service (PaaS), where the third party is responsible for providing APIs to the developers in order to run the application in the given computing environment. PaaS is based on the theory of virtualization, where resources can easily be added or removed according to variations in business. The PaaS applications are low-cost applications and sometimes freely available, allowing the utilization of the previously developed cloud organization in order to transfer or move the current application. With PaaS, the applications generated are bound to that platform, and developers may create new applications according to their requirements on the platform. The PaaS model allows working with the programming languages and functions provided by the selected platform.

The last one is IaaS (Laniepce et al., 2013), which stands for infrastructure as a service (IaaS). IaaS is a self-service model made up of expandable computing resources. This model provides various utilities, such as handling computers, networking, and repository services. The IaaS client is responsible for handling applications, middleware, and data, whereas the IaaS server handles repository, networking, and virtualization. The IaaS model is the most flexible in comparison to the SAAS and PaaS models. The hardware equipment is purchased according to their requirements and utilities, considering the size of the business organization. Small companies and startups follow the IaaS model because these companies lack monetary resources and cannot spend large amounts on purchasing hardware and software.

Cloud computing has proved its utilization in the computing industry and has been widely adopted by many organizations. The recent survey report shows that the revenue rate of companies has rapidly increased after investing in evolving technologies such as cloud and big data in comparison to other companies. The benefits of using a cloud computing platform are given below:

1. **Scalability:** The cloud environment supports scalability such that an organization or business may scale up or down according to its requirements. This causes changes in the operational and repository needs of the organization. These changes are handled

by the cloud computing environment, and the user is not burdened with installing or updating the required resources (provided by the cloud provider). The user is only concerned with using their time to run and carry out business operations effectively.

2. **Collaboration:** This feature facilitates association among employees and creates a work culture in a typical organization. This is particularly helpful for those employees who are actively working on one project across different locations, allowing them to use the same file for a particular project.
3. **Work From Home:** Cloud computing supports a "work from home" culture, where the only requirement is to have a proper internet connection.
4. **Latest Technologies:** Cloud computing follows the latest trends in the computing world and keeps its users informed about recent upgrades in the market.
5. **Consistency:** The cloud computing environment is responsible for providing consistent data because the same data is used at different locations by different employees working on a single project in an organization. The cloud environment provides consistent data, ensuring that data integrity is maintained and human errors are minimized.
6. **Recovery:** The cloud also provides important services for recovery during disaster situations (Ujjwal et al., 2019), such as power outages or even natural disasters.
7. **Prevention of Data Loss:** Data loss is a serious issue in the computing environment. This can be prevented with the help of a cloud-based server. The locally stored information on a particular system is vulnerable; therefore, it is a safe practice to upload the information to a cloud server, which is safer than local storage. The uploaded information in the cloud can be accessed from anywhere, provided there is a working computing device and a stable internet connection.
8. **Environment-Friendly:** In the present situation, the world is making all efforts to lessen pollution in all forms and create a

healthy Earth for generations to come. The cloud environment follows this goal with less usage of carbon imprints.

The cloud computing platform has some key issues (Branco Jr. et al., 2017) discussed below:

- The service provider has the job of allocating and de-allocating resources from the cloud once the user finishes its execution. The service provider is bound to keep low operational costs, and the resource provisioning decisions are required to be made dynamically to satisfy the quick demand variations.
- All the infrastructure developers are concerned about improving energy efficiency in the cloud computing environment.
- The cloud environment requires efficient management and analysis of network traffic so that network operators can make quick planning decisions by analyzing the varying network flow.
- Security (Subramanian and Jeyaraj, 2018; Zissis and Lekkas, 2012) is an impending topic in the cloud computing platform. The service providers rely on the infrastructure providers to attain data security. Confidentiality and data integrity are the major issues in the cloud computing environment.
- The virtual network is vulnerable to threats (Brohi et al., 2012); therefore, it is important to form a safe and secure network among all the elements of the cloud.
- Some factors, such as power failure, poor internet connectivity, and lack of maintenance at the data computing center, can lead to a situation called temporary downtime in the cloud environment.
- Security breaches are one of the primary concerns of cloud computing developers because the stored data available on the cloud is online and can be compromised if proper security mechanisms are not imposed.

8.2.5 FOG COMPUTING

In the computing industry, data has been increasing unexpectedly, and the world will see billions of connected machines by the end of this decade (Evans, 2011). The network designers have a tough job managing the magnitude and movement of data because there has been an enormous amount of work. The constraints in network bandwidth often pose problems in moving bulk data from IoT machines to the cloud effectively. Sometimes, privacy (security) constraints restrict sending data to the cloud environment. The problems of bandwidth and security constraints of cloud computing platforms can be overcome by a new computing paradigm known as fog computing (Hu et al., 2017; Upadhyay, 2018). In fog computing, computing services, data management, and storage services are allowed over the network nodes within proximity to IoT devices. The computation is not carried out solely in the cloud; rather, the computation happens on the route of data movement from IoT to the cloud.

In a fog model, two platforms are available: horizontal and vertical (Mouradian et al., 2017). The horizontal function enables the circulation of computing services among various platforms and industries. The vertical platform is designated for a specialized application, but there is zero interaction between different platforms. The vertical function is aimed at providing a flexible platform to meet the data-driven demands of fog computing developers and users.

Though fog computing (Yousefpour et al., n.d.) has several resemblances to cloud computing, there are notable differences addressed below:

- The security mechanism of fog computing is completely different from that of cloud computing. The security structure of cloud computing is centralized and located in designated buildings for data centers, whereas security in the fog computing environment must be provided at the edge or in the designated areas of fog nodes.
- The cloud's data centers are centralized in nature, whereas the fog nodes are organized in less centralized areas. Because of the decentralization in the fog computing environment, the nodes in fog can serve as fog computing nodes and fog resources can serve as fog clients.
- In terms of power utilization and resource availability, cloud computing is quite ahead of fog computing (Mukherjee et al., 2018).
- The operating environments of both computing technologies are different from each other. The cloud environment has massive data computing centers, while fog computing works on small-scale gateways, switches, and routers.
- Internet connectivity is a prime requisite to operate in the cloud environment, whereas fog computing does not have such

requirements. No continuous or stable internet connection is required to work in the fog computing environment.

Some of the benefits of fog computing are listed below:

- In fog computing, the nodes are heavily populated at the edge because the fog nodes at the network edge are ready to acquire the data generated by the machines and sensors. This helps in lessening the transit of data across the Internet and provides quality services.
- The bandwidth is saved because the computation of data and storage is performed between the cloud and the edge nodes.
- The fog computing model supports the mobility of several devices such as smartwatches and phones, whereas devices like traffic cameras located at the network end remain static in their position. A fog node might operate as a static resource or a mobile resource. The communication between mobile devices does not require data transmission to the cloud or any other base station.
- The multiple node distribution across geographical regions has the ability to document and determine the position of nodes to facilitate support for mobility. It eventually helps in making real-time decisions, fast data analysis, and achieving better location-oriented services.
- Node heterogeneity is supported in the fog computing model. A good variety of fog nodes are present, such as switches, gateways, servers, routers, and base stations. Virtualization has also been favored by the fog computing model in such a manner that virtual nodes and computational nodes are operational here and can be considered as fog nodes.
- Effective data encryption, integrity checks, and isolation measures have been undertaken to avoid security breaches.

The Fog Computing platform is modeled to support the Internet of Things (IoT). The IoT devices often help in reducing the gap between the cloud and the end devices. The major shortcomings of the fog model are written below:

- Trust and authentication are the two alarming issues in the fog computing environment. A fog node is the central element of the fog computing model. The fog node guarantees secrecy and obscurity for the users. End users are required to be aware of the authorization because the fog node carries out the global concealing process and non-diabolical actions. Hence, the fog nodes must maintain a level of trust in each other.

- It is really crucial to identify unauthorized access in order to prevent real data from being hacked (Mandlekar et al., 2014). Security issues, such as cooperation among nodes, need to be addressed.
- A fog node is vulnerable to malicious attacks (Mahmud et al., 2018) because fog nodes are located in different regions, with some regions having weak security arrangements. One such example is that a malicious node user can misuse and alter readings or may cause IP spoofing. Security issues (Zhang et al., 2018), such as IP address spoofing and eavesdropping, need to be addressed in the fog computing platform.
- Data consistency has been achievable using possible efforts. Everyone in the network is concerned about the confidentiality of their data (Koo et al., 2016). Hence, the preservation of privacy is an important aspect of the fog computing environment.
- Two types of communication channels have been used in transmitting data: (i) between IoT devices and fog nodes; and (ii) among fog nodes. The communication channel in either of the two cases is required to be secure. An intruder might send fake messages that get circulated in the network during communication (Soleymani et al., 2017).
- Task scheduling is complex in the fog computing model.
- Currently, service level agreements (SLAs) are designed for cloud computing platforms and not for the fog computing model.
- The design of the fog computing model is concerned with a few objectives, such as offloading and load balancing of the fog network.

8.2.6 EDGE COMPUTING

Edge computing (Tu et al., 2019) is one of the latest computing technologies that has acquired huge popularity in the last five years. This computing technology has served as a computing model for advanced technologies such as the IoT and vehicle-to-vehicle communication, and it provides a number of services to the user community. The last decade has seen a substantial increase in the number of communicating devices with the growth of IoT applications. The rise of IoT applications has led to the introduction of a number of communicative devices. The data generated by IoT devices are enormous, and therefore processing such data requires running several IoT services.

The edge computing (Ahmed and Rehmani, 2017) model is designed to produce data computation at the network edge rather than sending unprocessed data to data centers. This leads to bandwidth reduction and a decrease in computational complexity required by clouds. The edge computing model cleans, preprocesses, and collects IoT data using cloud services and builds a combination of IoT devices and the cloud.

Opportunistic edge computing (Olaniyan et al., 2018) creates a scalable foundation using resources supplied by the end users.

The benefits of edge computing are stated below:

i. Important networking issues like latency and confidentiality are easily handled using edge computing. A great reduction has been observed in cyber-attacks, and data security has also improved to a good extent due to the decentralized structure of the edge model.
ii. Connected devices are not required to wait for a centralized platform to provide a service, and the service availability is also relatively higher than in cloud computing.
iii. There is a reduction in operational costs because the preprocessing of data takes place at the network edge rather than transferring it to cloud data centers. This will lead to a reduction in infrastructure costs.
iv. The edge computing paradigm is scalable in nature and can create hybrid structures with the cloud computing model.

The section presented below deals with the open issues or challenges (Cao et al., 2018; Varghese et al., 2016) in edge computing.

- An efficient resource discovery mechanism is required to locate the resources and services at the edges of the network because of the large number of devices present on the network edge.
- The data being processed at the network edge only forms a subset of data and not the complete data. Therefore, it becomes necessary for enterprises to decide on a tolerable level of information loss.

- The hardware specifications of the edge computing model are high.
- An effective fault recovery mechanism is required to deal with imprudent faults on the edge node.
- Though job partitioning is not new in a distributed computing environment, however, it becomes troublesome in edge computing platforms because a scheduler is needed to assign partitioned jobs over nodes present at network edges.
- The risk factor must be comprehensively related to service providers and enterprises owning these devices. A cost-effective computational model must be constructed in such a way that edge nodes will be accessed by the expected user community.
- The traditional authentication protocols are not relevant for emerging computing platforms because of the heterogeneity of computational nodes.

An edge computing framework that is capable of making automated complex decisions in real-time directly on edge devices using AI-based techniques is called edge intelligence. The integration of edge computing and AI has given birth to the notion of edge intelligence in the computing world.

The physical closeness between the processing and data-generation sources provides various advantages compared to the traditional cloud-based computing framework, including minimum latency, energy efficiency, improved security, less bandwidth consumption, on-premises capabilities, and situational awareness.

8.2.7 UTILITY COMPUTING

Computing (Fortino and Palau, 2012) has become an integral part of implementing basic activities such as using computers or mobile phones to interact with one another, reading newspapers online, managing financial activities, and many more. The ever-growing demand for computing has presented questions to computer scientists and service providers to ensure service availability and provide secure services to all intended users. Computing, however, is required in the same manner that other basic utilities, such as water and electricity, are required because of its current demand in daily life activities. It is a kind of computing where complexity, as well as maintenance costs, can be easily divided equally among all its users. The intent of utility computing (Adhikari et al., 2016; Mondal and Sarddar, 2015) is to provide a technology that allows enterprises to provide and retain resources and different functionalities according to the requirements.

It aims to support a kind of infrastructure that can provide information technology (IT) services according to the demands of customers. Utility computing (Canali et al., 2005) differs from outsourcing because outsourcing focuses on location and resource management, whereas utility computing is related to resource management, resource consumption, and its utilization. The utility model is suitable for both corporate and outsourcing data centers. It intends to break down the huge IT foundations into several independent segments. A classification has been made in accordance with the business processes that are readily supported by the independent segments. The utility model strives to help the idle resources that are not currently being used and are non-functional. These resources can easily be supplied to other business processes as per requirement. Additionally, it is possible to turn these resources on or off according to requirements.

Utility computing has several advantages, which are listed below:

- This model is cost-effective because it allows the mutual sharing of resources among the users in an organization.
- There is no need to buy a resource because of the improved ability to match the resource specifications with varying space specifications over time.
- There is less complexity due to improvements in the management and maintenance of the system.

Some of the limitations of the utility computing model are given below:

- The machines or computers in the utility model are vulnerable to hacking. A hacker might attempt to access the private files of the clients, which poses a potential threat to their privacy.
- Reliability is also an issue in the utility model because an organization might curtail its services due to a financial crisis. Although the customers have been paying for the services, they may be deprived of the requisite services.

8.3 SUMMARY

Everyone wants a hassle-free computing experience, which brings various types of challenges for software developers and owners. Though there are many challenges, there are some possible solutions and recommendations that can certainly help in handling such challenges and problems, as described below:

- In a fog computing network, it is necessary to state appropriate SLAs and SLA management techniques.
- In a multi-objective fog model, several objectives, such as latency, security, availability, bandwidth, and energy, can be incorporated together to utilize the potential of a multi-objective fog network.
- Developing fast protocols and machine learning algorithms could help facilitate high-speed users.
- A proper scheduler is needed to schedule the partitioned jobs over the edge nodes in the network. Also, a support mechanism is required to verify the accuracy of the partitioned tasks by the receivers.
- A new set of authentication and trust protocols is required to handle the heterogeneity of the resources in a computing model.

The emerging computing platforms have transformed the notion of IT and presented a view of utility computing as a reality. The growing rate of the Internet and IoT has boosted the development of emerging computing models, which we have discussed in this chapter. We have also discussed the potential challenges and some promising solutions for these computing models. These computing platforms have been recognized worldwide and are widely used in the areas of e-governance, disaster management, education, and business organizations. These computing paradigms are still in the exploration phase, and it has been estimated that billions of computing users and devices will be connected to the Internet. The idea of market-based global clouds is to facilitate trading services by connecting the clouds and forming market clouds. In the future, a secure, unified, and interoperable platform can be developed by assembling all the computing platforms to provide seamless services to the user community and organizations.

KEYWORDS

- **Average machine utilization**
- **cluster resource utilization**
- **conventional algorithmsgrid scheduling problem**
- **hybrid algorithms**
- **load distribution uniformity**
- **resource utilization**
- **total completion time**

Bibliography

Abraham, A., Buyya, R., & Nath, B. (2000). Nature's heuristics for scheduling jobs on computational grids. In *Proceedings of the 8th IEEE International Conference on Advanced Computing and Communications (ADCOM 2000)* (pp. 45–52).

Adhikari, M., Das, A., & Mukherjee, A. (2016). Utility computing and its utilization. In *Emerging Research Surrounding Power Consumption and Performance Issues in Utility Computing* (pp. 1–21). IGI Global.

Ahmed, E., & Rehmani, M. H. (2017). Mobile edge computing: Opportunities, solutions, and challenges. *Future Generation Computer Systems, 70*, 350–361. Elsevier.

Ali, K. E., Mazen, S. A., & Hassanein, E. E. (2018). A proposed hybrid model for adopting cloud computing in e-government. *Future Computing and Informatics Journal, 3*(2), 286–295.

Alyaseri, S., & Ku-Mahamud, K. R. (2013). Bee foraging behavior techniques for grid scheduling problems. *International Refereed Journal of Engineering and Science (IRJES), 2*(4), 39–45.

Ambursa, F. U., & Latip, R. (2013). A survey: Particle swarm optimization-based algorithms for grid computing scheduling systems. *Journal of Computer Science, 9*(12), 1669–1677.

Amiri, E., Keshavarz, H., Ohshima, N., & Komaki, S. (2014). Resource allocation in the grid: A review. *Procedia-Social and Behavioral Sciences, 129*, 436–440.

Attiya, H., & Welch, J. (2004). *Distributed Computing: Fundamentals, Simulations, and Advanced Topics* (Vol. 19). John Wiley & Sons.

Balaton, Z., & Gombás, G. (2003). Resource and job monitoring in the grid. In *Proceedings of the European Conference on Parallel Processing* (pp. 404–411).

Belfiore, J., Campbell, D., Capps, S., Cellini, S., Fitzgerald, C., Gundotra, V., Lucovsky, M., Maritz, P., Mital, A., & Rudder, E. (2006). Distributed computing services platform. *Google Patents*. U.S. Patent No. 20060031020.

Berman, F., Fox, G., Hey, T., & Hey, A. J. (2003). *Grid Computing: Making the Global Infrastructure A Reality* (Vol. 2). John Wiley & Sons.

Binitha, S., & Sathya, S. S. (2012). A survey of bio-inspired optimization algorithms. *International Journal of Soft Computing and Engineering (IJSCE), 2*(2), 137–151.

Blum, C. (2005). Ant colony optimization: Introduction and recent trends. *Physics of Life Reviews, 2*(4), 353–373.

Blum, C., & Merkle, D. (2008). *Swarm Intelligence: Introduction and Applications*. Springer Science & Business Media.

Branco Jr, T., de Sá-Soares, F., & Rivero, A. L. (2017). Key issues for the successful adoption of cloud computing. *Procedia Computer Science, 121*, 115–122.

Brohi, S. N., Bamiah, M. A., Brohi, M. N., & Kamran, R. (2012). Identifying and analyzing security threats to virtualized cloud computing infrastructures. In *Proceedings of the 2012 International Conference on Cloud Computing Technologies, Applications and Management (ICCCTAM)* (pp. 151–155).

Buyya, R. (1999). *High-Performance Cluster Computing: Architectures and Systems* (Vol. 1). Prentice Hall.

Buyya, R., & Murshed, M. (2002). Gridsim: A toolkit for the modeling and simulation of distributed resource management and scheduling for grid computing. *Concurrency and Computation: Practice and Experience, 14*(13–15), 1175–1220.

Buyya, R., & Venugopal, S. (2005). A gentle introduction to grid computing and technologies. *Database, 2*, R3.

Buyya, R., Abramson, D., & Giddy, J. (2000). Grid resource management, scheduling, and computational economy. In *Proceedings of the International Workshop on Global and Cluster Computing* (pp. 2002–2040).

Buyya, R., Abramson, D., Giddy, J., & Stockinger, H. (2002). Economic models for resource management and scheduling in grid computing. *Concurrency and Computation: Practice and Experience, 14*(13–15), 1507–1542.

Buyya, R., Chapin, S., & DiNucci, D. (2000). Architectural models for resource management in the grid. In *Proceedings of the International Workshop on Grid Computing* (pp. 18–35).

Buyya, R., Yeo, C. S., Venugopal, S., Broberg, J., & Brandic, I. (2009). Cloud computing and emerging IT platforms: Vision, hype, and reality for delivering computing as the 5th utility. *Future Generation Computer Systems, 25*(6), 599–616.

Canali, C., Rabinovich, M., & Xiao, Z. (2005). Utility computing for internet applications. In *Web Content Delivery* (pp. 131–151). Springer.

Caniou, Y., & Gay, J. S. (2009). Simbatch: An API for simulating and predicting the performance of parallel resources managed by batch systems. In *Proceedings of the Euro-Par 2008 Workshops on Parallel Processing* (pp. 223–234). Springer.

Cao, J., Spooner, D., Turner, J. D., Jarvis, S., Kerbyson, D. J., Saini, S., & Nudd, G. (2002). Agent-based resource management for grid computing. In *Proceedings of the 2nd IEEE/ACM International Symposium on Cluster Computing and the Grid (CCGRID'02)* (pp. 350–350).

Cao, J., Zhang, Q., & Shi, W. (2018). Challenges and opportunities in edge computing. In *Edge Computing: A Primer* (pp. 59–70). Springer.

Chang, R. S., Chang, J. S., & Lin, P. S. (2009). An ant algorithm for balanced job scheduling in grids. *Future Generation Computer Systems, 25*(1), 20–27.

Chen, C. C., & Liu, Y. T. (2018). Enhanced ant colony optimization with dynamic mutation and ad hoc initialization for improving the design of a TSK-type fuzzy system. *Computational Intelligence and Neuroscience, 2018*, 1–16. https://doi.org/10.1155/2018/4981035.

Chen, T., Zhang, B., Hao, X., & Dai, Y. (2006). Task scheduling in grid based on particle swarm optimization. In *Proceedings of the 2006 Fifth International Symposium on Parallel and Distributed Computing* (pp. 238–245). IEEE. https://doi.org/10.1109/ISPDC.2006.36.

Chu, S. C., Tsai, P. W., & Pan, J. S. (2006). Cat swarm optimization. In *PRICAI 2006: Trends in Artificial Intelligence: 9th Pacific Rim International Conference on Artificial Intelligence* (pp. 854–858). Springer. https://doi.org/10.1007/11801603_98.

Coello, C. A. C., Lamont, G. B., & Van Veldhuizen, D. A. (2007). *Evolutionary Algorithms for Solving Multi-Objective Problems* (Vol. 5). Springer.

Cusumano, M. A. (2010). Cloud computing and SaaS as new computing platforms. *Communications of the ACM, 53*(4), 27–29. https://doi.org/10.1145/1721654.1721667.
Czajkowski, K., Foster, I., & Kesselman, C. (1999). Resource co-allocation in computational grids. In *Proceedings of the Eighth International Symposium on High Performance Distributed Computing* (pp. 219–228). IEEE. https://doi.org/10.1109/HPDC.1999.805291.
Darwish, A. (2018). Bio-inspired computing: Algorithms review, deep analysis, and the scope of applications. *Future Computing and Informatics Journal, 3*(2), 231–246. https://doi.org/10.1016/j.fcij.2018.06.001.
Dave, M., & Choudhary, K. (2016). Job shop scheduling algorithms—A shift from traditional techniques to non-traditional techniques. In *Proceedings of the 2016 3rd International Conference on Computing for Sustainable Global Development (INDIACom)* (pp. 169–173). IEEE.
Deb, S., Fong, S., & Tian, Z. (2015). Elephant search algorithm for optimization problems. In *Proceedings of the 2015 Tenth International Conference on Digital Information Management (ICDIM)* (pp. 249–255). IEEE. https://doi.org/10.1109/ICDIM.2015.7381882.
Deb, S., Fong, S., Tian, Z., Wong, R. K., Mohammed, S., & Fiaidhi, J. (2016). Finding approximate solutions of NP-hard optimization and TSP problems using the elephant search algorithm. *The Journal of Supercomputing, 72*, 3960–3992. https://doi.org/10.1007/s11227-016-1778-1.
Dobre, C., Pop, F., & Cristea, V. (2008). A simulation framework for dependable distributed systems. In *Proceedings of the 2008 International Conference on Parallel Processing-Workshops* (pp. 181–187). IEEE. https://doi.org/10.1109/ICPP-W.2008.63.
Dong, F., & Akl, S. G. (2006). Scheduling algorithms for grid computing: State of the art and open problems. Technical Report No. 2006–504. *School of Computing, Queen's University*.
Dorigo, M., & Blum, C. (2005). Ant colony optimization theory: A survey. *Theoretical Computer Science, 344*(2–3), 243–278. https://doi.org/10.1016/j.tcs.2005.05.020.
Dorigo, M., Maniezzo, V., & Colorni, A. (1996). Ant system: Optimization by a colony of cooperating agents. *IEEE Transactions on Systems, Man, and Cybernetics, Part B: Cybernetics, 26*(1), 29–41. https://doi.org/10.1109/3477.484436.
Evans, D. (2011). The Internet of Things: How the next evolution of the Internet is changing everything. *Cisco White Paper, 1*(2011), 1–11.
Faris, H., Aljarah, I., Al-Betar, M. A., & Mirjalili, S. (2018). Grey wolf optimizer: A review of recent variants and applications. *Neural Computing and Applications, 30*, 413–435. https://doi.org/10.1007/s00521-017-3272-5.
Fibich, P., Matyska, L., & Rudová, H. (2005). Model of the grid scheduling problem. In *Exploring Planning and Scheduling for Web Services, Grid and Autonomic Computing* (pp. 17–24). Springer.
Fidanova, S., & Durchova, M. (2005). Ant algorithm for grid scheduling problem. In *Proceedings of the International Conference on Large-Scale Scientific Computing* (pp. 405–412). Springer. https://doi.org/10.1007/11408877_45.
Flórez, E., Barrios, C. J., & Pecero, J. E. (2015). Methods for job scheduling on computational grids: Review and comparison. In *Proceedings of the Latin American*

High Performance Computing Conference (pp. 19–33). Springer. https://doi.org/10.1007/978-3-319-14690-5_2.

Fortino, G., & Palau, C. E. (2012). Next generation content delivery infrastructures: Emerging paradigms and challenges. *International Journal of Distributed Sensor Networks, 2012*, 1–10. https://doi.org/10.1155/2012/170634.

Foster, I. (2003). The grid: Computing without bounds. *Scientific American, 288*(4), 78–85. https://doi.org/10.1038/scientificamerican0403-78.

Foster, I., & Kesselman, C. (2003a). *The Grid 2*. Morgan Kaufmann.

Foster, I., & Kesselman, C. (2003b). *The Grid 2: Blueprint for a New Computing Infrastructure*. Elsevier.

Foster, I., Kesselman, C., & Tuecke, S. (2001). The anatomy of the grid: Enabling scalable virtual organizations. *The International Journal of High-Performance Computing Applications, 15*(3), 200–222. https://doi.org/10.1177/109434200101500302.

Gadir, O. M., Subbanna, K., Vayyala, A. R., Shanmugam, H., Bodas, A. P., Tripathy, T. K., Indurkar, R. S., & Rao, K. H. (2005). High-availability cluster virtual server system. *U.S. Patent No. 6,895,457*. U.S. Patent and Trademark Office.

Gharehchopogh, F. S., & Gholizadeh, H. (2019). A comprehensive survey: Whale optimization algorithm and its applications. *Swarm and Evolutionary Computation, 48*, 1–24. https://doi.org/10.1016/j.swevo.2019.03.004.

Gharehchopogh, F. S., Ahadi, M., Maleki, I., Habibpour, R., & Kamalinia, A. (2013). Analysis of scheduling algorithms in a grid computing environment. *International Journal of Innovation and Applied Studies, 4*(3), 560–567.

Ghosh, T. K., Goswami, R., Bera, S., & Barman, S. (2012). Load balanced static grid scheduling using the Max-Min heuristic. In *Proceedings of the 2012 2nd IEEE International Conference on Parallel, Distributed and Grid Computing* (pp. 419–423). IEEE. https://doi.org/10.1109/PDGC.2012.6449856.

Goldberg, D. E. (1989). *Genetic Algorithms in Search, Optimization, and Machine Learning*. Addison-Wesley.

Goswami, S., & Das, A. (2015). Deadline stringency-based job scheduling in a computational grid environment. *2015 2nd International Conference on Computing for Sustainable Global Development (INDIACom)*, 531–536.

Grover, R., & Chabbra, A. (2016). Bio-inspired optimization techniques for job scheduling in grid computing. *2016 IEEE International Conference on Recent Trends in Electronics, Information & Communication Technology (RTEICT)*, 1902–1906.

Hamscher, V., Schwiegelshohn, U., Streit, A., & Yahyapour, R. (2000). Evaluation of job-scheduling strategies for grid computing. In *International Workshop on Grid Computing* (pp. 191–202).

Hu, P., Dhelim, S., Ning, H., & Qiu, T. (2017). Survey on fog computing: Architecture, key technologies, applications, and open issues. *Journal of Network and Computer Applications, 98*, 27–42.

Ihsan, R. R., Almufti, S. M., Ormani, B., Asaad, R. R., & Marqas, R. B. (2021). A survey on Cat Swarm Optimization algorithm. *Asian Journal of Research in Computer Science, 10*(2), 22–32.

Izakian, H., Ladani, B. T., Zamanifar, K., & Abraham, A. (2009). A novel particle swarm optimization approach for grid job scheduling. In *International Conference on Information Systems, Technology and Management* (pp. 100–109).

Jiang, C., Wang, C., Liu, X., & Zhao, Y. (2007). A survey of job scheduling in grids. In *Advances in Data and Web Management* (pp. 419–427). Springer.

Jiang, H., & Ni, T. (2009). PB-FCFS-a task scheduling algorithm based on FCFS and backfilling strategy for grid computing. *2009 Joint Conferences on Pervasive Computing (JCPC)*, 507–510.

Jones, W. M., Ligon, W. B., Pang, L. W., & Stanzione, D. (2005). Characterization of bandwidth-aware meta-schedulers for co-allocating jobs across multiple clusters. *The Journal of Supercomputing, 34*, 135–163.

Kandagatla, C. (2003). Survey and taxonomy of grid resource management systems. *University of Texas, Austin*.

Kant, A., Sharma, A., Agarwal, S., & Chandra, S. (2010). An ACO approach to job scheduling in a grid environment. In *International Conference on Swarm, Evolutionary, and Memetic Computing* (pp. 286–295).

Karaboga, D., Gorkemli, B., Ozturk, C., & Karaboga, N. (2014). A comprehensive survey: Artificial bee colony (ABC) algorithm and applications. *Artificial Intelligence Review, 42*(1), 21–57.

Kavis, M. J. (2014). *Architecting the Cloud: Design Decisions for Cloud Computing Service Models (SaaS, PaaS, and IaaS)*. John Wiley & Sons.

Kennedy, J. (2006). *Swarm Intelligence*. Springer.

Kennedy, J., & Eberhart, R. (1995). Particle swarm optimization. *Proceedings of ICNN'95-International Conference on Neural Networks, 4*, 1942–1948.

Kfatheen, S. V., & Banu, M. N. (2015). MiM-MaM: A new task scheduling algorithm for grid environment. *2015 International Conference on Advances in Computer Engineering and Applications*, 695–699.

Kfatheen, S. V., & Marimuthu, A. (2017). ETS: An efficient task scheduling algorithm for grid computing. *Advances in Computational Sciences and Technology, 10*(10), 2911–2925.

Kleinrock, L. (2005). A vision for the Internet. *ST Journal of Research, 2*(1), 1–5.

Klusáček, D., & Rudová, H. (2010). Alea 2: Job scheduling simulator. *Proceedings of the 3rd International ICST Conference on Simulation Tools and Techniques, 61*.

Kokilavani, T., & Amalarethinam, D. D. G. (2011). Load balanced min-min algorithm for static meta-task scheduling in grid computing. *International Journal of Computer Applications, 20*(2), 43–49.

Kokilavani, T., & Amalarethinam, D. G. (2010). Applying Non-Traditional Optimization Techniques to Task Scheduling in Grid Computing: An Overview. *International Journal of Research and Reviews in Computer Science, 1*(4), 33.

Kondo, D. (2007). SimBOINC: A simulator for desktop grids and volunteer computing systems.

Koo, D., Shin, Y., Yun, J., & Hur, J. (2016). A Hybrid Deduplication for Secure and Efficient Data Outsourcing in Fog Computing. *2016 IEEE International Conference on Cloud Computing Technology and Science (CloudCom)*, 285–293.

Krause, J., Cordeiro, J., Parpinelli, R. S., & Lopes, H. S. (2013). A survey of swarm algorithms applied to discrete optimization problems. In *Swarm Intelligence and Bio-Inspired Computation* (pp. 169–191). Elsevier.

Kurowski, K., Nabrzyski, J., Oleksiak, A., & Weglarz, J. (2007). Grid scheduling simulations with GSSIM. *2007 International Conference on Parallel and Distributed Systems*, 1–8.

Laniepce, S., Lacoste, M., Kassi-Lahlou, M., Bignon, F., Lazri, K., & Wailly, A. (2013). Engineering intrusion prevention services for IaaS clouds: The way of the hypervisor. *2013 IEEE Seventh International Symposium on Service-Oriented System Engineering*, 25–36.

Legrand, A., Marchal, L., & Casanova, H. (2003). Scheduling distributed applications: The sim grid simulation framework. *CCGrid 2003. 3rd IEEE/ACM International Symposium on Cluster Computing and the Grid, 2003. Proceedings.*, 138–145.

Liu, X., Xia, H., & Chien, A. A. (2004). Validating and scaling the microgrid: A scientific instrument for grid dynamics. *Journal of Grid Computing, 2*(2), 141–161.

Lu, B., Zhong, J., & Lam, J. (2010). Job-centric scheduling in a grid environment. *Google Patents.*

Lyytinen, K., & Yoo, Y. (2002). Ubiquitous computing. *Communications of the ACM, 45*(12), 63–96.

Mahmud, R., Kotagiri, R., & Buyya, R. (2018). Fog computing: A taxonomy, survey and future directions. In *Internet of Everything* (pp. 103–130). Springer.

Maipan-uku, J. Y., Muhammed, A., Abdullah, A., & Hussin, M. (2016). Max-Average: An extended Max-Min scheduling algorithm for the grid computing environment. *Journal of Telecommunication, Electronic and Computer Engineering (JTEC), 8*(6), 43–47.

Mandlekar, V. G., Mahale, V., Sancheti, S. S., & Rais, M. S. (2014). Survey on fog computing mitigating data theft attacks in the cloud. *International Journal of Innovative Research in Computer Science & Technology, 2*, 13–16.

Mareli, M., & Twala, B. (2018). An adaptive Cuckoo search algorithm for optimization. *Applied Computing and Informatics, 14*(2), 107–115.

Marini, F., & Walczak, B. (2015). Particle swarm optimization (PSO): A tutorial. *Chemometrics and Intelligent Laboratory Systems, 149*, 153–165.

Mathiyalagan, P., Dhepthie, U. R., & Sivanandam, S. N. (2010a). Grid scheduling using enhanced ant colony algorithm. *ICTACT Journal on Soft Computing, 2*, 85–87.

Mathiyalagan, P., Dhepthie, U. R., & Sivanandam, S. N. (2010b). Grid scheduling using enhanced PSO algorithm. *International Journal of Computer Science and Engineering, 2*(2), 140–145.

Menasce, D. A., & Casalicchio, E. (2004). A framework for resource allocation in grid computing. *MASCOTS 2004: 12th International Symposium on Modeling, Analysis, and Simulation of Computer and Telecommunication Systems*, 12th.

Meng, X., Liu, Y., Gao, X., & Zhang, H. (2014). A new bio-inspired algorithm: Chicken swarm optimization. In *Advances in Swarm Intelligence: 5th International Conference, ICSI 2014, Hefei, China, October 17–20, 2014, Proceedings, Part I* (pp. 86–94).

Merkle, D., Middendorf, M., & Schmeck, H. (2002). Ant colony optimization for resource-constrained project scheduling. *IEEE Transactions on Evolutionary Computation, 6*(4), 333–346.

Messina, P. (1998). Distributed supercomputing applications. In *The Grid: Blueprint for a New Computing Infrastructure* (pp. 55–73).

Mirjalili, S. (2015). Moth-flame optimization algorithm: A novel nature-inspired heuristic paradigm. *Knowledge-Based Systems, 89*, 228–249.

Mirjalili, S., & Lewis, A. (2016). The whale optimization algorithm. *Advances in Engineering Software, 95*, 51–67.
Mirjalili, S., Mirjalili, S. M., & Lewis, A. (2014). Grey wolf optimizer. *Advances in Engineering Software, 69*, 46–61.
Mishra, M. K., Patel, Y. S., Rout, Y., & Mund, G. B. (2014). A survey on scheduling heuristics in a grid computing environment. *International Journal of Modern Education and Computer Science, 6*(10), 57.
Molaiy, S., & Effatparvar, M. (2014). Scheduling in grid systems using ant colony algorithm. *International Journal of Computer Network and Information Security, 6*(2), 19.
Mondal, R. K., & Sarddar, D. (2015). Utility computing. *International Journal of Grid and Distributed Computing, 8*(4), 115–122.
Mouradian, C., Naboulsi, D., Yangui, S., Glitho, R. H., Morrow, M. J., & Polakos, P. A. (2017). A comprehensive survey on fog computing: State-of-the-art and research challenges. *IEEE Communications Surveys & Tutorials, 20*(1), 416–464.
Mukherjee, M., Shu, L., & Wang, D. (2018). Survey of fog computing: Fundamental, network applications, and research challenges. *IEEE Communications Surveys & Tutorials, 20*(3), 1826–1857.
Murshed, M., & Buyya, R. (2002). Using the GridSim toolkit for enabling grid computing education. *International Conference on Communication Networks and Distributed Systems Modeling and Simulation*, 27–31.
Neshat, M., Adeli, A., Sepidnam, G., Sargolzaei, M., & Toosi, A. N. (2012). A review of artificial fish swarm optimization methods and applications. *International Journal on Smart Sensing and Intelligent Systems, 5*(1), 107–148.
Nseef, S. K., Abdullah, S., Turky, A., & Kendall, G. (2016). An adaptive multi-population artificial bee colony algorithm for dynamic optimization problems. *Knowledge-Based Systems, 104*, 14–23.
Olaniyan, R., Fadahunsi, O., Maheswaran, M., & Zhani, M. F. (2018). Opportunistic edge computing: Concepts, opportunities, and research challenges. *Future Generation Computer Systems, 89*, 633–645.
Overeinder, B. J., Sloot, P. M., Heederik, R. N., & Hertzberger, L. O. (1996). A dynamic load balancing system for parallel cluster computing. *Future Generation Computer Systems, 12*(1), 101–115.
Ozturk, C., Hancer, E., & Karaboga, D. (2015). A novel binary artificial bee colony algorithm based on genetic operators. *Information Sciences, 297*, 154–170.
Pahl, C. (2015). Containerization and the PaaS cloud. *IEEE Cloud Computing, 2*(3), 24–31.
Panda, S. K., Bhoi, S. K., & Khilar, P. M. (2013). A semi-interquartile min-min max-min (SIM2) approach for grid task scheduling. In *Proceedings of International Conference on Advances in Computing* (pp. 415–421).
Panwar, P., Sachdeva, S., & Rana, S. (2016). A genetic algorithm-based scheduling algorithm for grid computing environments. In *Proceedings of Fifth International Conference on Soft Computing for Problem Solving* (pp. 165–173).
Patel, P. S. (2014). Multi-objective job scheduler using genetic algorithm in grid computing. *International Journal of Computer Applications, 92*(14).

Pazhaniraja, N., Paul, P. V., Roja, G., Shanmugapriya, K., & Sonali, B. (2017). A study on recent bio-inspired optimization algorithms. *In 2017 Fourth International Conference on Signal Processing, Communication and Networking (ICSCN)* (pp. 1–6).

Peleg, D. (2000). *Distributed Computing: A Locality-Sensitive Approach*. SIAM.

Phelps, S., & Köksalan, M. (2003). An interactive evolutionary metaheuristic for multi-objective combinatorial optimization. *Management Science, 49*(12), 1726–1738.

Prajapati, H. B., & Shah, V. A. (2014). Scheduling in a grid computing environment. *In 2014 Fourth International Conference on Advanced Computing & Communication Technologies* (pp. 315–324).

Qureshi, M. B., Dehnavi, M. M., Min-Allah, N., Qureshi, M. S., Hussain, H., Rentifis, I., Tziritas, N., Loukopoulos, T., Khan, S. U., & Xu, C. Z. (2014). Survey on grid resource allocation mechanisms. *Journal of Grid Computing, 12*(2), 399–441.

Rechenberg, I. (1973). *Evolution Strategy: Optimization of Technical Systems by Means of Biological Evolution*. Fromman-Holzboog.

Sahana, S. K., & Ankita. (2019). A comprehensive survey on computational grid resource management. *Proceedings of the Second International Conference on Microelectronics, Computing & Communication Systems (MCCS 2017)* (pp. 97–108).

Sahana, S. K., & Ankita. (2019). An automated parameter tuning method for ant colony optimization for scheduling jobs in a grid environment. *International Journal of Intelligent Systems and Applications, 11*(3), 11.

Shanthini, J., Kalaikumaran, T., & Karthik, S. (2015). Hybrid scheduling model for independent grid tasks. *The Scientific World Journal, 2015*, 1–9.

Shehab, M., Abualigah, L., Al Hamad, H., Alabool, H., Alshinwan, M., & Khasawneh, A. M. (2020). Moth-flame optimization algorithm: Variants and applications. *Neural Computing and Applications, 32*, 9859–9884.

Singh, M., Sholiya, S., & Gupta, P. (2014). Scheduling in grid computing—A review. *International Journal of Computer & Mathematical Sciences, 2*(1), 1–8.

Singh, S., Sarkar, M., Roy, S., & Mukherjee, N. (2013). Genetic algorithm-based resource broker for the computational grid. *Procedia Technology, 10*, 572–580.

Smarr, L., & Catlett, C. E. (1992). Meta computing. *Communications of the ACM, 35*(6), 44–52.

Soleymani, S. A., Abdullah, A. H., Zareei, M., Anisi, M. H., Vargas-Rosales, C., Khan, M. K., & Goudarzi, S. (2017). A secure trust model based on fuzzy logic in vehicular ad hoc networks with fog computing. *IEEE Access, 5*, 15619–15629.

Subramanian, N., & Jeyaraj, A. (2018). Recent security challenges in cloud computing. *Computers & Electrical Engineering, 71*, 28–42.

Takefusa, A., Matsuoka, S., Nakada, H., Aida, K., & Nagashima, U. (1999). Overview of a performance evaluation system for global computing scheduling algorithms. *Proceedings of the Eighth International Symposium on High-Performance Distributed Computing (Cat. No. 99TH8469)* (pp. 97–104).

Tiwari, P. K., & Vidyarthi, D. P. (2016). Improved auto control ant colony optimization using lazy ant approach for grid scheduling problem. *Future Generation Computer Systems, 60*, 78–89.

Tu, W., Pop, F., Jia, W., Wu, J., & Iacono, M. (2019). *High-Performance Computing in Edge Computing Networks*. Elsevier.

Ujjwal, K. C., Garg, S., Hilton, J., Aryal, J., & Forbes-Smith, N. (2019). Cloud computing in natural hazard modeling systems: Current research trends and future directions. *International Journal of Disaster Risk Reduction*, 101188.

Upadhyay, N. (2018). Fogology: What is (not) fog computing? *Procedia Computer Science, 139*, 199–203.

Uymaz, S. A., Tezel, G., & Yel, E. (2015). Artificial algae algorithm (AAA) for nonlinear global optimization. *Applied Soft Computing, 31*, 153–171.

van Steen, M., & Tanenbaum, A. S. (2016). A brief introduction to distributed systems. *Computing, 98*(10), 967–1009.

Varghese, B., & Buyya, R. (2018). Next generation cloud computing: New trends and research directions. *Future Generation Computer Systems, 79*, 849–861.

Varghese, B., Wang, N., Barbhuiya, S., Kilpatrick, P., & Nikolopoulos, D. S. (2016). Challenges and opportunities in edge computing. *2016 IEEE International Conference on Smart Cloud (SmartCloud)* (pp. 20–26).

Wei, L., Zhang, X., Li, Y., & Li, Y. (2012). An improved ant algorithm for grid task scheduling strategy. *Physics Procedia, 24*, 1974–1981.

Weiss, A. (2007). Computing in the clouds. *Networker, 11*(4), 16–25.

Werstein, P., Situ, H., & Huang, Z. (2006). Load balancing in a cluster computer. *2006 Seventh International Conference on Parallel and Distributed Computing, Applications, and Technologies (PDCAT'06)* (pp. 569–577).

Xhafa, F., & Abraham, A. (2008). Meta-heuristics for grid scheduling problems. In *Metaheuristics for Scheduling in Distributed Computing Environments* (pp. 1–37). Springer. https://doi.org/10.1007/978-3-540-69260-7_1.

Xhafa, F., Carretero Casado, J. S., & Abraham, A. (2007). Genetic algorithm-based schedulers for grid computing systems. *International Journal of Innovative Computing, Information and Control, 3*(5), 1053–1071.

Xu, Y., Li, K., Hu, J., & Li, K. (2014). A genetic algorithm for task scheduling on heterogeneous computing systems using multiple priority queues. *Information Sciences, 270*, 255–287.

Yan, H., Shen, X. Q., Li, X., & Wu, M. H. (2005). An improved ant algorithm for job scheduling in grid computing. *In 2005 International Conference on Machine Learning and Cybernetics* (Vol. 5, pp. 2957–2961).

Yang, X. S. (2010). *Nature-Inspired Metaheuristic Algorithms*. Luniver Press.

Younis, M. T., & Yang, S. (2017). Genetic algorithm for independent job scheduling in grid computing. *MENDEL, 23*, 65–72.

Younis, M. T., Yang, S., & Passow, B. (2017). Meta-heuristically seeded genetic algorithm for independent job scheduling in grid computing. *Applications of Evolutionary Computation: 20th European Conference, EvoApplications 2017, Amsterdam, The Netherlands, April 19–21, 2017, Proceedings, Part I, 20*, 177–189.

Yousefpour, A., Fung, C., Nguyen, T., Kadiyala, K., Jalali, F., Niakanlahiji, A., Kong, J., & Jue, J. P. (2019). *All One Needs to Know About Fog Computing and Related Edge Computing Paradigms*.

Yousif, A., Nor, S. M., Abdualla, A. H., & Bashir, M. B. (2015). Job scheduling algorithms on grid computing: State-of-the-art. *International Journal of Grid and Distributed Computing, 8*(6), 125–140.

Yu, J., & Buyya, R. (2006). A budget-constrained scheduling of workflow applications on utility grids using genetic algorithms. *In 2006 Workshop on Workflows in Support of Large-Scale Science* (pp. 1–10).
Yu, X., & Gen, M. (2010). *Introduction to evolutionary algorithms*. Springer Science & Business Media.
Zhang, L., Chen, Y., Sun, R., Jing, S., & Yang, B. (2008). A task scheduling algorithm based on PSO for grid computing. *International Journal of Computational Intelligence Research, 4*(1), 37–43.
Zhang, P., Zhou, M., & Fortino, G. (2018). Security and trust issues in fog computing: A survey. *Future Generation Computer Systems, 88*, 16–27.
Zhang, Q., Cheng, L., & Boutaba, R. (2010). Cloud computing: State-of-the-art and research challenges. *Journal of Internet Services and Applications, 1*(1), 7–18.
Zhao, H., Pei, Z., Jiang, J., Guan, R., Wang, C., & Shi, X. (2010). A hybrid swarm intelligent method based on genetic algorithm and artificial bee colony. *In Advances in Swarm Intelligence: First International Conference, ICSI 2010, Beijing, China, Proceedings, Part I, 1* (pp. 558–565).
Zissis, D., & Lekkas, D. (2012). Addressing cloud computing security issues. *Future Generation Computer Systems, 28*(3), 583–592.
Zouache, D., Arby, Y. O., Nouioua, F., & Abdelaziz, F. B. (2019). Multi-objective chicken swarm optimization: A novel algorithm for solving multi-objective optimization problems. *Computers & Industrial Engineering, 129*, 377–391.

Glossary

Academic Grids: Grids can be useful for sharing information among educational institutions in different geographical locations. Students from different places might get involved in a common project and can collaborate and exchange information while working in a grid environment.

Alea: Alea is a grid scheduling simulator developed by Dalibor Klusacek and Hana Rudova to evaluate different scheduling algorithms in the grid environment. The Alea simulator used here is Alea 3.0, which is an improved version of Alea 2.1, based on a popular grid simulation toolkit called GridSim toolkit. This simulator is able to handle common scheduling problems in the grid environment, such as resource and job heterogeneity, resource failure, and dynamic job arrival. The simulator uses two interfaces called Scheduling Policy and Optimization Algorithm to add a new scheduling algorithm to the simulator. The first interface handles the job arrival and job selection for execution. The latter interface is implemented when the users create their own method.

Ant Colony Optimization (ACO): Marco Dorigo and his colleagues developed Ant Colony Optimization (ACO) as a powerful metaheuristic to solve NP-complete problems at the beginning of the 1990s. Inspired by the indirect communication capability of ants, ACO is treated as the subgroup of system of social insect approaches. The pheromone deposition of ants forms a pheromone trail, which is sensed by the other ants in the search space to find food sources. ACO is a probabilistic approach because the path that leads the ants to the food source is highly dependent on the quantity of pheromones.

AppleS: The AppleS (Application Scheduling) is a grid middleware project developed at University of California, San Diego to support application scheduling.

Application Layer: The lower layer provides interfaces and programming environment to build grid applications and portals. The grid portals support web-enabled application services which enables a user to submit and get results for their submitted jobs on the remote resources.

Artificial Algae Algorithm (AAA): As the name suggest, the AAA is inspired from living habits and nature of microalgae. It is a new bio-inspired algorithm which draws its inspiration from lifestyles of algae such as reproduction, algae habits and adaptation to neighboring environment to modify the main species.

A Scheduling Problem: A scheduling problem consists of a set of jobs, resources, optimality condition, working environment and other constraints specified by the user and the resource provider.

Asia Pacific Grid: The Asia Pacific Grid popularly known as APGrid, is an international collaboration, has initiated the testbed development in the Asia Pacific region. The aim of APGrid is to allow sharing of resources, technologies and knowledge as well as developing new grid techniques and technologies.

Autonomy: The resources of the grid are spread across multiple locations for organizational use and are owned by different resource owners. It is very important to maintain a cordial relationship between the resource owners and the organizational bodies using the resources for continuous and effective usage of resources.

BeoSim: The BeoSim designed for analyzing job scheduling algorithms running in parallel at different scheduling sites for a multi-cluster computational grid. It can work with synthetic or real workload traces. It also gives visualization tools based on Java.

Bioinformatics Research Network (BIRN): BIRN is a kind of testbed in bio-medical science which facilitates data sharing stored in several repositories around America.

Boltzmann Selection: The selection rate is handled by a continuously changing temperature.

Bricks Simulation System: The Bricks simulation system is designed to facilitate simulation of client-server computing model where remote access is provided to libraries and packages executing on supercomputers. It has a centralized scheduling mechanism developed at the Tokyo Institute of Technology in Japan.

Cactus: The design of Cactus framework makes it an excellent choice as a testbed for a grid computing environment. It is another project funded by the European Union. This testbed mainly supports scientific programming.

Cat Swarm Optimization (CSO): The CSO algorithm is a new optimization algorithm that impersonates the behavior of cats. In the last few years, CSO has been used to solve optimization problems. There are different modes of cats in the CSO algorithm. The seeking mode signifies that the cats are resting but they are still alert. In the tracing mode, the cats performs local search to find the good (optimal) solution of given optimization problem.

Chicken Swarm Optimization Algorithm (CSOA): CSOA is a new swarm optimization algorithm that imitates the nature of chicken swarms and their ranking order. Lately, the literature study suggests that these algorithms have proven their potential in solving multi-objective optimization problems.

Cluster Computing: In cluster computing, various machines are combined together to execute an application or individual job. A typical illusion of one virtual machine (server) is presented before the user in such a manner that the user believes that it is interacting to a single system. A high-performance cluster contains a good number of computing machines called nodes. These nodes are further classified as general computing nodes and master nodes.

Cloud Computing: Cloud computing can be considered as a next-generation computing technology whose nodes are virtualized through "hypervisor" technologies to meet explicit service-level agreements. The cloud environment can be accessed using web service technologies such as SOAP (Simple Object Access Protocol) and REST (Representational State Transfer). The service model's setup relies on user requirements that can be public, private, community, or hybrid.

Collective Layer: This layer consists of protocols such as Grid Resource Information Protocol, which enables information across a group of resources. This layer includes resource brokers for resource management and scheduling jobs (applications) on the global computational resources.

Commercial Grids: In business world, the demands of the customers are increasing rapidly which requires instant and fast response serve the customers and understand the market dynamics to stay competent in this area.

Communication Resources: Resources that specify the network bandwidth of the grid, that is, the data transfer rate of the machines and other communication paths of the grid, are called communication resources.

Computation Resources: Resources that specify its processing capacity in a grid network are called computation resources. They are also known as processing resources.

Computational Grids: These are the compute-intensive grids which serves the computational needs of the clients. The CPU cycles are the main resources provided by computational grids. These grids provide combined CPU cycles of various resources located at different sites to satisfy user requirements. Applications such as weather forecasting, nuclear simulation, complex business analysis uses computational grids for implementation.

Condor: Condor is a grid middleware project developed at University of Wisconsin, Madison that supports high efficiency and throughput computing methods. This supports conversion of collection of workstations and dedicated clusters into a distributed super-computing facility.

Connectivity Layer: The authentication and communication protocols are provided by the connectivity layer for secure network transactions. It provides secure mechanisms to identify users and resources of the grid. Other services such as access to storage resources, remote process management and QoS constraints are handled at this layer.

Crossover: The genetic information of the selected individuals are combined together to form a new offspring. It enables exploration of the search space and finds unexplored regions to give better quality of solutions that can survive to the next generation. The selection of the crossover technique depends on the type of genetic representation chosen to represent the solutions in GA.

Data Grids: The data-intensive grids are useful in performing operations on massive amounts of distributed data. Different types of data around the globe are placed in data repositories, digital libraries, and data warehouses and are scattered over multiple administrative sites located in different geographical regions. Data grids are intended to provide a safe and reliable mechanism for data transfer, data filtering, and overall data management systems. CERN is a widely known data grid that deals with the development of huge data organizations.

Distributed Computing: It is a kind of computing that enables the users to access the required services without disclosing the existence of several autonomous computers. The mode of interaction between the communicating entities in a network is known as message passing based on standard protocols.

Edge Computing: The edge computing model is designed to produce data computation at the network edge rather than sending unprocessed data to data centers. This leads to bandwidth reduction and computational complexity requirements by clouds. The edge computing model cleans, preprocesses, and collects IoT data using cloud services and builds a combination of IoT devices and cloud. This computing technology has served as a computing model for advanced technologies such as the Internet of Things (IoT) and vehicle-to-vehicle communication and provides a number of services to the user community.

Elephant Search Algorithm (ESA): The ESA is a member of heuristic optimization algorithms, and it imitates the behavior and traits of elephants.

Enabling Grids for e-Science Projects: Enabling Grids for e-science projects popularly known as the EGEE project is one of the major grid initiatives in the development of grid computing infrastructure in current times. The European Union has funded this major data grid project which associates more than 250 computing (resource) centers of 48 different countries to generate a reliable source of computing for European and global research groups.

Enterprise Schedulers: These schedulers are viable in an enterprise which depends on local schedulers of the enterprise for job-resource management.

Evolutionary Algorithms: Evolutionary algorithms are a subset of non-conventional algorithms which are based on the principles of Darwinian theory of evolution. Like swarm algorithms, these algorithms are also problem independent and do not require any prior information about the problem being solved. They involve several control parameters which affect the nature of the search process and their effectiveness.

Fabric Layer: This layer is composed of resources such as networks, storage devices and processors distributed across different grid sites. The computational resources such as servers and supercomputers are required for running various operating systems. Other scientific devices such as sensor networks are helpful in providing real-time data for direct transmission to the intended computational sites.

First Come, First Serve (FCFS): FCFS is one of the simplest and most conventional scheduling approaches, and scheduling decisions are made on the basis of the arrival time of jobs. FCFS is non-preemptive in nature, such that a job, once assigned a resource, will never be preempted (leave the resource) until it finishes its execution. The sequence of arrival of jobs decides the running sequence of jobs, which means the job that arrives first (first come) will be scheduled first (first serve).

Fish Swarm Algorithm (FSA): The FSA algorithm is one of the intelligent swarm optimization algorithms that have important attributes such as quick convergence speed as well as deep and efficient search mechanisms.

Fitness Function: The objective function is also called the fitness function. The fitness function evaluates the fitness of the candidate solutions for a problem. It determines the closeness of a given design solution in achieving certain objectives. In this case, the objective is to minimize the total completion time of jobs and enhance resource utilization. A fitness function is decided by the scheduler according to the requirements of the application.

Fog Computing: In fog computing, the computing services, data management, storage services are allowed over the network nodes within close proximity to IoT devices. The computation is not carried out alone in cloud; rather the computation happens on route of data movement from IoT to cloud. The Fog Computing platform is modeled to support Internet of Things. The IoT devices often help in reducing the gap between cloud and the end devices.

GARUDA: GARUDA is an Indian National Grid Computing initiative launched by Centre for Development of Advanced Computing (C-DAC) with an aim to provide solutions to different scientific and engineering problems. GARUDA is a collaborative effort of engineers, compute scientists and researchers to develop a nation-wide grid consisting of large number of computational nodes, data storage resources and other scientific instruments.

Genetic Algorithm: The invention of GA is attributed to John Holland in Michigan in the 1960s. A candidate solution in a GA is represented by chromosome. The GA operates on a group of solutions called population rather than a single solution. Selection, Crossover and Mutation are the three important parameters of GA.

Genetic Bee Colony (GBC) Algorithm: GBC algorithm is a nature inspired evolutionary algorithm which is capable of solving machine learning problems such as classification and selection problems.

Grid: A grid is defined as a collection of resources such as servers, databases, processors, and networks. These resources (homogeneous or heterogeneous) are scattered over different geographical regions.

Grey Wolf Optimization (GWO): The GWO algorithm belongs to group of latest meta-heuristic algorithms and has been motivated by the hunting and leadership attributes of grey wolves. These wolves are related to the Canidae family. The grey wolves tend to live in group which is led by the alpha wolf of the group.

Grid Application Development Software: The Grid Application Development Software project popularly known as GrAds, intents to create a framework to use grid resources in a much simpler manner.

Grid Computing: The Grid Computing is defined as a computing paradigm designed to meet the dynamic demands of users by providing common access to computational resources which are networked together and act as a virtual supercomputer.

Grid Datafarm: The Japanese research and scientific community has developed the Grid Datafarm (Gfarm) project to support Petascale data-intensive computing, enabling distributed resources in a vast area. The salient features of this framework are to (1) dedicate a Grid file system for integrating local disks of computing systems in the computational grid. (2) facilitate distributed and parallel computing linking Data Grid and Computational Grid.

GridLab: The European Union has funded the GridLab project that aims at developing a Grid Computing Software Infrastructure to serve the application communities. This project has collaborated efforts of system scientists, astrophysicists and other researchers from different domains to enhance effective usage of resources in the grid environment.

Grid Scheduling: Scheduling is a central part of a grid computing environment. The jobs of the grid are scheduled over appropriate resources according to the propriety of job and resource. A scheduling technique is adopted which finds right matching of job to resource with an objective to reduce the total completion time of jobs that eventually elevates the performance of the job and the grid.

GridSim – GridSim is a Java-based and platform independent simulation toolkit which provides support for designing and simulating various scheduling models in the grid environment. This toolkit is developed by Rajkumar Buyya and his team at Grid Computing and Distributed Systems (GRIDS) lab. New scheduling methods can be easily integrated into GridSim.

GridSphere : GridSphere is one of the eminent grid initiatives funded by the European Union which aims at creation of web portal environment to facilitate the grid users.

GSSIM: The GSSIM (Grid Scheduling Simulator)is a GridSim-based simulator that was put into operation in 2009. GSSIM aims to provide a simple scheduling framework for simulating and testing scheduling algorithms in the Grid environment. The slow rate of execution and bad visualization outputs are the problems encountered in GSSIM.

Health Science Grids: The role of grid computing in health science is significant in terms of finding new, accurate and fast methods of diagnosis. The doctors are having huge amount of data and their analysis will greatly help in finding cure and treatment to the patients irrespective of their geographical locations.

High-Efficiency Schedulers: The high efficiency schedulers aim to achieve maximum efficiency of the system and hence they are focused on elevating the job performance which eventually enhances the efficiency of the grid environment.

Hybrid Grids: There are several grids which are not dedicated to single application. Instead of providing services to specific applications, some grids are diverse in nature and provide services in multiple domains. TeraGrid is a kind of grid which is used in academic, health-science and research activities.

Job: A job submitted by the grid user to the grid system has a specific requirement of resources. The resource requirement can be storage, processing, software libraries etc.

Load Balancing: The workload distribution among the resources of the grid must be done in a uniform manner so that neither of the resources in the grid becomes overutilized nor underutilized. The utilization of all the resources in the grid should be uniform for effective resource utilization.

Local Schedulers: The local schedulers, sometimes called cluster schedulers is responsible for assigning jobs to the resources in the same regional or local network.

Meta-Schedulers: The meta-schedulers or the meta-brokers are used for the management of jobs/applications which is scheduled at multiple resources across various grid systems. These schedulers also help in maintaining uniform load across different systems.

Microgrid: It is an emulator designed using the Globus toolkit. It uses the Globus API to execute its applications. Since a microgrid is an emulator, it takes more time to run applications on emulated resources. Though the output of the emulator is explicit, the design of the application and scheduling environment is also time-consuming. It can be used as a verification tool to check the simulation results with other real applications.

Modular Computing: Grid computing supports a model of modular computing. A computing paradigm with no single point of failure is considered modular where multiple resources are available and can handle a job in the case of single resource failure in grid environment.

Monarc 2: The Monarc 2 aims at providing a modeling as well as optimization tool for large distributed computing systems. It is mainly designed to support data processing architectures and provide a flexible environment for evaluating their performance. The Monarc 2 is an extension of Monarc Simulator. Monarc 2 is developed by enhancing the flexibility and performance of Monarc.

Moth Flame Optimization (MFO): The MFO is a recent search optimization algorithm. Moths are identical to butterflies in their behavior. The moths follow their own way of navigation and fly towards moonlight during nighttime.

Mutation: The last operator, mutation, is optional which randomly modifies the offspring (child) generated in the crossover step of the GA. Mutation brings diversity in the GA which is required for the exploration of the search space.

National Research Grid Initiative: The National Research Grid Initiative (NAREGI) is a popular grid program developed by the Japanese scientific and research community that aims at building an R&D center of high performance to escalate scientific and engineering applications

NEESGrid: This grid is meant to assist the scientists and researchers working in earthquake engineering society to demonstrate and perform experiments in diverse locations and investigate data through a common terminal.

NetSolve: The NetSolve or GridSolve is a grid middleware project developed at University of Tennessee, Knoxville aims at bringing together the different resources interconnected by computing network. This middleware is a RPC based client/server structure that facilitates a user to access the software as well as hardware components remotely.

Nimrod: Nimrod is an Australian grid initiative project developed at Monash University. This project is designed to handle the complexities related to parametric computing on groups of distributed systems. Nimrod gives an elementary declarative language to express a parametric experiment. The plans of parametric computing can be created by domain experts, and the Nimrod run time system can be used to execute different applications such as bio-informatics, business process simulations, and operational research.

Ninf: Ninf is a Japanese programming middleware solution based on GridRPC (Remote Procedure Call) programming structure. This middleware provides a user friendly interface to access various software, hardware and data resources such as scientific data.

One point crossover: A random position is selected in the two parent solutions which serves as the swap point and divides the parents into two parts. The two-child solutions are generated by swapping the two parts of the parents.

Open Grid Service Architecture Data Access and Integration: The Open Grid Service Architecture Data Access and Integration, popularly known as OGSA-DAI, is a middleware solution that facilitates the application developers by providing easy access to distributed data at multiple sites along with various local access mechanisms. Integration of data can also take place at server site and deliver the output with the help of several protocols and policies within OGSA-DAI. This middleware is able to accommodate data resources, such as relational databases, files, or XML databases, and can handle multiple operations, such as changing to disparate formats with the help of a highly malleable and extensile framework.

Particle Swarm Optimization: Keneddy and Eberhart has developed Particle Swarm Optimization (PSO) by simulating the social (collective) behavior of living organisms such as flocks of birds or fish school. Later, after much simplification of the algorithm, it is found that PSO works well for the optimization problems and can be applied to large and complex data sets.

Parallel Computing: The property of parallel computation allows complex simulations to break into various sub-parts and run them in parallel during scientific computation. This yields faster results in comparison to the entire computation performed in the series mode

Public Grids: These are the non-commercial grids offering services to general public issues. The concept of public grids depends on the availability of unused CPU cycles and data storage to solve public problems.

Quality of Service (QoS): It consists of functional and non-functional properties that measure the nature of service from several viewpoints. These properties are different performance metrics like scalability, response time, reliability, and availability. The Service Level Agreement (SLA) sets an accord between the service provider and the service user over minimum values for QoS performance attributes, which are required to be met once a service is called.

Rank Selection: In this method, the individual solutions are arranged in the order of their fitness values. Later, a rank is assigned to the individuals where the most fit individual has rank N (N is the highest rank) and the rank 1 is assigned to the least fit individual.

Real-Time Grids: The real-time applications have various requirements which are not supported by traditional computational or data grid. These real-time grids provide virtual workspace to enable the interactions between the clients and applications. Real-time applications such as disaster management are handled by real-time grids.

Resource: A resource is a scheduling entity where a job is scheduled and processed according to its requirements. There are several properties of a resource such as its processing speed and memory. Resources in grid are distributed across multiple sites where each site has its own access rights and usage policies.

Resource Allocation: Resource allocation makes use of available resources of the resource repository in the most efficient manner. The resource manager must have a complete report of available resources to make effective resource allocation.

Resource Forecasting: This technique allows the resource manager to make a prediction of future resource requirement before the actual start of the project. It also unveils the potential risks and unexpected costs that may incur after the completion of the project.

Resource Layer: This layer consists of resource-specific protocols such as Grid Resource Access and Management Protocol (GRAMP) for allocation and monitoring of resources. It also contains some information and management protocols. The information protocol helps to inquire the state of the resources (by making a call to fabric layer) and the management protocol helps in managing the access to shared resources in the grid.

Resource Leveling: This technique helps to uncover the underused resources whose potential has not been realized completely in the organization.

Resource Management: Resource management is the efficient utilization of resources in the best possible manner. It involves deep planning and analysis of the job requirement as well as resource availability to make appropriate job-resource assignments in any working environment. Resource management consists of several approaches that can be used to handle resources.

Resource Monitoring: It is important to keep track of the status of the resources in a dynamic grid environment. It is possible that a new resource can be added to an existing grid infrastructure or an existing resource may become unavailable at any point of time.

Resource-Oriented Schedulers: The goal of these schedulers is to escalate the resource utilization in a computing network.

Resource Utilization: Resource utilization is an important factor which affects the performance of the grid environment. Resource management enables the resources to the users, which considers both user and resource provider satisfaction. Optimal resource utilization helps in achieving improved system performance.

Robustness: A dynamic environment like grid keeps on changing with time, in terms of its resources, networks and job heterogeneity. Hence a robust scheduler is an extreme need to maintain the performance of the grid environment. The literature study of the metaheuristics shows that they are robust in nature.

Roulette Wheel Selection: This is a simple method of selecting an individual from the population of solutions. The chances of selection of an individual depend on its fitness. The probability of selection of an individual is high for fitter individuals. The slots in the wheel indicate the fitness value of the individuals.

Scheduler: The job of a scheduler is to place the job over the resource based on the requirement of a job and track the status of the job and resource until it finishes its execution.

Scientific Grids: Grid computing has made remarkable contribution in the field of science and technology and it is creating new advancements and developments till date. Standard scientific projects related to astronomy, quantum physics and nuclear science are having their grid systems exclusively for their needs.

Selection: The process of selection selects solutions (parents) from the original population of solutions. The idea is to select good parent solutions that can survive into the next generation and reproduce new offspring

Service-Oriented Computing: It forms the backbone of a popular distributed computing system, i.e., Cloud computing. The underlying principle is to embrace the notion of services for application and system development. Service itself is an abstraction that has the capability to perform basic to complex tasks based on requirements and irrespective of the programming language or computing platform. Service-oriented (SOA) is a logical approach to organizing software systems and providing services to users through observable interfaces.

Shortest Job First (SJF): SJF belongs to conventional family of scheduling algorithms which can be preemptive or non-preemptive. The jobs, in this case, are scheduled over the available resources on the basis of their processing requirements. The jobs with low processing requirement are favored over jobs with high processing requirements.

SimGrid: The SimGrid is designed for modeling the distributed applications and testing them in a distributed environment with real life scenarios. It is C based simulator which consists of various tools such as MSG, GRAS and SMPI. The MSG tool of SimGrid supports testing of scheduling algorithms in the simulation environment. The other two tools, GRAS and SMPI, are used in the development and analysis of real applications.

Simbatch: The Simbatch is designed for the batch schedulers and provides simulation for scheduling. The design of Simbatch is based on MSG tool of SimGrid.

SimBOINC: The design of SimBOINC (Berkley Open Infrastructure for Network Computing) is also based on SimGrid simulator. SimBOINC supports simulation of heterogeneous and volatile computing systems. It follows a client server model where many clients make a request to the central server. The client request contains simulation inputs such as speed and workload availability.

Software-as-a-Service (SaaS): The SaaS method enables the distribution of complicated business processes in the form of service to the user which can be accessed from every location.

Specification: The job requirements are written in a high-level language.

Storage Resource Broker (SRB): The SRB, led by the Supercomputing center in San Diego, is a renowned grid middleware project that organizes dissimilar data repositories and handles data storage, access management, and data replication

Super-Schedulers: The super-schedulers performs centralized scheduling approach where the scheduler manages the selection of resource and execution of job over the chosen resource. The jobs are assigned to a single computing resource during their execution.

Swarm Intelligence: The field of computer science which is driven by the behavior of swarm of living organisms is known as swarm intelligence. It is a subset of artificial intelligence. It is generated in a decentralized and distributed environment with the help of the intelligence of the members of the swarm by replicating their behavior. This intelligence helps in designing more efficient algorithms that can find solutions to complicated real-world applications.

TeraGrid: The United States' National Science Foundation has funded a grid infrastructure called TeraGrid that gives computing power of 40 teraflops and storage capacity of 2 PB across eight grid sites in the United States. Grid3 is a major testbed covering 25 geographical sites in US and Korea that are being used for operational areas such as Astronomy, Computational Biology and High Energy Physics.

Threshold Probability (p_0): It is a minimum probability value set by the scheduler. Initially, the conventional ACO is run several times and the value of transition probability is calculated using Equation 1 for every iteration. The value of threshold probability is randomly selected from set of transition probability values using conventional ACO.

Total Completion Time (TCT) of Jobs: The TCT of jobs is defined as the time taken by all the jobs of the workload to complete their execution

The Globus Toolkit: The Globus toolkit is a very popular grid middleware project developed by the Global Alliance conducted by the Argonne National Laboratory.

The Grid Scheduler: The grid scheduler is the most important entity in a grid system. It is responsible for selecting and allocating a resource from a set of resources for particular job under given constraints.

Tournament Selection: The tournament selection is a popular selection method because it is easy to implement and gives better solutions to the problems. This method involves selection of individual from the population of solutions which are set to compete against each other.

Utility Computing: It aims at supporting a kind of infrastructure which can provide information technology services according to the demand of customer. Utility computing differs from outsourcing because outsourcing focuses on location and resource manager whereas utility computing is related to resource management, resource consumption and its utilization. The utility model is suitable to corporate as well as the outsourcing data centers. It intends to break down the huge IT foundations into several independent segments.

Utility Grids: The job of utility grids is to pool the dynamically accessible resources to meet the needs of the given application. This helps in combining resources from multiple machines dynamically and providing services which is not possible by a single machine.

Whale Optimization Algorithm (WOA): The WOA is another metaheuristic providing solutions for complex engineering problems. Whales are smarter than humans because whales have twice the amount of cells that humans have, which contributes to their smartness. Whales are capable of thinking, communicating, learning, and developing their own dialects. A type of hunting technique by humpback whales known as the bubble-net feeding technique is a special feature of these whales.

Zewura Workload: MetaCentrum, the Czech National Grid Infrastructure (NGI), has provided the workload called zewura workload for testing new algorithms and comparing its performance with the other reference algorithms. The workload traces are produced from TORQUE traces, which contain 17256 jobs. These jobs were gathered between January and May 2012. The workload is in Standard Workload Format (SWF). The workload requires two files, namely, the job description file and the machine description file.

Index

W

X

Y

Z